I, UNIV█████

M000036555

DEMOLISHING AND REBUILDING SPIRITUALITY FOR A SCIENTIFIC AGE

DARRYL SLOAN

SKYLIGHT PRESS

First published in Great Britain in 2018 by Skylight Press,
210 Brooklyn Road, Cheltenham, Glos GL51 8EA

Publisher: Daniel Staniforth

Printed and bound in Great Britain by Lightning Source, Milton Keynes.

British Library Cataloguing in Publication Data:
A catalogue record for this book is available from the British Library.

ISBN 978-1-910098-04-2

CONTENTS

In memory of Aristarchus

INTRODUCTION

THE search for truth is not for everyone. It is not for those who accept without question the beliefs they inherited by accident of birth. It is not for those whose natural tendency is to mimic the thoughts and attitudes of their peers. It is not for those who are afraid to be different. It is not for those who need the approval of others to maintain their own happiness. It is not for those who only have ears for what makes them feel good. It is not for those who think they already *know* and need never change their minds. In short, it's not for a lot of people.

This book is primarily for anyone who feels frustrated, angry, or confused in the task of figuring out what life is all about. It is a love letter to the person I used to be, someone whose anxieties and sorrows are undoubtedly mirrored in the experiences of others – perhaps you. This is my attempt to lend a helping hand to anyone who has intuitively felt (to borrow a line from the movie *The Matrix*) "a splinter in your mind."

In the following pages you will not find a dogmatic, unchangeable belief system. In fact, you will come to understand that the notion of an ideological endpoint is untenable. I offer nothing that will transform you from unenlightened to enlightened, asleep to awake, or lost to saved. Learning is a curve, not a switch that flips from off to on, and you will shortly see that the idea of salvation (by whatever name it is called) is an illusion.

That said, the level of your understanding has a powerful effect on your personal happiness, ethical values, and sense of purpose. If you see man as little more than a speck of dust in a vast impersonal Universe, that's going to affect your whole outlook on life. If you view yourself as a poor sinner, dependent on the mercy of a divine lawgiver, that will also mould your life in a dramatic way. It is of no small importance to figure out where man stands in relation to the wider Universe, for the sake of your happiness and, in some extreme cases, your very sanity.

My broad aim is to state a rational case for a philosophical viewpoint known as monism (sometimes called non-dualism or non-duality). This is the idea that everything is one; nothing is truly separate from anything else. Beyond appearances, the Universe is *one singular essence*, not a collection of many separate things. The mind is not separate from the body, nor is the body separate from the Universe, nor is the Universe separate from whatever we mean by God. At present, you may be sceptical of how we might arrive at such a conclusion without a reliance on mysticism or an intuitive leap of faith. You might also wonder what practical benefit there would be in holding such an unusual worldview. Wait and see.

Our first task will be to undo the social conditioning we've all inherited. Each person is, to one extent or another, a product of his upbringing. How many of us have thoroughly examined the veracity of all that we were conditioned to believe as children, through our parents, local religious institution, education authority, media, and culture? A quest for truth must begin with the unmasking of our unconscious assumptions and the withdrawing of our trust in unquestioned ideas. We must also identify, and armour ourselves against, the many psychological ploys that are used to manipulate our minds.

After freeing ourselves, the challenge is then to rationally examine the world as it truly appears to us, not as we would like it to be. Using philosophy and science, putting aside all prejudice and wishful thinking, we will attempt to synthesise a perspective that has the potential of getting closer to the truth than anything on offer within the various dogmatic belief systems of the world.

I will share insights about the mind and the nature of reality that most people are entirely unaware of. Some big surprises are in store, especially regarding what you take for granted as your identity. Perhaps most surprisingly of all, I will delve into parapsychology and the occult, principally as an attempt to demonstrate that consciousness plays a much more significant role in the Universe than contemporary science is willing to entertain. Extrasensory perception, psychokinesis, magic – are such phenomena real, and if so, what do they teach us about who we are and how the Universe works?

It's rare to find someone whose belief system hasn't become like a stone inside his mind, hard and non-malleable. But guess what? It's really just a choice. When you hear new and challenging information, don't say, "How can I somehow bend this to fit into what I already believe?" Say, "What do I currently believe that I need to amend in light of this new information?" When my cherished beliefs are attacked, my natural response is to jump to their defence, with stubbornness, pride and fear cheering me on. It's right there that I need to reel myself back in and say, "Hold on a minute. Maybe it's *me* who needs to learn something from *you*."

The most productive mentality you can have is simply this: always, always, *always* have a worldview that doesn't resist change. Go wherever the information leads you, without fear, because surely the truth is never something to dread.

If you employ this approach to learning, there is no guarantee, nor any necessity, that you will end up embracing exactly the same worldview that I hold. In fact, it may help me if you differ. Then you can show me the points where I've got it wrong and we both benefit. Isn't that refreshing?

PART ONE
REALITY CHECK

The individual has always had to struggle to keep from being overwhelmed by the tribe. To be your own man is a hard business. If you try it, you'll be lonely often, and sometimes frightened. But no price is too high to pay for the privilege of owning yourself.

Rudyard Kipling

Man is the only creature who refuses to be what he is.

Albert Camus, *The Rebel*

BORN TO BE BRAINWASHED

WHAT's life all about? I imagine most people have asked themselves that question. Some, like me, have obsessed over it. It's funny that there are so many different answers floating around, so many people in so many varying cultures supremely confident that their answer is the real one.

"We're here to love God and our fellow man," the Christian might say.

"There is no meaning to life," the atheist counters. "You die, it's game over. Get used to it."

"Our spirit is on a journey of evolution as we reincarnate from life to life," claims the New Ager.

"Listen to yourselves," the agnostic says. "How the hell are we supposed to know anything? I doubt we were ever meant to."

In my boyhood, my mother brought me to church, where I learned something about the Christian religion and the idea of worshipping a supreme being called God. This sense of reality was reinforced by prayers in school assembly alongside the singing of songs like "He's Got the Whole World in His Hands." Religious Education classes taught me about Jesus, the Son of God, who died on a cross to save mankind from the penalty of sin.

If you are told that something is true from your earliest years, before you have developed any critical thinking ability, and you are told it over and over again, and you are never given any encouragement to question that information, and never presented with any other view of reality, that is not *education*, it is *indoctrination*. Add to this the fact that you are surrounded by many people who believe the same things and it becomes easy to think, "Well, everybody knows this; it must be true." This is how one generation indoctrinates the next, over and over, and it can be observed everywhere you look in the world. Christian culture keeps on churning out more Christians; Jewish culture keeps on producing Jews; Muslim culture generates Muslim children.

When I was a child, Christianity sat in the back of my mind as a casual, inherited belief system that wasn't really making any demands of me, because I had never been confronted with the whole story in clear terms. Then, when I was seventeen, a friend informed me that unless I became a Christian – that is, a true, committed, born-again Christian – I would be going to hell for all eternity. And so I committed my life to the Lord, to serve him.

If you had asked me back then why I did it, I would have told you that I recognised there was nothing to fear and nothing to lose in becoming a Christian. God was the source of all wisdom, so his way would be the best way for my life. But the real underlying reason why I believed was because I had been primed for this belief all my life. It never occurred to me, even at seventeen, to ask myself, "Hey, am I sure this is all true?" I lived in a culture where it was generally accepted to be true, and that was good enough for me. I never noticed that my culture represented only a fraction of humanity, and there were many other cultures that believed dramatically different things with the same degree of confidence. In fact, just a few miles from my Protestant community was a Roman Catholic community which I was certain had got the wrong end of the stick about Christianity (even though I was only vaguely aware of what the differences were). I held this confidence for no other reason than I was raised in a Protestant community and heard only Protestant ideas again and again.

Almost all of us are born gravely disadvantaged, unless we are lucky enough to have parents who encourage sons and daughters to think their own independent thoughts instead of implanting beliefs into them. Wherever we live in the world, we are all born into the *zeitgeist*, a word that means "the spirit of the age." The zeitgeist isn't one particular worldview; it is any worldview that puts people into a herd and says, "This is the way it is. No need to question it."

The zeitgeist isn't specifically religious in nature. I'll give you an example that might seem funny. I don't use anti-perspirant. That's right, never. And I happen to ride a bicycle to work every day. "Ugh! You stink!" I hear you cry. Actually, I don't. Did it ever occur to you that when you expend energy physically, your body is supposed to sweat and there's a physiological reason for this? Have you ever considered that it's probably detrimental to your health to prevent an area of your skin from doing what it's designed to do? No? Well, *think* about it. If you're going to use anti-perspirant, do it for a better reason than merely noticing that everyone else is using it.

Nature endows men and women with armpit hair. Modern aesthetic values dictate that women should shave theirs off. But the purpose of this hair is to wick moisture away from the skin, so that the skin will remain dry enough to minimise the growth of bacteria. Given the fact that the armpit is the most consistently warm area of the body, nature is pretty smart to provide an abundance of hair in that spot. Shaving the hair off, not so smart. "But wait," you say. "We can use anti-perspirant to prevent sweating altogether." I see. Never mind the fact that the purpose of sweat is to provide a vital cooling effect. Furthermore, when you wash your body in alkaline pH soap, your skin loses its natural acid mantle, making it susceptible to bacterial colonisation. If you're worried about perspiration causing a nasty smell, the truth is it's actually odourless until it's fermented by bacteria that thrive in hot, humid environments – like a hair-free armpit with a high pH, caused by shaving and soap.

The female obsession with removing underarm hair, as well as leg hair, is the result of a sustained advertising campaign that began in the early twentieth century. Despite men and women joyously mating for countless millennia without hair removal wax, in the past hundred years it has suddenly become unthinkable for a woman to leave her legs alone. Men, would it bother you to feel a slight fuzz underneath your palm as you caress a woman's thigh? Why? It doesn't bother you to sense it when you caress her arm, does it? Or should women wax their arms next? The whole affair is ridiculous.

Kids have a sweet tooth. Nobody much objects to giving sweets to a child as a little treat once in a while. But have you ever stopped to consider what sweets are? Often they're lumps of chemically treated sugar. Did you ever stop to consider that humans were not meant to ingest artificial chemical substances as food? There is no nutritional value in artificial flavourings whatsoever and their only purpose is to fool the brain into thinking, "Hey, this is delicious!" Did you ever think that maybe, just maybe, it might not be good for a young developing child to eat this junk? So why do we give children these things? Because everyone else is doing it, so it must be okay.

On the same theme, a child reaches fourteen and the dentist says, "Ah-ha. You've got some nasty tooth-decay going on in there. Three fillings should clear that right up." You would think the penny would drop when we see that we're having dental surgery done on children. Let me say that word again, with emphasis, in case it slipped by unnoticed: we're doing *surgery* on children, and we don't bat an eyelid. Something is very wrong with the world when nobody senses the abnormality of a high percentage of people needing surgery before they reach adulthood. We all know that nobody with any sense would hand a cigarette to a five-year-old and say, "There you go, Pete. Light up." How did we come to believe that it's unacceptable to destroy a child's lungs, but acceptable to destroy his teeth? Why do we think this is normal? Because we're constantly looking at society around us to tell us what's normal – to tell us what's right.

Look at how we eat, in general. Our foods are typically mixed with all manner of artificial additives. Sometimes the ingredients label on a product will feature an unintelligible list of chemical substances. I once noticed a television advertisement that said, "No artificial colours." This is the perfect example of the way companies will try to deceive the public into believing their product has a healthy side. Here's how you tell: when a product says "No artificial colours," that means there *are* artificial *flavours*, otherwise the label would proudly display "No artificial flavours or colours." I see this all the time and I try to steer clear of foods like that. Some ingredients lists bear the mysterious solitary word "flavouring," which gives the company a licence to put who knows what in the food.

A popular artificial additive is monosodium glutamate (MSG). It does not serve any digestive function whatsoever. It is, quite simply, a drug, and its purpose is to affect the brain. MSG is called a flavour enhancer. It is designed to fool your brain into thinking that what you're eating is tastier than it really is. Maybe it's just me, but somehow the idea of bombarding my body with brain-altering drugs on a regular basis does not sound like a good idea. On the plus side, I'm happy to see that public consciousness of this issue has risen to the extent that the phrase "No MSG" printed on a food product can be used as a sales pitch. Even so, it's hard to know what sales pitch you can trust. If you see "Low fat" on the packaging, look carefully at the ingredients, especially the one marked sugar. The sad truth is that the vast majority of processed foods are unhealthy, designed in a laboratory to dope us. That's not an exaggeration. Sugar releases the pleasure chemical dopamine in the brain. So an easy way to sell a food product is to lace it with excess sugar. Just read the labels.

Here's how common modern eating habits work. The unhealthy foods are shoved in our faces through television advertising; they're calling out to us as we walk through the supermarket. So we buy them and eat them. And we find that they taste super-delicious, because they have been engineered to affect us in that way – much more appealing than the "bland" products in the whole foods section. Unfortunately, the major health problems that result from this habitual way of living don't announce themselves with a sudden fanfare; they creep up on you almost imperceptibly over a period of many years.

We need to stop playing copycat with society and realise that our eating habits are radically at odds with mankind's natural relationship with the Earth. We've come to accept that heart disease, diabetes, and cancer are diseases over which we have no control, when diet is a prime factor in all these cases. We have an amazing ally, who fights illness on our behalf every day: the immune system. All it asks is that we nourish it with food that has real nutritional value: unprocessed meats, fruits, vegetables, nuts. The human race has a very long history of thriving on this sort of diet.

When I communicate this kind of information, I'm struck by how difficult it can sometimes be to affect people. When we eat junk, we don't notice how we're increasing the toxicity of our bodies and compromising the effectiveness of our immune systems. The effects progress so slowly as to be unnoticeable on a day-to-day basis, and that's as far as people are prepared to gaze. "I feel the same today as I felt yesterday, so what's the problem?"

We gravitate to what is familiar instead of doing what we really need to do, which is revolutionise our thinking.

The harm we do doesn't begin and end with our bodies, but extends to the rape of the planet itself. Every two weeks I move a bin full of rubbish to the front of my house for collection. A portion of that refuse is not bio-degradable, mostly packaging from products, occasionally some items from the house that have broken. These will be taken to landfill sites where they remain indefinitely. Consider how big these sites must be when everyone in the modern world is doing the same, all the time – an ever-flowing river of waste that has nowhere to go and just keeps building.

I sometimes imagine what it might be like for a native American Indian from centuries ago to set foot in our modern world and observe our culture. In contrast to that simple way of life which took from the Earth only what it needed, he would witness us getting drunk on materialism. We sacrifice so much of our lives, working forty or more hours per week for what we call a living, only to invest what little free time we have staring zombie-like into a rectangle in the corner of the room, in an attempt to fill a void inside us. Hypnotised by television, victims of our own culture, we behave like reckless spendthrifts, cluttering our houses with junk that we don't need and barely even want. I think our homes and our shopping malls would look like incomprehensible insanity to that Indian. We don't see that truth, because we blindly accept the structure of our lives without question. And it's a structure that is ever-so-gradually assassinating the planet.

Look at how many cars are on our roads. Every day we take fossil fuels from the ground and turn them into pollution on a grand scale. In some cities there is so much traffic that permanent smog hangs in the sky. It's not just cars that are at fault. Most of the electricity in our homes comes from fossil fuels, the pollution from which is released into the air on a grand scale at the power plants. I recall a girl from Sheffield, England, who came to live here in Northern Ireland, telling me that the air here was noticeably fresher. People are forced to live in places where they aren't even permitted to breathe properly, and we call this normal life!

I'm not saying we should never purchase a car, never buy a new stereo, never do anything nice for ourselves. But we need to wake up to what we are all, collectively, doing to the planet and make changes for the better that will allow the Earth to recover. The way that mankind has been living since the dawn of the Industrial Revolution is simply not sustainable in the long run, because it is all based on turning finite resources into pollution. There's a saying: "No snowflake in an avalanche ever felt responsible." Our personal contribution to the destruction of the planet appears tiny, because we fail to recognise that personal irresponsibility is the basis of collective irresponsibility.

What is normal life? Normal life, according to the zeitgeist, is whatever the majority around you decide is normal life. We might like to think we're so much more civilised than the ancient Romans, who clapped and cheered at the gladiators battling to the death, all in the name of sport. But the truth is, if you lived in those ancient times, you would more than likely have adopted the same value system as your peers, because most people get their values by copying those around them. They are sheep and they follow the flock. Only when you start asking questions, only when you start *thinking* for yourself, can you see things for what they really are. Suffice it to say, here in twenty-first century Western civilisation, we haven't reached any sort of pinnacle of enlightened behaviour, not by a long shot.

We have all been conditioned to believe certain things. It happens from the cradle, long before we have any ability to think for ourselves. For some people, it lasts until the grave. For others, who decide to do their own critical thinking, that endeavour often starts too late, when they have already made certain assumptions about life. One assumption might be "The Bible is the word of God," or it could equally be "The physical Universe is all there is." Those assumptions then guide their thinking from that point on.

When you ask yourself what life is all about, and you start off with certain assumptions already made, what hope have you of finding the real truth? Those assumptions will immediately dictate your sense of what's possible and impossible. Worse still, your assumptions may be so subtle that you're not even consciously aware you're making them. Later, I'm going to go very deep down the rabbit hole on this point, and it's going to pack a few surprises.

It may be tempting to think that there's no hope of finding any real enlightenment in life. When you look at how many different belief systems exist in the world, and how many people are certain that their way is the One True Way, who the hell is this guy Darryl Sloan to say he's found it? Well, I haven't found it. Enlightenment is always a matter of degree and there is no finish line in the quest for truth; you would have to be omniscient for that. It would also be a miracle if nothing in this book needed revision in a few years. If my mind is truly active, then the things I learn in the future are bound to cause me to reassess some of what I'm expressing now. But that's the joy of learning. I'm merely one of many voices heading in a particular direction that appears correct.

As we all individually search for truth, that search is taking us somewhere, however slowly it may seem and however many wrong turns we might make along the way. My personal search was never a journey of going round in circles. Even when I look back to when my beliefs were certainly wrong, those experiences taught me things, helped me to eventually move forward with a clearer understanding. However confused you may be right now, don't allow cynicism to suffocate you; there *is* light at the end of the tunnel.

When we develop critical thinking in the latter part of childhood, we may start to ask questions and entertain doubts about some of the beliefs we've been conditioned to hold. Rarely do we ask enough questions. Unless you reassess *everything* (and in forthcoming chapters you're going to see exactly how much I mean by everything), you haven't a hope of finding the truth. If you assume at the outset that the basic view of reality you grew up with is on firm ground, then you unwittingly booby-trap the quest from the first step. Instead of seeking the truth, what many do is seek to defend what they inherited – which may never have been given enough scrutiny in the first place. When we hear challenging information, we so easily perceive it as a threat and gravitate back to what we already believe. But we are not gravitating to the truth, only to the familiar.

If you want to learn the truth about life, first begin by unlearning the lies, by questioning the zeitgeist and leaving no stone unturned. That's what makes this approach different from so many belief systems claiming that they're the real representatives of the truth. How many of them skipped the part about *unlearning*?

THE LAND OF CONFUSION

To any believer of any religion, let me be clear at the outset: you have every right to believe what you wish. It's not my place to dictate a version of reality and tell you, "This is the way it's got to be, or else." If, after reading this book, you move forward with your faith intact, that's your prerogative. This is about all of us, as individuals, taking personal responsibility for what we think. I may feel disappointed or frustrated when I fail to make someone see what has become so clear to me, but when all is said and done, your mind is your own.

When I first became a Christian, aged seventeen, there were several reasons why I made the commitment. (1) I was conditioned to believe Christianity was true by my upbringing, so it seemed like there was really no choice; (2) I was threatened with damnation if I neglected it, so there was no time to waste; (3) I believed God was perfectly wise, so there was nothing to lose by doing his will; (4) I felt that this could be the missing link that would make my life fulfilling, so there was everything to gain.

During my many years as a Christian, when asked why I gave my life to Christ, I was inclined to leave out number 2, the fear-based reason. When asked the same question today, now that I have rejected religion, I tend to emphasise number 2. The truth, in complete fairness, is all four reasons and probably more. There was some wisdom and some naïvety and some fear involved in my decision. We're all different. One person may be scared out of his wits by a fire-and-brimstone preacher; another may have been raised in a Christian home and feels the pressure of his parents' expectations; another may feel rotten inside and yearn for forgiveness and acceptance; another might possess a longing for the sense of family that comes from joining a fellowship where people love each other; another may seek enlightenment and notice something in Christianity that allows him to make better sense of his life. The list goes on.

When I became a Christian, my natural response was to join a local church and begin reading the Bible in my personal life. At church I was taught that the Bible was the infallible word of God. This meant that I should consider everything I found within it to be absolutely true. I didn't investigate that claim; I didn't really know how. I simply knew that the Bible was an ancient text, and I had to assume that the people in charge of putting it together, translating it, and declaring its authenticity, knew what they were doing. Not so different from sitting in History class at school and taking it on trust that the Battle of Hastings took place in 1066. But in truth, assumptions are dangerous things. It makes no difference to my life to place some trust that my History teacher is giving me correct information, but it's a much bigger deal to place unquestioning faith in a book that seeks to control my life.

These factors didn't occur to me at the time. I put my trust in the Bible and hoped that I was on the verge of filling some kind of void in my life – although if you had asked me to define exactly what that void was, I would have been hard pressed to do so. In practical terms, I thought I might finally gain the ability to quit masturbating and thus bring an end to my vague feelings of guilt about it. It sounds funny now, but it seemed like a big deal to a bewildered teenager trying to cope with his awakened sexuality in a world where sex is viewed as forbidden or dirty in so many contexts.

Things did not go well for me as a Christian from the get-go. One of my close friends was a staunch atheist. We would debate while walking to college in the mornings. As a newcomer to any serious critical thinking, I was no match for him, and my faith in God was soon lying in ruins. I did pick up the pieces fairly quickly and I continued being a Christian, but something had changed. For my whole life, I had believed that Christianity was the true religion because I had been surrounded by that viewpoint. It wasn't so much something that I had *learned* as something I had been *conditioned* to accept. Now that this conditioning had been challenged, it ceased to be something I could unthinkingly place confidence in. The claims of Christianity seemed profound and I wanted to believe, but now this could only be a personal belief, not something I could hold with unshakeable assurance.

I would sit in church and see certainty shining in the faces of other believers. When I asked some of them if they knew Christianity was absolutely true, they would assert, "Yes, I know it's true." Whereas I could only say, "I *believe* it's true." I felt like I was on the outside of something that seemed easily grasped by others. The experience with my atheist friend seemed to have scarred me in a way that I couldn't recover from. But looking back, it was actually an invaluable gift. The fact that I was never sure prevented me from closing the door on inquiry. And asking questions is vital to any quest for truth. At the time, I didn't dare think that maybe the people who seemed so sure about Christianity were only brimming with confidence because they had stopped asking questions, or perhaps had never started. It's not my place to judge what way they were thinking, but I had experienced the zeitgeist's grip on me, and no one is exempt. If there ever was a Big Answer that made it crystal clear why Christianity was true beyond reasonable doubt, no one was ever able to communicate it to me.

The more that I learned, the more problems I encountered. Consider the account of the Garden of Eden (Genesis 1-3). We may choose to interpret this as literal history, or as a mythological approximation of obscure prehistoric events. Either way, the character Adam should be regarded as an actual person, because he is referenced in several genealogies listed later in the Bible (Genesis 5:1-5; 1 Chronicles 1; Luke 3:23-38). If I am to believe that Adam lived, as the first ever man, I have to calculate that the human race has only been around for six to ten thousand years. You get that sort of figure when you add up all the generations from Adam to Jesus, plus two thousand years to take us to the present day. Suddenly the cost of believing in the Bible was the rejection of science.

In 1 Samuel 15 I encountered a disturbing passage where God commands his people, the Israelites, to undertake the mass slaughter of men, women, children, infants and animals:

This is what the LORD Almighty says: "I will punish the Amalekites for what they did to Israel when they waylaid them as they came up from Egypt. Now go, attack the Amalekites and totally destroy everything that belongs to them. Do not spare them; put to death men and women, children and infants, cattle and sheep, camels and donkeys."   1 Samuel 15:2-4

When the New Testament influences you to believe that life is sacred, something is seriously wrong when this same God once commanded his people to kill countless babies. I have debated this issue with Christians and heard all the arguments. Some will say that we don't always understand God's ways, which is really just a refusal to look squarely at what is in front of you. Another will say, "God has the right to do what he wants because he's God." My problem is not with God's actions; it's with the radically changing standard of behaviour he demands of his people. Someone once offered me this justification: "Those Amalekite children would grow up to be adults, learn of their people's history and of what the Israelites did to them. They would seek revenge, and so it was appropriate to wipe the whole nation out there and then." I see. So now we believe it's fair to enforce the death penalty in infancy for the mere *possibility* of committing a crime later in life, and never mind the fact that the judging of a person by his race alone is, well, *racism*.

Some answer the dilemma by pointing out: "All mankind is under God's condemnation as a result of the Fall. God is under no obligation to be merciful, so we are in no position to object when he chooses to display his wrath. We're so accustomed to his mercy that we forget what it is – *undeserved* favour." It's a good argument until you realise that the text has already stated why God desired the children to be killed – not because they were sinners, but because they were Amalekites. The universal sinfulness of mankind is no justification for the abandonment of social justice.

Exodus 20 contains the Ten Commandments. In verse 5 we have a brief commentary on the second commandment, which is a prohibition on bowing down before images: "I, the LORD your God, am a jealous God, punishing the children for the sin of the parents to the third and fourth generation of those who hate me." Close variations on this statement are also made in Exodus 34:7, Numbers 14:18, and Deuteronomy 5:9. The Lord's idea of justice is clear and quite horrific to modern ears. It boils down to: "If your dad was bad, then I'm blaming *you*, too." And yet, in complete contradiction to this, in Deuteronomy 24:16 God commands his people to execute a very different form of justice: "Parents are not to be put to death for their children, nor children put to death for their parents; each will die for their own sin."

Regarding the slaughter of the Amalekite children, put yourself in the place of an Israelite soldier. Imagine yourself holding a sword over a baby and recall that the Lord commanded you to strike. Do you obey? Unconscionable, isn't it? It may belong to the Old Testament era, but what does that matter? This is supposed to be the same God that Christians worship today. Is it realistic to suggest that God was once psychotic but he's all better now? Of course not. But that's what Christians are really stating when they seek to brush aside the unpalatable elements of the Old Testament. The answers that might look acceptable on paper don't really do you much good when you face the reality of it. And the reality is that the God of the Bible is a God who pushes his people into the biggest extreme of racism – genocide – and calls it good.

As if this wasn't bad enough, we read later of King David preparing to build a temple for the Lord (1 Chronicles 22), when God informs him: "You have shed much blood and have fought many wars. You are not to build a house for my Name, because you have shed much blood on the earth in my sight. But you will have a son who will be a man of peace and rest, and I will give him rest from all his enemies on every side. His name will be Solomon, and I will grant Israel peace and quiet during his reign. He is the one who will build a house for my Name." On the one hand, the Lord commands his people to go to war, and on the other, he holds it against them. The cherry on top of this staggering hypocrisy is found in the words of Jesus, as he answers his critics: "You belong to your father, the devil, and you want to carry out your father's desires. He was a murderer from the beginning" (John 8:44). When someone with a record of mass murder accuses another of being a murderer, that's just plain hilarious.

I never had such clear and strong opinions about this in the early days, of course. What I had was a shelf in my mind upon which I stored all the stuff that I couldn't make sense of – or didn't dare to make sense of. I could never understand how a preacher could stand on a pulpit and talk about "the infallible word of God" when we were using multiple translations of the Bible, each of which had differences of opinion on how to translate this or that passage. These modern translations were an attempt to correct many of the known errors that had been discovered in the popular centuries-old translation, the King James Version. Not so infallible back then, it seems. If you have a New International Version of the Bible and you look in the footnotes of any New Testament book, you will see the words "Some manuscripts" over and over again, as in "Some manuscripts do not have verse 47" (Matthew 12:47). I didn't understand how we could claim that the Bible was the divinely inspired word of God when it was full of question marks about whether this word or that phrase was truly in the original text. I've heard it said in defence of the Bible that none of the discrepancies affect any of the teachings of the Bible. But once you find corruption, you have no way of knowing how much or how little is there, or whether any teachings are affected, because you simply haven't got the original to compare. So I put this problem on the shelf along with all the other questions I couldn't answer. The trouble was, rarely did anything come down from the shelf and get resolved. Instead of using these problems as pointers to the idea that Christianity might be a false religion, I pushed them out of mind.

The everyday experience of living the Christian life was difficult, to say the least. As a teenager, it was impossible to adhere to Christianity's strict no-sexual-thoughts-allowed policy. Jesus said, "Anyone who looks at a woman lustfully has already committed adultery with her in his heart" (Matthew 5:28). But here's the problem. We're wired for sex; it's biological. You can't switch it off. Boys are supposed to feel attracted to girls and vice versa. It isn't some wicked desire. It's your body telling you what it wants to do, no different in principle from our appetite for food. Obviously, if you're a responsible person, you'll act responsibly and not just follow your every sexual whim, just as it's not sensible to eat too much food and become overweight. The misuse of our bodily appetites might be termed sinful, but the urges themselves are a natural part of life. This is plain to me now, as an adult, but as a young Christian, all I could understand was that I was such a disappointment to God because I couldn't control my sexual feelings.

Imagine a perfect world, with Adam and Eve having never sinned. Think of yourself born into this paradise. You grow up, walking around naked every day, and you eventually marry. Is your marriage night supposed to be the first time you ever experience an erection? "Eek! What's happening to me? I feel so strange. Is this what it means to be horny?" The idea is just plain ridiculous. There is nothing unholy about a hard-on. I'm sorry, Christians, but the sex-is-dirty attitude just has to go. Young people have suffered enough.

It wasn't just sexuality that gave me problems. Christian morality in general was a hard thing to figure out. You try to do God's will by keeping the Sabbath holy and avoiding work. You hear of one Christian who thinks it's wrong to play sports on a Sunday, while another thinks it's okay. You start to think it's probably wrong to do any shopping on a Sunday because you are encouraging others to work – encouraging them to *sin*. You even begin to wonder if you're offending God by washing the dishes on a Sunday. Besides all this, no one ever explained why the Sabbath changed from the Jewish Saturday to the Christian Sunday. Maybe we should keep both days holy, just to be sure?

The confusion quickly multiplies. The Baptist denomination claims that no one should be baptised until they make a conscious decision to become a Christian. The Presbyterian denomination claims that the infants of Christian families should be baptised. The Roman Catholics go as far as saying that an infant cannot receive the grace of God *until* he is baptised. Let's assume, hypothetically, that the Catholics happen to be the ones who got it right: Baptist parents, who think they are serving God by *withholding* baptism from their children, are actually compromising their lives.

Consider the Eucharist, the ritual of eating bread and drinking wine in remembrance of the death of Jesus. Roman Catholics believe that the bread and wine become the actual body and blood of Christ. Protestants believe that the bread and wine only figuratively represent the body and blood of Christ. Each side accuses the other of terrible sacrilege.

Not only are we poor bewildered humans charged with deciphering which religion on the planet is the right one to follow, but which particular sub-division of which religion. And if we get it wrong, there may be dire eternal consequences for us and our children. I hated struggling to figure out what God really required of me. It's all well and good to understand that God wants your love, but when it comes to the business of showing that love through obedience, that's where things get confusing and frustrating.

In my later years as a Christian, I couldn't face doing any missionary activities. I thought, "I've made a choice to believe this, but how can I say to other people that they must believe it, too? I believe that God will judge the world, but it's just a belief. I don't *know* it. How then can I shove a message in someone's face and say, 'You must believe,' as if I can prove what I'm claiming?"

Being a *thinking* Christian leaves you in a real mess, doesn't it? There are two ways out of that pickle: (1) give up thinking for yourself, or (2) dare to disbelieve.

THE BOGEYMAN FOR ADULTS

ROGER ran down the corridor and burst through the doors into the office. The two dozen employees, hearing the clatter, looked up from their desks and saw his panicked expression. "Quick!" he yelled. "We need to get out! The building's on fire!"

Pulses raced. Everyone jumped to their feet and made a beeline for the emergency exit. Once on the street, they gazed back into the building, looking for the first signs of smoke and flames. They waited ... and waited. Nothing happened.

Eventually, Roger walked towards the building, pushed open the door, and looked back over his shoulder with a mischievous grin. "Suckers!"

Roger had manufactured a believable threat and made the others invest in that belief. Once implanted, the belief manipulated their emotions (fear), which then controlled their behaviour (running). Of course, the scam was over after they had been standing outdoors for a few minutes, but for the duration of the experiment Roger got his colleagues to do what he wanted them to do. He essentially mind-controlled them. It's especially important to note that they would have felt completely in charge of their own actions during the whole episode. This is the genius of mind control: to influence a person's behaviour while the intended target unwittingly believes he's completely in control.

Now, imagine Roger had changed one variable in his experiment. Let's say the words he used were: "Quick! We need to get out! There's a werewolf down the corridor and boy is he pissed!" It wouldn't have had quite the same effect, would it? For a threat to be effective, it must be believable – not true, not provable, just *believable*.

One of my chief objections to Christianity is its use of the threat of damnation. The fear of hell is a believable threat to a society already steeped in a religious ideology. A warning must have credibility to work effectively, and that's where the zeitgeist comes in: "Everybody knows this, so it must be true." It's all well and good to warn someone of a *real* threat, but how often is the threat of God's judgement presented without any evidence to back it up? Instead, it relies on the zeitgeist. It depends on people being exposed to Christianity *en masse*, conditioned from birth to think, "It must be true, because I've heard it so often and everybody else around here believes it." Imagine no one had ever heard of Christianity and an archaeologist today suddenly unearthed the Gospels and told the world, "I've just learned that there's a God who holds us all in condemnation, but if we do what these scrolls say, we'll be saved." How much impact do you think that would have?

Sometimes the words are dressed up in a positive fashion – how God, in his love, sent his Son to die as a sacrifice to save us from his judgement. But the underlying message is always the same: "Unless you do what we tell you, you will be damned to hell for all eternity." The word *gospel* means "good news," but it relies on us first knowing about the "bad news" of God's judgement. The whole message boils down to love at gunpoint: "Accept the 'free gift' of my love, or face the consequences."

The bottom line is this: without evidence, the gospel doesn't mean anything. And the onus is really on the "salesman" to present you with the evidence. It's not the responsibility of those on the receiving end to go looking. I mean, do we really have to investigate the claims of every religion on the planet, just in case one of them might be true and we may miss our tiny window of opportunity to obtain salvation?

Christianity presents a message that everybody needs to hear in order to be saved from some terrible fate, but only a portion of the world ever gets to hear it. It's a game of eternity-by-postcode. If you're not lucky enough to be born in a locale where the "one true religion" gets a hearing, then it would have been better for you if you were never born. Furthermore, according to Christianity, we're born with *original sin*, a fallen nature that ensures we cannot get through life without committing sins. Despite never having a choice about whether we wish to be born, we discover that we have no choice but to become sinners, no choice about falling under God's judgement, no choice about being born in a country where we never hear the message of salvation, and no choice about suffering in hell for all eternity. Is it possible that this rigged game is a true and credible picture of what lies behind human existence?

When these problems started to finally become clear to me, after almost twenty years of experience as a Christian, I started to see what the whole game of religion was about: mind control. Christianity uses an unsubstantiated threat to control your thinking and thus dictate your behaviour. There's no other way to describe what I did when I became a Christian. I no longer had any freedom to think for myself. I could never say, "Original sin? I'm not sure about that. Maybe there's another reason for all the trouble in the world." The word of God declared it to be the truth, and so I had to believe it. Original sin and an assortment of other "truths" then shaped my character and actions.

Having the freedom to think your own thoughts means being able to make your own judgement calls on what is possible and impossible, true and untrue, right and wrong – to formulate a worldview that you have worked out with your own mind. Christianity takes that freedom away and says, "No need to think for yourself. In fact, it's perilous to do so. But never mind; we've worked it all out for you." Pre-packaged, ready-made "truth."

I recognise that not all Christians come to believe by being made afraid of judgement, and to them what I'm saying may sound offensive. You don't live in fear. I know you don't, because I didn't live in fear for most of my Christian life, either. I felt safe and secure under God's protection. But just wait till you experience doubt. It's not a comfortable spot to be in, when your mind starts seeing a different picture and you sense your faith ebbing away. When doubt grows to the extent that you think Christianity is probably false and you make the leap into disbelief, it's not pleasant to consider what might happen to your soul if you've unwittingly made a bad decision. A voice in your head cries in panic, "What if I'm wrong?" And another soothing voice says, "Look, it's much more comfortable over there. Don't think. Just believe, and you won't have to feel afraid any more." The fear of God's judgement is Christianity's big magnet, designed to pull you in and *hold* you in. God becomes the adult version of the bogeyman, a repackaging of the myth that cruel parents use to keep their children from sneaking out of bed during the night. "I don't *know* that there's a monster in my closet," muses the child. "But Daddy says there is, and I don't think he would lie, so I had better do as I'm told." Similarly, the adult says to himself, "I don't know that there's a hell. But the Church and the Bible say there is, and I don't think they would lie, so I had better do as I'm told."

French philosopher Blaise Pascal (1623-1662) crystallised this predicament in what is called Pascal's Wager. When the existence of God can neither be proved nor disproved, there is much to be gained from wagering that God exists (everlasting life) and little to be gained from wagering that he does not (annihilation at death). Conversely, one has nothing to lose in believing (the worst case scenario for the believer is annihilation), but everything to lose in disbelieving (where the worst case scenario is eternal punishment). Belief in God is therefore the best bet.

The first problem with Pascal's Wager is that it is entirely motivated by the desire for security, not truth. It is the way of the coward, who runs for cover at the first sign of danger. This mental attitude is utterly toxic to the pursuit of truth, because one's course is guided not by logic, but by emotional pressures. The reason why our beliefs are so easily shaped by our emotions can be understood by looking at prehistory. Back when we were hunter-gatherers living in the wild, the scientific method of disbelieving in something until you have sufficient evidence wouldn't have served us very well. If a man heard a bush rustling a few feet away, he had a greater survival advantage if he assumed that there was a predatory animal just out of sight beyond the leaves. That belief would cause him to act accordingly and retreat from the danger, real or imagined. There would have been a distinct survival disadvantage in taking the stance: "I will not believe there is a predator behind the bush until I part the leaves and see for myself." Evolution gave us brains that are wired for survival, not objectivity. Pursuing truth objectively requires us to overcome emotional pressures that attempt to shape our beliefs.

The next problem is that the wager fails to ask: "Which God – the God of the Christians, or the God of the Muslims?" It could be argued that both are the same God, but Christianity and Islam each claim exclusive status as the one true route to God; both warn of hell and damnation for rejecting the offer of salvation; both cannot be true. The security that Pascal's Wager proposes is an illusion. How one reacts to it depends entirely on which religion is the most familiar to the individual.

Thirdly, if one chooses to believe only because he is afraid to disbelieve, is that even genuine belief? Would an all-seeing God not see the base motive behind the outer appearance of religious conviction?

Fourthly, if Christians are having a personal relationship with God, as they often claim, how can they simultaneously speak of his existence as nothing more than the safest bet? If they know him, then no wager is needed, because he is real in personal experience. If they want to use the wager, they have to be willing to admit that they don't know God personally. They can't have it both ways.

Lastly, it is simply not true to say that there is little to be gained from wagering that God does not exist. One's whole outlook on life is determined by his philosophical and religious perspective. Make the wrong choice and you face an earthly existence (which could be your only one) that will be poisoned by falsehood.

I refused the easy route. I thought to myself, "If the threat of damnation were taken away and I had a simple choice right now of what to believe, would I continue to believe in Christianity?" The answer was no. If the only reason I had left to believe was because I was being coerced into it, then that was no good reason at all.

The judgement of God is very hard to truly believe in, even for a Christian. It's one thing to tell yourself that you believe in the reality of hell, but quite another to *actually* believe it. Looking back on my own Christian experience, I can see this self-deception in action. In 2005 my mother was dying of cancer and she was not a Christian. As she lay in hospital, I wrestled with myself: "If you don't say something to her now, before it's too late, you'll never forgive yourself." So a couple of days before the end, when she was drifting in and out of consciousness on morphine, I spoke to her briefly about my concern for her soul, asking her to get right with God. She mumbled, "I will, son," and fell right back into a drug-induced slumber. Was this genuine religious conviction, or merely comforting words from a loving mother who could not bear to see her son in distress? I never knew. And for some reason, it never became a worry for me. I remained a Christian for several years after her death, and in all that time I never had an anxious thought about the possibility that she was suffering in hell for all eternity. Such a scenario was simply unreal, even as a remote possibility. My emotions were telling me that I didn't believe in the judgement of God, while my mind was telling me I did.

If what you think and what you feel are in conflict, it may be a signal that you're lying to yourself. The next time you hear a Christian talking about hell and judgement, pay careful attention to his emotions, not just his words. You might glimpse a very revealing contradiction.

There are those who warn me about hell as if they're talking about the weather. On the opposite extreme are those who seem to take a sadistic delight in vividly describing the bodily tortures I will suffer in the lake of fire. If such persons truly believe in the judgement of God, they must be entirely without compassion for the plight of human beings. I suspect, rather, that they have as much compassion as anyone else, but are putting on a big act – to me and to themselves. Perhaps that's just as well. For how could anyone truly believe that such a horrific fate awaits the majority of the human race without it driving him insane?

SEVEN DEADLY SCHEMES

IT's not just fear of damnation that keeps a person tied to a belief he has outgrown. The fear of what others think of us is another powerful influence. A teenager with Christian parents may worry about what they will think of him if he abandons his faith, or he may not be able to face breaking their hearts. Christian parents also need to look squarely at the way they manipulate their own children by the expectations they place on them and the emotional blackmail they unconsciously subject them to. For some Christian parents, the idea of their child using his own free thinking to form his unique individual view of life is out of the question; the child must be taught only Christian views and protected from hearing anything that calls them into question, for fear that he should damn his soul to hell. In other words, he must be indoctrinated instead of educated.

When I abandoned Christianity, several close friends ostracised me from their lives. The retired pastor of the church I had attended angrily said, "You've trampled underfoot the Son of God!" – a reference to Hebrews 10:26-31, a passage condemning those who return to their sin after having known the "truth." My great sin was daring to have a metaphysical difference of opinion, and this was enough to transform me into the enemy of God. I was stunned as I watched a warm friendship of almost two decades disintegrate in the space of a few minutes. He told me he could not accept me in his home any longer because I was now under discipline by the church (whatever that meant). His wife burst out crying because of my decision, but agreed with her husband that I was no longer welcome. These people were almost like a second family to me at one point in my life, so I know what it's like to pay a high price for sticking to your convictions.

Another friend calmly told me that because I had spoken against Christianity, the friendship was over. "May God have mercy on you" were his final words. He took offence because, in his view, I was mocking his God. From my perspective, I did no such thing. I cannot mock someone I don't believe exists. This is how people react when they allow their view of life to become so *sacred* that they feel they should deny anyone else the right to call it into question. Furthermore, when a person chooses to view something as sacred, this attaches a reverence – a holy respect – to the belief that emotionally restricts the holder from ever questioning it himself. Christianity has all exits covered.

I listened to another Christian friend label me as arrogant and accuse me of lying, with angry outbursts and snide remarks. His expression of spirituality appeared anything but spiritual. What I was seeing was a dear friend determined to poison his life with bitterness. At an unconscious level, it was also emotional blackmail: the holding of a friendship to ransom unless the other party agrees to submit.

Losing friends was hard, but when I abandoned Christianity it felt like I had taken a broom and swept a big ball of dirt out of my mind. It was a breath of fresh air to finally take responsibility for my own thoughts and actions, instead of continually looking outside of myself for something else to tell me what to do.

I have no malicious agenda against Christianity. All I'm interested in is letting the truth speak for itself. If I honestly thought Christianity were true, I would be first in line to dedicate my life to Christ. But apparently I'm going to end up in hell because I'm too stupid to see the truth. Hypothetically, if I were to die and find myself face-to-face with a God who is going to judge me, what would I say in my defence for the "blasphemy" that I've written here? "I did what I thought was right" – which is all any of us can do.

I will not be as bold as to condemn all religion outright, nor even to slam Christianity in its entirety. There is value in studying religion, because religion is essentially man reaching out to something beyond the world of his senses (which tends to be labelled God). That is a noble quest, and it's the very same preoccupation of this book. Things only go wrong when religion is turned backwards and asserted as God reaching out to man. Then come claims of divinely inspired texts and divinely instituted human authorities. Religion becomes a dictatorship rather than a source of useful, if imperfect, knowledge. Unfortunately, this reversed approach constitutes the vast portion of organised religion in the West.

Authoritarian religion narrows your vision into a sharp focus by dictating "truth" and denying you the right to think anything contrary. Once you commit yourself to looking at life through that tunnel, you lose any ability to see outside of those confines. And outside might be where the real truth lies, but you'll never know unless you let yourself look. The whole manipulation game is so plain to me. When you finally see the bars on the cage you've been living in, you can't unsee them.

Based on my own experience of Christianity and my observation of it in the lives of others, I've come up with the following list of coercion tactics regularly employed by believers:

1. Implant the desired belief system in others from as young an age as possible, long before they are able to think critically.

2. Exploit the tendency of people to follow the herd. Surround them with like minds and encourage uniformity of thought.

3. Protect people from access to "dangerous" information that challenges the belief system, lest the hearers should be swayed and damn their souls.

4. Declare the belief system to be sacred, thus protecting it from examination and the potential of criticism. To think freely and depart from orthodoxy is to commit heresy.

5. Terrify unbelievers using threats of judgement, so that they will bend to your wishes. Encourage them to act immediately, rather than taking time to weigh the evidence.

6. Indulge in emotional blackmail to ensure that your loved ones don't choose a different path. Let them be aware that it would break your heart if they went their own way.

7. When loved ones reject your belief system, bully them back into submission with insults, accusations, and threats of ostracism.

The perpetrators of all of these tactics are rarely aware of the manipulative aspects of their actions. Those who act in these ways are not bad people; they are themselves victims of brainwashing. If they became aware of the harm they were doing, they would cease. Some are partially aware. This is why one Christian might shout, "Turn or burn!" to everyone in sight, while another might seek to first learn what his opponent believes then attempt to reason with him. My complaint is not that all Christians are guilty of all seven coercion tactics; this is clearly not the case. My complaint is that I never have to look very far in organised religion to see these mind games happily and blindly employed in the ongoing manipulation of humanity.

To those on the receiving end of these attempts at mind control, I suggest the following antidotes, point for point:

1. Take no opinion of another on blind trust, but start asking questions from as young an age as possible.

2. Resist your tendency to follow the herd, since the world is full of diverse herds, each one contradicting the others and clamouring for followers. Do your own individual thinking instead.

3. Seek out challenging information, because it holds the potential of exposing your errors, thus guiding you to greater truth.

4. View no assertions as sacred. It is only through criticism that we can discern truth from error.

5. Fear no claims without evidence.

6. Do what you think is right, even when it causes distress to yourself and others. Giving in to emotional blackmail means handing over control of your life to someone you think is wrong.

7. Don't give in to bullies, or you will spend your life being a victim.

I must clarify that the above points are addressed primarily to adult readers. I will add one important caveat for those living under the care of their parents. Children and teenagers cannot always afford to be quite as bold as adults. Be careful about telling your Christian parents that you're not a believer. Your mother and father may be entirely reasonable people, or they may not. Use your own judgement here. There is no value in causing your parents unnecessary emotional distress, or in provoking friction in your relationship, or in getting yourself kicked out of your own home. The latter is a rarity, but it has been known to happen. I can afford to weather the storm of broken relationships, because I'm an independent adult. But to young people I would advise: there is no need to turn your life upside down purely on principle. You may feel the urge to stand up for what you believe. I'm not saying you shouldn't; I'm only saying it may be pragmatic to bide your time.

Christian apologists like to present Christianity as a *reasonable* faith, one that is based first and foremost on an allegedly firm historical record of God's dealings with mankind. They live in a bubble of intellectual fantasy that is utterly divorced from the reality of the Christian life in the real world. They like to think that the common man rejects Christ purely out of pride and attachment to sin. The reality is that most people, whether Christian or not, have little knowledge of the historical case for Christianity. Prideful rebellion is unavoidably woven with superstitious fears of an unproven threat. In the absence of reliable facts, the dilemma of accepting or rejecting the gospel is more a matter of psychological warfare against subtle forms of coercion.

Christians, by and large, fall far short of the mark of expressing a reasonable faith. Often unable to offer a rational defence of their religion, they are certainly not using reason when they seek to convert others. Christian intellectuals need to raise their eyes from the apologetics books, emerge from their colleges, take a hard look at the *real* manner in which their religion is advanced in the world *en masse*, and stop indulging in this false ideal of Christianity's intellectual superiority, because it's nowhere to be found in practice. Over the years, I have debated with hundreds of Christians on the Internet, and a productive discussion with a rational Christian is the exception rather than the rule.

Of course, a statistical observation about bad Christian behaviour does not make Christianity false. I could rant about fire-and-brimstone fundamentalist preachers, televangelist swindlers, fraudulent faith healers, and paedophile priests. All of that may raise concerns over whether Christianity can truly live up to its claim that it changes lives for the better. But I'm not a fan of *ad hominem* arguments. Christianity ultimately stands or falls on whether its claims reflect reality as we find it. I will state my case on that issue in subsequent chapters.

My aim, presently, is to raise awareness of the mind games that are employed in the field of religion, where our natural weaknesses are exploited in order to manipulate us. Overcoming such weaknesses is vital in the pursuit of truth.

PARADIGM SWING

I was a Christian for almost two decades of my life, from ages seventeen to thirty-five. I call this my Christian period, although it might be better termed my pendulum period, because during this time I abandoned and reaffirmed my faith more times than I can remember. Sometimes the psychological squeeze of how I was supposed to think and act would become too painful, leading me to seek relief from somewhere. And escape was just too easy. All I had to do was pull down some of the unresolved questions from the dusty shelf in my mind and shine a light on them.

It's funny how one can always find a reason to believe in Christianity, or a reason to disbelieve, depending on personal needs. For some, a conversion to Christianity can initiate a life-changing experience that brings an end to alcohol abuse, drug-taking, wife-beating, or some other destructive behaviour. Such persons have so powerful a reason to believe that no argument against it can compete. However, it should be noted that for each individual who transforms his life through religion, there is someone else who makes the same positive changes without it.

Just as one person can use an emotional reason to believe, another can use an emotional reason to disbelieve. My reasons to disbelieve, I admit, were sometimes emotional rather than rational. I just couldn't take it any more. I was tired of my religion not working properly in my life. I felt confused about what was true, shackled by life-denying demands, depressed by my failure to change my life for the better, painfully aware of the constant surveillance of a divine parent that I regularly disappointed, jealous that others around me seemed to be happier.

Christians may think that I was merely victimised by a seriously imbalanced form of Christianity and that this is no reason to criticise the religion as a whole. But my experiences cannot be dismissed so easily. While my primary experience of Christianity was of a fairly strict Calvinism taught in a traditional Baptist environment, I also spent significant time under Presbyterianism and Pentecostalism. What *is* a balanced form of Christianity? I have never encountered it. Whatever the sect, the issues I was dealing with seemed to have their source in the common core of Christian belief.

I had to get out. It was either that, or continue going steadily insane. So I took a look at the Garden of Eden again, and I allowed the scientific difficulties with it to come to the fore of my mind. The more I thought about this Bible narrative, the more like a fairytale it seemed. Equipped with this, and other scriptural problems, I felt I had good grounds for abandoning ship. It seemed like I was making a rational decision, and in part this was so, but the underlying force behind it was emotional.

Our minds have this unfortunate tendency towards self-deception. Rather than seeking the truth without bias, we believe what we want to believe, then look for evidence to back up our decision while ignoring evidence to the contrary. Of course, it also has to be stated that a large part of the reason why I embraced Christianity in the first place was emotional need. If we're going to get to any real truth about life, we've got to get past our emotions and look impartially at information, even when it's painful to do so. And we've got to force ourselves to look at *all* the data, instead of cherry-picking what we like from our preferred side of the fence.

Each time I abandoned Christianity, and each time I returned to it, I felt like I was doing the right thing for the right reasons. In a sense, the reasons could only be emotional, because the rational arguments seemed inconclusive, and could support or tear down either position, depending on what angle you looked at them.

Regardless of the whys and wherefores, the lessons I learned from living a period of my life from the atheist perspective were invaluable. When I stopped being a Christian, the first thing that hit me was blissful relief, because all the psychological difficulties that came as a result of Christian teachings could now be thrown in the bin. This did not mean: "Hooray! Now I can sleep around with girls and not feel guilty. Two bottles of vodka, please, thanks very much. Hey, roll me a joint, will you?" Nothing in my lifestyle changed for the worse. On the contrary, things improved. As a Christian, I was taught that we have original sin, and if not for the grace of God we would all be running around revelling in every wickedness under the sun. Interestingly, as soon as I stepped out of the shackles of religion, I started taking *more* responsibility for my actions, not less. No longer able to fall back on God and his promise of forgiveness for every wrongdoing, I realised that it was all up to me. Any consequences, for myself or others, that would result from my actions would be real consequences that I could not take back. I did not become the monster that Christianity indicated I ought to be without God's help.

It was also a relief to be able to stop categorising everyone around me as either one of the saved or the unsaved. As a Christian, I had based my opinions of people more on what compartment they fitted into than on what their actions told me about their characters. Heaven-bound Christians by default were The Good, and hell-bound unbelievers were The Bad – maybe not bad in any overt way that you could put your finger on, but they had unclean hearts and could not be trusted in the way that a Christian could.

This attitude of mind was certainly not unique to me. It is expressed in every Christian who seeks exclusively Christian friendships. Now that I was on the outside, I could begin to see that this division of mankind was not true. There were trustworthy and untrustworthy Christians, just as there were trustworthy and untrustworthy non-Christians. I had non-Christian parents, and I'm sorry to say that to some extent I allowed my attitude to affect how close we could be. As a Christian, I always saw myself as different – an outsider in society and, to some extent, an outsider in my own family. It was good to be able to rid myself of such a mentality.

In determining how to live my life, what a breath of fresh air to be able to make a decision and not have to consult some mental list of dos and don'ts, wondering how much God was smiling or frowning upon me for my choices. Right and wrong were no longer based on lists of commandments, but on considering the consequences of my actions. I've heard Christians argue that to abandon religion is to abandon any meaningful basis for morality. But what are we – robots? Do we really need to be programmed with a list of rights and wrongs to have a meaningful sense of right and wrong? I think it seems that way to the Christian because he has been taught to believe mankind is inherently evil. Therefore to be without guidance from a higher authority is to be lost in a sea of wickedness. But is love not just as much a part of our nature as hatred? Does your pet Labrador need to consult some Doggie Bible before knowing that it's good to lick the face off you? Likewise, when a Christian says, "Oh, you don't believe in God. Why don't you lie, cheat and steal your way through life? Because if there's no one to judge you, you can do anything and get away with it." Well, if we love others only because we're afraid of what will happen to us if we don't, that's not much of a basis for morality. How about loving because we *want* to love, because it's in our nature?

I went through a joyous honeymoon period when I abandoned religion, but a honeymoon was all it was, because there were certain realities I had to face. Without religion, it seemed I had to let go of certain concepts that were tied to religion. Now there could be no answers to prayer, no divinely guided plan for my life; I had no soul, and there was no afterlife. All of these were religious ideas and they had to go. The world quickly became a cold and impersonal place. But maybe that was okay, and maybe that was something that ought to be faced.

The problem was that my own future death was going to make a mockery out of all my accomplishments in life; nothing would have any lasting significance. Thousands of precious memories would die as soon as my brain switched itself off. An unfortunate consequence of my atheistic outlook was depression. It wasn't a big deal, just a minor irritation that gnawed at me. I would be out on my bicycle, enjoying a ride through beautiful countryside on a warm summer day. All five senses in my body are feeding me pleasure, but my joy is poisoned by a subtle sense of gloom that never quite goes away. A nagging inner voice says, "Someday you will be dead, and none of this will have mattered."

Consider a scientist who dedicates his life to improving the world. Let's say he makes some great discovery that revolutionises all our lives for the better. This would seem to inject a great deal of meaning into his life, significance that certainly continues long after his death. But where is the world heading? To oblivion, just as every human organism heads to oblivion. All matter is subject to decay. Even if humanity gets through the next few hundred years without bringing about some global apocalypse, one day the sun is going to perish. What becomes of the human race then? What becomes of that great body of scientific knowledge we've dedicated a staggering amount of time and energy into creating? It will be as if the human race never existed. Not even the memory of it will remain, because there isn't a mind left to house it.

As an atheist, this was my reality. I said to myself, "It doesn't matter. We humans have an inflated view of our own importance in the Universe. Mortal is what we are, what we're supposed to be, and all we'll ever be. And mortality is enough." But is it enough? Why did I feel a continual sense of urgency that I was running out of time? Why did I find my most pleasurable experiences continually tainted with sorrow? Why was there always a feeling of emptiness nagging at me? It's because I had faced reality. Never was life defined better than in Shakespeare's *Macbeth*: "It is a tale told by an idiot, full of sound and fury, signifying nothing."

"Well, face it," says the atheist. "Wishing it otherwise doesn't make it so." I did face it. And it depressed the hell out of me. It became the emotional trigger that made me yearn for the sense of meaning that Christianity provided.

Now that I had been away from religion for a period, I was able to look back with rose-tinted glasses, forgetting all the negative aspects of the experience. Christianity wasn't all bad. I enjoyed some great times of fellowship, and learned some genuine insights about life from the Bible, amid all the other confusion. And so, I placed all my unresolved problems with Christianity back onto the shelf in my mind, and I returned home like the prodigal son.

But nothing had been fixed. All the same issues I had before I left were waiting to leap back into my experience. There was no solution, no peace to be had. And so, over the years, I became like a swinging pendulum, pulled back and forth by opposing forces, never able to sit still and accept one position or the other. A Christian one month, an atheist the next – back and forth.

Aside from letting my heart rule my head, the futility of life without God was a strong *rational* indicator that atheism was wrong. Let's assume for a moment that atheism truly is the enlightened viewpoint. By implication, then, the enlightened man is the depressed man. But that didn't make any sense. Was it rational to think that man, in his most enlightened state, would be depressed by his own existence? Or was the depression nature's way of telling me: "You're not seeing this correctly." The Universe is teeming with vitality; are we really supposed to spend our days battling sorrow over our mortality? It seemed an absurd predicament. So, if nihilism was absurd, and nihilism was the direct consequence of atheism, wouldn't that make atheism absurd?

Where I had been going wrong all this time was in assuming that I had only two choices: Christianity or atheism. On the one hand, I inherited all the trappings of authoritarian religion, which caused me so much suffering. On the other hand, atheism seemed to lead inevitably to a nihilistic outlook on life, which was intolerable in the long run. What I was also doing, without realising it, was gravitating towards an established belief system – seeking to align myself with an existing herd. Each time I changed my mind, I was making a huge paradigm shift at a totally unconscious level.

We find a useful analogy of this in the "snap to grid" feature from computer drawing programs. Let's say you want to draw a rectangle that's exactly 5.3 by 8.2 cm. When "snap to grid" is active, the program forces your rectangle into either 5.0 by 8.0 or 6.0 by 9.0, refusing you access to any position in between. Our lazy brains seem inclined to play "snap to grid" with our beliefs.

The failure of a particular religious ideology to live up to its claims is an entirely distinct question from the matters of whether there is a creator, whether we have souls that survive death, whether the supernatural or miraculous ever invades human experience. Yet when a person rejects Christianity, entire modes of thinking are transformed. The theist becomes the atheist; the religionist becomes the secularist; the supernaturalist becomes the naturalist; the transcendentalist becomes the material minimalist. These changes often occur at an unconscious level, as we pull ourselves away from one ready-made system and snap to another. Perhaps some of these shifts are right and proper. My only point is that they should not be happening without your conscious awareness.

Eventually I came to see that the truth was not on one side or the other. In fact, the root of all my problems was an underlying issue that was prevalent in both worldviews: the belief in mind-body dualism, the view that the mind is an actual entity distinct from the body (distinct even from the material of the brain). Regardless of religious influence, we tend to believe this because it reflects how we intuitively feel about ourselves. Meanwhile, science, at the basic high school level, doesn't refute it. So it's no surprise that many atheists are dualists. From a human perspective, dualism provokes feelings of loneliness, urgency, and depression, as the mind views its position as a very real entity, stuck inside a dying body, living in a hostile Universe. The Christian deals with this by indulging in the fantasy that the mind is divinely protected and will live forever, while the atheist deals with it by becoming saddened over the fact that the mind is as vulnerable and mortal as the body. But strange as it may sound, dualism is dead. I don't expect the reader to accept that statement at face value, but a large portion of this book will be devoted to convincing you of it. Some esoteric forms of ancient religion express the fallacy of dualism, as does quantum physics (a branch of science that examines the strange behaviour of subatomic particles). Unfortunately, most of us only get to see the exoteric side of religion and science, both of which ensnare us in a purely dualistic view of the human condition. Looking back, I can see clearly that this was the source of all my confusion.

To be fair, not all atheists are dualists. Those with an understanding of quantum physics might view reality as a *field*, where no part (including mind) is separate from the whole at a fundamental level of being. This provides a radically different framework for understanding one's own existence from the Newtonian mechanics that we learn at school. Most of us finish our education and go forth into the world viewing the Universe as an unconscious machine made out of bits and pieces. Absolute reality consists of particles of matter that are fundamentally separate from each other, stacked together like LEGO blocks in three-dimensional space. Contrasted with the whole Universe, a person seems very small and insignificant. Whether I chose the church or the classroom, I couldn't make sense of my existence, because I was seeing my mind, my body, and the Universe in terms of duality, separateness, alienation.

How does an appreciation of the Universe as non-dual change anything? In short, because there is no *you* separate from the whole. But a mere anecdote will not suffice. We will tackle this question comprehensively in part 2.

A rational atheist with a high school education might assert: "I believe in science. I've got no time for any mystical mumbo-jumbo." It's easy to see why such an attitude prevails, because science has provided us with an ever-increasing understanding of reality. We feel that it's only a matter of time before we find all the answers. This is a subtle trap, because when we look deeply at reality, we observe that there are particular areas in which a scientific approach fails us. There are places where we come across the infinite, and the infinite simply refuses to be bound and measured. There isn't a box big enough to fit infinity. For instance, the trillionth, trillionth, trillionth decimal place of the number pi (π) is a particular digit between zero and nine, but it would take much longer than a human lifetime to work it out, and even then you're barely getting started with the actual value of pi. If you had enough time, you could go on uncovering another trillion, trillion, trillion, trillion, trillion decimal places. Pi has no end, and yet paradoxically every single one of its decimal places has a discrete value that is in no sense random, no matter how deep you go.

This simple mathematical example shows that infinity is something quite real, yet utterly ungraspable within space-time. No matter how hard you try, you can't get hold of it in its entirety. And yet infinity is an aspect of reality. It follows logically that a complete picture of reality cannot be uncovered by sciences that are able to deal only with finite categorisations. The acceptance of this logic is the heart of metaphysics.

By contrast, the failure to grasp this breeds the sort of rationalist who thinks that the Big Bang explains the origin of the Universe. But when carefully examined, what it really does is confront us with the mystery of the infinite. And so, the need to develop a metaphysical model of reality becomes inescapable.

It's vital to understand that science is a process, not an endpoint. What we often think of as truth in science is merely a point in this process. Consider the transition from Newtonian mechanics to quantum mechanics. It really was a case of back to the drawing board – a complete rethinking of the entire nature of reality in a new and unfamiliar framework.

There are those who feel that we are on the cusp of understanding everything, and there are those who feel that what we currently know about reality is merely the tip of the iceberg. Which perspective is the more accurate? The scientist tends to favour the former, while the mystic favours the latter. But how would we possibly know? We are simply at a point in the process of science. If we say it is a point close to the finish line, how do we justify that? We would have to be in possession of a Theory of Everything to know how close we are to attaining a Theory of Everything. And that's logically absurd.

We can now begin to see the value of more abstract ways of reasoning, because they allow us to think far ahead of the point in science where we happen to be stuck at present. We permit our minds to take intuitive leaps, to play with ideas that cannot be proved empirically, but which allow us to theorise in ways that make greater overall sense of the Universe than the picture that emerges from our present scientific proofs alone. Later, our more daring theories may be proved right or wrong. A lack of certainty in the present is not reason enough to hold oneself back from creative thinking. Judging by the amount of science that ends up being amended or replaced, we can hardly claim that our present point in the process is the ultimate irreplaceable truth, can we? Furthermore, should we say that the ancient Greeks were wrong to theorise about the existence of the atom, just because they didn't have the advantage of an electron microscope? Among the great minds in science I see a willingness to think outside the box, but among the educated public I perceive a deadness of creativity born out of a one-dimensional mode of thinking.

Another stumbling block for the unwary in the field of science stems from how we use language. When we attach a label to something, it's tempting to assume that we now know what that thing is. If I ask the question, "What is life?" I can only give an answer by contrasting life with what is not life. So I might note the differences between a rock and a creature, and talk about such aspects as movement, growth, replication, mutation, DNA. This comparison lulls me into thinking that I've grasped what life is, but if I pause for a moment and really think about the question, it hits me that I have no idea what life is. I can describe observable characteristics, but ultimately I'm faced with the fact that life is a fundamentally mysterious thing.

Science boils down to a self-referencing system of symbols relating to the world of experience. Simply put, we understand A in relation to B, and B in relation to A, and then we pretend to ourselves that we know absolutely what A is and what B is. We're really dealing with a mass of abstractions that are all relative to each other. We never get to the *essence* of anything. The tragic result of a reliance on any single self-referencing system is a loss of awareness that there is a fundamental mystery behind the Universe itself.

When Albert Einstein famously said, "God does not play dice with the world," this was not an admission that he was a Christian, or even a believer in a divinity with a personality and character, as God is depicted in so much of religion. He clarified: "I believe in Spinoza's God who reveals Himself in the orderly harmony of what exists, not in a God who concerns Himself with fates and actions of human beings" (*Albert Einstein: Philosopher-Scientist* [1949], edited by Paul Arthur Schilpp). Einstein appreciated the term God as an abstraction. He had an awareness of the abstract nature of language. In defending his "religious" inclinations, he explained: "Try and penetrate with our limited means the secrets of nature and you will find that, behind all the discernible concatenations, there remains something subtle, intangible and inexplicable. Veneration for this force beyond anything that we can comprehend is my religion. To that extent I am, in point of fact, religious" (*Einstein and Religion* [1999] by Max Jammer).

Behind all our science is an inability to get to the bottom of the fundamental mystery of existence. The failure to recognise this results in the erroneous sense that you *know* more than you know, breeding a misplaced confidence that scientific investigation alone can answer every question we could possibly ask. What is life? We don't know. Furthermore, we *can't* know, because we are stuck with a self-referencing system of abstractions.

Science tends to operate under an assumption of determinism, the view that the Universe is totally explainable in mechanistic terms. This is understandable, because we are able to find clear patterns of order in the Universe that can be supported with mathematical equations. But is *everything* explainable in this way? We casually assume so, purely because of science's track record of ongoing successes. It lulls us into thinking that there is no limit on a human's ability to understand reality. Strictly speaking, we could only know that no such limit exists if we already possessed a Theory of Everything. In the absence of that, scientists sometimes make the *philosophical assumption* that determinism rules supreme. But in truth, the jury's out. Let's speculate for a moment that the nature of reality is ultimately non-deterministic. The startling implications of that would be that *science cannot completely explain reality*, because science deals only in what is mechanistic in nature. Science is fantastic, but you'd better make room for the philosophy of science, or you will end up making assumptions that you don't know you're making. Without a Theory of Everything, relying exclusively on science is like a runner shouting "I win!" while he's still running the race.

By science alone, we end up viewing the Universe as a lifeless automatic machine, where the Earth somehow became a life-infested rock. Life is viewed as an anomaly that just happened to sprout when certain conditions were met in the random flux of non-conscious energy; life is nothing more than an extremely complex arrangement of clockwork mechanisms craftily pretending that it's more. Feelings of insignificance, alienation and meaninglessness are the natural consequences of this view. Religion, for all of its problems, at least begins with an appreciation of transcendent mystery, and thus avoids the sort of myopic worldview that an exclusive reliance on science tends to stimulate.

When we're ready to admit that we can only know what life is by abstraction, it then becomes possible to model the Universe differently. Life (whatever that is) exists on Earth precisely because life is a property of the Universe. The Universe is, in some sense, alive. This position makes so much more sense than a fully automatic Universe containing a life-infested rock. Life does not come from non-life. If it did, then we're all technically zombies. When I say to an atheist, "The Universe is alive," he may ask, "Define what you mean by life." At this point, I am stumped for words, because I am alluding to something deeply mysterious. This failure to answer the question might be seen as a victory for the atheist, yet he is working under the false assumption that *he* understands what life is, merely because he can provide a description of it using the symbols of his self-referencing system.

The role of science is to figure out how the Universe works, while the concern of philosophy is to answer questions that are deemed metaphysical. The prefix *meta* means at a more abstract level. So metaphysics tackles issues that physics can't, such as the fundamental ground of being. Science may offer important data on philosophical issues, but it is shortsighted to assume from the outset that science can replace philosophy entirely. The scientist is compelled to think in a manner that demands evidence, while the philosopher is permitted to construct abstract models in an effort to best explain the mystery of existence. Those models must not be opposed to the clear findings of science, but they are allowed to be more speculative where science is silent. Actually, speculation does rear its head in the field of science, too. For instance, there is a theory that the Big Bang gave birth to many parallel universes, each one having different physical laws. This is one way of explaining why the laws of physics in our Universe are so finely tuned to support life. Give yourself a zillion universes to play with and among all the duds there will be at least one happy accident: ours. Since each of these universes is cordoned off from all others, there's no way to prove they even exist. So we see that the methods of philosophy and science are entwined, not just in the manner of good science replacing bad philosophy, but also scientists relying on the toolkit of philosophy (speculation) to get themselves out of a jam. Where science speaks, philosophy must concede; where science is silent, philosophy must press on.

Those who live by scientific investigation alone, to the exclusion of wider philosophical reasoning, are simply falling in line with the method of thinking they inherited through their schooling. They've got one tool in their box and they're shouting, "This is the only tool! All other tools are broken and useless!" Not so. They've got a really good tool, but it has particular limits in what it can accomplish. And when you reach those limits, you don't keep foolishly chipping away with the same tool; you grab a different one. The original name given to science was natural philosophy. It was viewed, not as our sole means of determining truth, but as a particular branch of philosophy concerned with examining the physical Universe.

When a religionist relies totally on an internally consistent self-referencing system that he calls, for instance, Reformed Theology, he has great confidence in the truth of his religion, because he sees how everything fits neatly together. Unfortunately, this same myopia can easily infect those who rely totally on an internally consistent self-referencing system called science. All things look true from a limited point of view. Getting to the real truth involves looking at the Universe from many more angles than the few that are handed to us in our particular cultural neck of the woods.

The herd mentality expresses itself in the field of science, just like it manifests in religion. It exists at a deep and unconscious level within us, but when we eventually see it – when what was unconscious becomes conscious – all its power to control us is gone. And finally we're in a position to pursue the truth with unclouded minds.

REASON VERSUS REVELATION

W HAT is authentic Christianity? There are many factions claiming to represent the true essence of the religion, from Roman Catholicism, to Eastern Orthodox, along with all the sects of Protestantism, and a handful of independent cults. Which one hits the bullseye? Do any of them? Perhaps the best way to answer this question is to step back from the clamouring voices and attempt to ascertain which modern expression of Christianity is most in keeping with the original religion of the first century.

In pursuing this line of enquiry, we discover that early Christianity took three centuries to fully crystallise into a definite shape – and the end product was Roman Catholicism. Protestants must understand that embryonic Christianity (to coin a term for the early period) was not based upon the principles of Protestantism. There was no New Testament to act as a governing authority in the lives of Christians; it hadn't yet been collated into a single volume. Nor was it entirely clear which writings in circulation were authentic and which fraudulent. Believers originally looked to the twelve apostles of Jesus for divine guidance. The apostles later passed this responsibility on to successors, who were called bishops. This is termed *apostolic succession*. Bishops carried exactly the same divine authority, when expressing collective agreement on matters of faith and morals. The original Christian religion was an institution rooted principally in the authority of *men*, not scripture. This is why the Catholic Church has always emphasised the importance of its traditions, alongside the Bible.

The leadership of the Church held authority over the minds of its followers because it was believed that Jesus himself had instituted this organisation, giving the apostle Peter the position of prime leadership: "You are Peter, and on this rock I will build my church, and the gates of Hades will not overcome it" (Matthew 16:18). There's a subtle play on words in this verse, which is lost in the translation from the original Greek into English. The name Peter in Greek means rock. So when Jesus says "this rock," he is referring directly to Peter, not to some physical rock in his vicinity. From this verse, Catholics believe that St. Peter was the first pope, and his authority has ever since been handed down to successors.

By contrast, Protestants deny the supreme authority of the magisterium of the Church (that is, the pope and bishops), making it subordinate to the scriptures. Divine authority is enshrined in the New Testament as the final revelation of God. This principle is called *sola scriptura*, Latin for "by scripture alone" – the view that the Bible is the inerrant word of God and the supreme authority for the Christian religion.

I grew up in a Protestant subculture and found the ideas of Catholicism strange: the veneration of Mary as the mother of God, the use of images in worship, the role of a priest absolving a confessor of sin. I could find no evidence for these practices in the Bible. "How can Catholics fall for this rubbish?" I wondered. What I failed to understand was that Roman Catholicism was not based on *sola scriptura*, but on traditions established by the allegedly infallible teachings of the apostles' successors.

Protestants are often highly critical of Roman Catholicism, sometimes to the point of asserting that Catholicism is not legitimate Christianity. How does the Protestant account for the fact that embryonic Christianity was not based on the principles of Protestantism, nor did it evolve into Protestantism, but into Catholicism? From the fourth to the sixteenth century, Christianity *was* Roman Catholicism. During this period of more than a millennium, Protestantism did not exist, and nothing like it existed. The Bible was not revered as the supreme rule of Christianity. The magisterium of the Church was equally supreme, and this included the power to decide which books should be included in the New Testament and which should not. It was also the bishops' business to interpret the Bible on behalf of the masses.

In the fourth century, various writings were collected into what we call the New Testament. This volume is regarded as authoritative because, and only because, the Church declared it so. What I mean by authoritative is that the New Testament contains an accurate historical record of the teachings of Christ and the apostles. In Catholicism, the matter of infallibility rests with the apostles and their successors, right down to the present day, and is restricted to collective agreement on matters of faith and morals alone. A maverick bishop expressing a pet theory is not said to be infallible, nor is infallibility to be confused with impeccability; a pope may still be a villain (as history attests). Infallibility in matters of faith and morals also lets the Church off the hook for any errors in other fields, such as cosmology.

Protestantism originated in the sixteenth century as an objection to corrupt practices in the Catholic Church. This protest, known as the Reformation, was a rebellion of the highest order, a questioning of the authority of the Holy Church itself. This move was completely understandable, as there was a huge gulf between the ideals of the New Testament and the corrupt practices of the magisterium. What else could the true disciple do but oppose a religion that had already divorced itself from the principles of its founder? It was necessary to pick a side – the bishops or the scriptures – and it was not possible to have both.

The only problem with this is that Christianity had never, in its entire history, been based solely upon the authority of the New Testament. That authority had always been on an equal footing with magisterial authority. Ideally, the magisterium and the scriptures were supposed to complement each other. But they didn't, and that was the crux of the whole crisis. The original protest that would evolve into Protestantism started, not as a rejection of the Roman Catholic Church, but as an attempt to reform it. When this failed, it then became necessary to abandon the Church altogether and reinvent Christianity in a new form – not its original form, but a form never before seen. *Sola scriptura* was a new move.

Protestants deny the infallibility of the Church leadership, but affirm the infallibility of the words of the Bible. The unfortunate tendency is to treat the New Testament like a document that fell out of heaven, straight from God to man. Some Protestants take this position to such an extreme that they regard the King James Version of the Bible alone as authoritative, refusing to see any value in modern translations. So, which Bible was authoritative *before* the KJV (completed in 1611)? Seemingly, the question has never occurred to them, nor are they willing to take notice of the fact that the modern translations have corrected many errors in the KJV.

A slightly more defensible Protestant view is that only the original texts were inspired by God. These are, unfortunately, lost, since they were commonly written on papyrus, a material that degrades easily over time. The copies are subject to accidental transcription errors, deliberate editing, and imprecision of translation. So today's Bible is regarded as imperfectly inspired.

Then there is the matter of ascertaining how we should determine which particular books are inspired, since many were excluded from the canon. Authorship of the gospels of Matthew and John is traditionally ascribed to the apostles of Jesus so named, but neither Mark nor Luke was among that group. So we cannot appeal to apostleship as the signature of divine inspiration. The Protestant is in the unfortunate position of having to concede that the "correct" canon of the New Testament was ultimately decided by a bunch of Catholic bishops, whose divine authority he curiously doesn't recognise. Generally speaking, Protestants tend to blindly trust that the providence of God oversaw the selection of the books. Mind you, that didn't stop the founder of Protestantism, Martin Luther (1483-1546), attempting to have Hebrews, James, Jude and Revelation removed.

Christian apologist Josh McDowell, in *The New Evidence that Demands a Verdict* (1999), writes at length on the issue of how the Christian can defend the New Testament as the word of God. He states his case by going right back to the first centuries of Christianity, but fails to make a single mention of apostolic succession, creating a false impression that Protestantism's *sola scriptura* was in effect from the beginning.

If the claims of Protestantism, at its origin, were correct, then the previous fifteen hundred years was a long, long expanse of time for Christianity to be in the wrong. Protestants must face up to the shocking historical implications of their viewpoint: God chose to keep his Church in spiritual darkness for one and a half millennia before finally putting it on the right track. Think of all the generations that have come and gone, knowing nothing but this darkness, then attempt to reconcile that with Jesus' prophecy: "I will build my church and the gates of Hades will not overcome it"?

Regardless of what the Protestant finds contemptible about Catholicism, he is faced with the insurmountable problem of being unable to trace Protestantism back to Christ without it *becoming* Catholicism in the process. The first Protestants shook their fists, understandably, at the Catholic Church's abuses of power. Even so, there is no denying that historical Christianity *is* Roman Catholicism.

* * *

Martin Luther was Protestantism's prime mover and is hailed as a hero by Protestants to this day. But I suspect that few of them have read his actual words. So, without further ado, take it away, Martin:

Reason is the Devil's greatest whore; by nature and manner of being she is a noxious whore; she is a prostitute, the Devil's appointed whore; whore eaten by scab and leprosy who ought to be trodden under foot and destroyed, she and her wisdom ... Throw dung in her face to make her ugly. She is and she ought to be drowned in baptism ... She would deserve, the wretch, to be banished to the filthiest place in the house, to the closets.

Martin Luther (Erlangen Edition)

There is on earth among all dangers no more dangerous thing than a richly endowed and adroit reason ... Reason must be deluded, blinded, and destroyed.

Martin Luther, quoted by Walter Kaufmann, *The Faith of a Heretic*

Christianity, whether Catholic or Protestant, places revelation on a higher platform than reason. This means that direct communication from God trumps anything that man might figure out with his brain. Many Christians today view science as important, but when man's reason clashes with God's revelation, the Christian will choose God every time. In the present climate, this is what accounts for the high proportion of Christians who deny the theory of evolution, for it flies in the face of the doctrine of original sin.

Of course, the problem with this argument is: how do you know the Bible is God's revelation, unless you arrive at that conclusion by a process of reasoning? In Luther's day, the divine inspiration of the Bible was considered a self-evident truth, by virtue of its widespread acceptance in Western civilisation under the Church's long-term dominance. To a lesser extent, this kind of conditioning is still prevalent today. People believe that the Bible is God's word and they don't know why, other than to admit that they've been taught this from the cradle. This is, of course, the very same trick that is played upon the citizens of Utah (the capital of Mormonism) with the Book of Mormon, Israel with the Tanakh, and Islamic countries with the Qur'an.

I've encountered Christians who deny the importance of reason. They will say something like, "The Holy Spirit speaks to my heart, and that's how I know. Nothing you say can change my mind." This is merely a convenient cop-out that allows them to excuse themselves from difficult debate without losing face. There is no greater a lost cause than a person who abandons the necessity of critical thinking while fully believing that he cannot be wrong.

Revelation cannot trump reason, because reason must be used to validate revelation. Unfortunately, reason *invalidates* revelation, as we will shortly discover. The best we might say about the Protestant Reformation is that it was an attempt to rescue Christianity, to restart a failing ideology in a new and different form. For a while, it was successful. But today, due to the positive impact of science upon human understanding, we can see that Luther's condemnation of reason was a grave error. It's high time for Christianity to undergo another reformation, to re-emerge in a new and fully science-affirming form. But could it survive such a transition?

What we have at present is a religion that survives by misrepresenting science. When reason confronts revelation, scripture is caught between a rock and a hard place. The dogma-defender is left with the choice of either moving deeper into irrationality, or bending science to fit scripture – which is a totally unscientific move. The notion that Christianity and science fit together as complementary branches of God's truth is untenable. Revelation and reason are sometimes in conflict, and this means that we are faced with the necessity of picking a side.

Some Christians may object: "We are not all Bible literalists. I do not believe in a literal seven-day creation. I recognise that the Bible was not written as a science textbook for twenty-first century humans. The original readers were much more primitive in their understanding of nature, and so the creation account was written in a manner relevant to them." I completely agree, but unfortunately St. Paul, author of most of the New Testament epistles, does not. He explicitly bases the following teaching about the role of women on his belief that the first man was literally created before the first woman, and the first ever sin was committed specifically by a woman, not a man, just like it says in the account of the Garden of Eden:

A woman should learn in quietness and full submission. I do not permit a woman to teach or to assume authority over a man; she must be quiet. For Adam was formed first, then Eve. And Adam was not the one deceived; it was the woman who was deceived and became a sinner.

1 Timothy 2:11-14

You'll rarely hear a sermon on those verses preached in church today. I can be a little sexist myself at times, in that I acknowledge there are some things men do better than women (and, importantly, there are other things women do better than men). St. Paul, however, knew how to take it to an extreme. But I'm not overly interested in condemning him for his cultural conditioning; my main point is that he was a literalist in his view of the creation account. And if literalism doesn't hold true, then any moral principles that are derived from literalism are void. If we accept that man was not literally created before woman, we can't then assert, "Man is boss because man came first." Yet that's exactly how St. Paul thought, and that's exactly what he said, under inspiration of the Holy Spirit, apparently. He was a literalist through and through, and his outdated logic is forever enshrined in the scriptures. So how can the Christian possibly defend the divine inspiration of the Bible or the infallibility of the apostles?

Literalism seems to serve Christians perfectly well until some scientific finding or cultural development ends up calling a Bible assertion into question. Then begins a process of cherry-picking and back-pedalling in an attempt to maintain credibility. Taking this approach, what you end up with is a lukewarm version of Christianity that is destined to suffer from ever increasing erosion.

As long as science continues to be appreciated as a vital means of determining truth, and as long as a high value is placed on the secular education of the public, it is inevitable that Christianity will ultimately be doomed to obsolescence. The more information that science reveals about reality, the more it becomes clear that the claims of Christianity do not reflect reality. This is *the* point on which Christianity stands or falls. We will discuss some poignant examples of the clash between science and scripture in forthcoming chapters.

A contemporary Christian who has never examined the history of his religion may have the rose-tinted perspective that Christianity is thriving in the modern world. But when compared to the dominance that the Church enjoyed in the Middle Ages, what we are seeing today, by comparison, could be something close to Christianity's last gasp.

HISTORY IN HIDING

CHRISTIANITY (before it was called Christianity) began as a sect of Judaism. The original intention of its founder Jeshua (Jesus) was not to start a new religion, but to reform the existing religion of the Jews. The religious leaders didn't take kindly to his interference, and in the end Jesus ruffled enough feathers to get himself killed. But that was not the end of Christianity. It was much more influential among Gentiles (non-Jews) and evolved into a religion entirely separate from Judaism.

The message of Christianity was communicated from place to place, and across time, as an oral tradition, the stories of Jesus being passed around by word of mouth. Later, these were written down as gospels. From 50 to 150 AD, a number of documents were circulating among churches, consisting of gospels, epistles, acts, apocalypses, homilies, and collections of teachings. Some of these were documents that made it into the Bible as we know it today; others were not included. In early Christian history, these documents were not yet regarded as authoritative scripture on par with the Old Testament. The Church was more concerned with practical and moral matters than with theology. Between 140 and 200 AD, Christianity began to organise its teachings. This was done as a defence against the rise of several alternative versions of Christianity (derisively referred to as heresies): Marcionism, Gnosticism and Montanism.

When it came time to decide on a definitive list of books (called a canon) that would become the New Testament, there was much debate over which books should be included and which discarded as fraudulent. Among the documents under consideration were the following (which may be unfamiliar to Bible readers, as they were ultimately rejected): Hermas, Wisdom, the Acts of Paul, 3 Corinthians, Barnabas, Didache, the Revelation of Peter, the Shepherd, the Gospel According to the Hebrews, the Gospel of the Egyptians, the Preaching of Peter, the Traditions of Matthias, the Sibylline Oracles, and the Oral Gospel. Several Church bishops suggested canons, but none were in complete agreement. There was widespread accord about certain books (the four gospels: Matthew, Mark, Luke and John), and much disagreement over others (especially the epistles of John and Revelation).

How did this entangled mess of information and misinformation get sorted out? A defining moment was the First Council of Nicaea (325 AD), under the leadership of Emperor Constantine of Rome. Constantine had become a Christian in 312 AD, and he later declared Christianity to be the state religion of Rome. This imbued Christianity with a power it had never possessed before. Bishops assembled for the First Council of Nicaea and decided upon what would become known as the Nicene Creed – a definitive statement of what Christianity was to be from then on. The significance of the fourth century (as opposed to the first) in defining the shape of Christianity is evidenced by the fact that, to this day, we refer to the *Roman* Catholic Church.

The final decision on which books would be included in (and excluded from) the New Testament canon was made at the Synod of Hippo (393 AD). The list included all the books found in our modern New Testament. The original Catholic Bible also included several inter-testamental apocryphal works, whereas Protestant Bibles today omit these as non-inspired. Protestant scholars will argue that the Church's original choice of "divinely inspired" books was correct because God's providence oversaw the decisions. How then do they justify the removal of several of them over a thousand years later?

Today's Christian apologists tend to assert that highly rational criteria went into judging whether a document should be canonised, as though the bishops of antiquity reasoned in the scientific manner of the modern age. This is a gross exaggeration of the reality. Consider the distinctly unscientific thinking of the early Church father St. Irenaeus in the second century, on the matter of why there ought to be four gospels:

The Gospels could not possibly be either more or less in number than they are. Since there are four zones of the world in which we live, and four principal winds, while the Church is spread over all the earth, and the pillar and foundation of the Church is the gospel, and the Spirit of life, it fittingly has four pillars, everywhere breathing out incorruption and revivifying men. From this it is clear that the Word, the artificer of all things, being manifested to men gave us the gospel, fourfold in form but held together by one Spirit. As David said, when asking for his coming, "O sitter upon the cherubim, show yourself." For the cherubim have four faces, and their faces are images of the activity of the Son of God. For the first living creature, it says, was like a lion, signifying his active and princely and royal character; the second was like an ox, showing his sacrificial and priestly order; the third had the face of a man, indicating very clearly his coming in human guise; and the fourth was like a flying eagle, making plain the giving of the Spirit who broods over the Church. Now the Gospels, in which Christ is enthroned, are like these.

St. Irenaeus, *Against Heresies*

St. Irenaeus's insistence on four legitimate gospels boils down to an entirely subjective game of join the dots, wherein he attempts to imbue the number four with mystical significance. When such blatantly irrational thinking was the norm in ancient times, it's difficult to have any confidence in the canon of the New Testament as divinely chosen.

Researching the history of Christianity reveals a minefield of potentially wrong conclusions. Part of the problem with getting to the truth is that some scholars approach history with the intention of making Christianity look as good as possible. Richard Bewes, author of *The Resurrection: Fact or Fiction?* (1989), asserts that the gospels of Matthew, Mark and Luke must surely reflect accurate history because three distinct authors recount the same events with astounding accuracy. This argument looks good on the surface, until you do a little more research. Most scholars tend to regard the Gospel of Mark as the earliest written of the three in question. It was then used as a source from which Matthew and Luke extracted material for their individual texts. The gospels of Matthew and Luke, written independently of each other, also feature common material not found in Mark, so scholars postulate that there was another source: Q, a hypothetical lost document containing sayings of Jesus. Matthew and Luke (but not Mark) drew information from Q. This scenario perfectly explains the commonalities in the three gospels; the resurrection was not corroborated by multiple sources in the way that Bewes suggests.

Bewes was also happy to quote the Jewish historian, Josephus (born 37/38 AD), as evidence:

Now there was about this time Jesus, a wise man, *if it be lawful to call him a man,* for he was a doer of wonderful works, a teacher of such men as receive the truth with pleasure. He drew over to him both many of the Jews, and many of the Gentiles. *He was the Christ,* and when Pilate, at the suggestion of the principal men among us, had condemned him to the cross, those that loved him at the first did not forsake him; *for he appeared to them alive again the third day; as the divine prophets had foretold these and ten thousand other wonderful things concerning him.* And the tribe of Christians so named from him are not extinct at this day.

Flavius Josephus, *Antiquities of the Jews*
[emphasis mine]

Christians sometimes use this passage as evidence that Jesus was a real man who did the miraculous deeds recorded in the New Testament. But with a little additional research we learn that this passage has been disputed since the 17th century, and from the 18th century the consensus view among historians has been that the references to Jesus were not in the original text but were deliberately inserted in a later edition. It's not hard to see the logic. Would a Jew really say of Jesus, "He was the Christ"? Clearly not, since the Jewish people rejected him as their messiah, except for those Jews who converted to Christianity. Josephus was not numbered among them. So how much or how little of the quoted passage was in the original edition? That's up for debate, but Christians will typically side with whatever allows them to best defend their position. In other words, they claim that only the bits

I've italicised were additions. The truth is, we just don't know. The passage was clearly tampered with for the purpose of defending Christianity. How much or how little is unknown. Since no firm conclusion can be made, no evidence for the historicity of Jesus can be drawn from it.

Knowledgeable Christians also like to use the example of the first century Roman historian, Tacitus (circa 55-120 AD), in defence of the historicity of Jesus. Tacitus recounts the great fire of Rome, for which some blamed Emperor Nero:

To get rid of the report, Nero fastened the guilt and inflicted the most exquisite tortures on a class hated for their abominations, called Christians by the populace. Christus, from whom the name had its origin, suffered the extreme penalty during the reign of Tiberius at the hands of one of our procurators, Pontius Pilate, and a most mischievous superstition, thus checked for the moment, again broke out ...

Cornelius Tacitus, *Annals*

The above reference certainly lends credibility to the view that Jesus was a real person, but does more harm than good to the notion that his miraculous deeds were well attested. Note that Christianity is referred to as a "mischievous superstition." Indeed, the only records we possess of the miracles of Jesus are the Gospels themselves. We might also mention the miracles in various apocryphal writings of the period, but Christian scholars themselves deny the veracity of these documents, so we needn't go there. On a side note: I can't help but smile when I hear a Christian apologist marvelling at the remarkable consistency of the Bible as a whole. Since the early Christian bishops gave themselves permission to exclude from the canon any book that proved inconsistent, of course the Bible would be consistent!

Even without the record of Tacitus, it's fair to say that there likely was a real Jesus, who was an influential teacher with a significant number of followers, and he was probably executed for his religious troublemaking. We can infer this on the grounds that Christianity did not spring from thin air. The most natural explanation for its existence is the reality of its founder, just as Buddhism originated with a man called Siddhartha Gautama, and Islam with Muhammad. The problem lies in separating the historical facts from the legends. Did Jesus' execution on the cross really fulfil Old Testament prophecies, or was it a great surprise to his followers, who then sought to account for it by manufacturing myths about their leader? For instance, it is recorded that Jesus was from Nazareth, but according to Old Testament prophecy (Micah 5:2), the Messiah would come from Bethlehem. In order to overcome this discrepancy, a story is invented about Mary and Joseph travelling to Bethlehem of Judea to take part in a census (one which is not confirmed by any extra-biblical source). While there, pregnant Mary gives birth to Jesus, conveniently fulfilling the messianic prophecy before returning home to Nazareth. The gospels of Matthew and Luke include this story, known as the Nativity, while Mark and John omit it. Another prophetic aspect of the Nativity is the virgin birth, included as a fulfilment of Isaiah 7:14. It is remarkable that two of the four gospel writers choose to omit something so vital to the Christian religion. Christians may be convinced of the historicity of the virgin birth and the resurrection, "for the Bible tells me so," but it is all too plausible that these details were retroactively fitted into the history of Jesus to make sense of his highly inconvenient death. Such suspicion is all the more justified when we learn that most scholars believe the original text of the Gospel of Mark ended at 16:8, with the discovery of the empty tomb of Jesus. Verses 9 to 20 contain an account of resurrection appearances. This section is missing from the earliest manuscripts, which suggests that it was a later addition to the text.

Christian apologist Josh McDowell, in *The New Evidence that Demands a Verdict*, objects to this kind of historical scepticism on the grounds that there is a wealth of other literature from antiquity that is accepted as factual with far less evidence available than what we possess for the New Testament. The sceptic is accused of allowing an unjust anti-supernatural bias to sway his opinion. But a prejudice against the supernatural is entirely understandable and rational. We base what we believe on our personal experience of life, where we find that the miraculous is notable by its absence. Through the repetitive nature of experience, we learn that gravity holds us down, and we trust that we will not unexpectedly rise up into the air. We learn that when a person dies, he stays dead; a three-day-old decomposing corpse is not going to just get up and walk. When faced with an astonishing claim, it is entirely reasonable to ask, "How sure can I be that this really happened?"

The history of the world is a complex tapestry and we are sometimes reliant on making best guesses based on varying qualities of evidence. Sometimes there are whole gaps where we have to make huge assumptions about what likely took place, to get us from A to B. And history is always open to reinterpretation through new archaeological findings; it does not have the rigidity of fields like mathematics and physics. There is nothing unfair or unjust about taking a sceptical stance to allegedly supernatural events in antiquity. Is the Bible the only historical record containing the supernatural? No. For instance, Siddhartha Gautama was probably a real person (born over half a millennium before Jesus). Just like the Jesus story, various miraculous deeds are recorded about the Buddha, but these are likely nothing more than exaggerated expressions of hero-worship. Are the supernatural events from any ancient document taken seriously by scholars? No. When dealing with the ancient world, truth and legend are unavoidably woven together.

When a Christian apologist makes a big noise about the undeniable historical "facts" of the miracles of Jesus in the Gospels, he has lost all perspective. Similar miracles are also found in the admittedly fraudulent apocryphal books. Consider this excerpt from one of the infancy gospels, regarding a very young Jesus with his mother in Egypt:

> And it came to pass, when the most blessed Mary went into the temple with the little child, that all the idols prostrated themselves on the ground, so that all of them were lying on their faces shattered and broken to pieces; and thus they plainly showed that they were nothing. Then was fulfilled that which was said by the prophet Isaiah: Behold, the Lord will come upon a swift cloud, and will enter Egypt, and all the handiwork of the Egyptians shall be moved at his presence.
>
> Pseudo-Matthew

This miracle is presented in a style identical to those in the canonical gospels. It even features the fulfilment of an Old Testament prophecy (a common trend in the New Testament), although in this instance we must conclude that it is a deliberately falsified fulfilment, since the writings of Pseudo-Matthew are not recognised as legitimately historical. We are expected to believe that all of the miracles in the canonical gospels are real, while all of the miracles in the non-canonical gospels are fictitious. It is abundantly clear from the evidence at hand that miracle-making and prophecy-fulfilling were popular writing exercises among Jesus' followers.

The most damning part of the story is that not a single supernatural act surrounding Jesus can be adequately verified by secular history. One of them in particular was as noticeable as a nuclear bomb. When Jesus was hanging on the cross, the following astronomical event allegedly occurred:

> It was now about the sixth hour, and darkness came over the whole land until the ninth hour, for the sun stopped shining. And the curtain of the temple was torn in two.
>
> Luke 23:44-45

This was no eclipse. Those last only a few minutes, not *three hours*. You would think that something so out-of-this-world would merit mention by numerous secular writers who directly experienced it. No such evidence exists, which is very telling. In fairness, the early historian Thallus mentions the darkness, attempting to explain it as an eclipse. But is he writing as an eyewitness of the event, or is he merely commenting on existing Christian writings? We can't be sure. This alone is certainly not sufficient to convince me that a supernatural event happened in the skies over first century Palestine. The overall climate of silence on the matter is far more convincing.

Even when sceptical of miracles, we should have nothing to fear by being open to their possibility. All it would take to change our minds is evidence.

Understandably, for a claim so contrary to experience, the evidence would have to be beyond reasonable doubt – like a historical record, free from the suspicion of embellishment and corroborated by multiple varied sources. The New Testament falls colossally short of that mark.

The similarities between the account of Jesus' life and the myths of many pagan sun gods is certainly significant. To merely scratch the surface of this, note that the traditional birth-date of Jesus is 25 December. It's common knowledge today that we have no information about an actual birth-date. Christmas Day on 25 December was first celebrated in the fourth century – the time of Roman Emperor Constantine. But the date already had massive significance in pagan religions. The winter solstice, which takes place on 21/22 December, is when the sun stops moving south and we experience the shortest day. On 25 December the sun visibly begins moving northward, heralding the coming of spring and new life. It is the birth, or rebirth, of the sun. Pagan history has many accounts of sun gods who are said to be born on 25 December, because ancient people were aware of the cycle of the sun. For instance, in Babylon, the feast of the Son of Isis (the goddess of nature) was celebrated on 25 December. Partying, gluttonous eating and drinking, and gift-giving were traditions of this feast. Ring a bell? In the early Christian era, the Roman god Sol Invictus (the Unconquered Sun) was born on 25 December. In 350 AD, Pope Julius I declared that Christ's birth would be celebrated on 25 December. This decision was clearly a deliberate concession to pagan beliefs, in an attempt to make Christianity easier to accept. In effect: "You can keep your religious festival, only change the name of your god." The fact that we continue to celebrate the birth of Christ on 25 December to this day just goes to show the power of religion to perpetuate a lie through century after century with the greatest of ease.

In considering whether the account of Jesus' life is based on earlier myth, it's not even necessary to venture outside the Bible. The Old Testament account of Joseph from the latter chapters of Genesis bears startling parallels to Jesus' life. To quote just a fraction of these: Joseph was one of twelve brothers; Jesus had twelve disciples. Joseph was brought to Egypt as a young boy, as was Jesus. Joseph was betrayed by his brother Judah; Jesus was betrayed by his disciple Judas. Joseph was sold for twenty pieces of silver; Jesus was sold for thirty. Joseph was tempted to sin by Potiphar's wife; Jesus was tempted to sin by Satan in the wilderness. Joseph was imprisoned with two criminals; Jesus was hung on the cross between two criminals. Joseph became the saviour of Egypt and the surrounding nations; Jesus became the saviour of the world. Christians themselves acknowledge the parallels and have a name for the phenomenon, stating that Joseph was a "type" of Jesus, that is to say, God specifically ordered the events of both lives to reveal this synchronicity. I would ask, is it more appropriate to jump to the supernatural explanation, or to consider the simpler one: both accounts are a mix of history and legend, telling the same symbolic story with different details?

Many astounding similarities are also reported between Christianity and other pre-Christian pagan religions, including accounts of miraculous births and resurrections. This was acknowledged by the early Church father, Justin Martyr, who said, "For when they say that Dionysus arose again and ascended to heaven, is it not evidence the devil has imitated the prophecy?" Again, jumping to the supernatural explanation, over the rather more straightforward view that aspects of the life of Jesus were retellings of older myths.

If you're feeling a little overwhelmed by information at this point, here's a thought that might help simplify matters: we are all being told to bet our lives on a historical probability. We are not being instructed to bow before fact. How reliable is the historical accuracy of the life of Jesus? Based on the level of research I have done, I would say not nearly reliable enough.

We can illustrate the same problem with the ancient Greek philosopher Socrates. Like Jesus, he left behind no writings of his own. We know something of his life and his philosophy only through the writings of others who spoke of him, principally Xenophon and Plato. The trouble is, they each said different things about him, one contradicting the other, and we may never be certain which account was the more honest. The historical Socrates is forever lost amid a mixture of truth and falsehood. What, then, makes the exploits of Jesus so factual, when we have no source besides the Gospels themselves for confirmation?

Unable to convince a person using reason and evidence, the Church then seeks to coerce through the fear of hell – the dread of a place that no one could possibly know is real ... unless the information had been communicated to man by God himself. Of course, if this God really has spoken to the human race in antiquity, then that changes *everything*, and people like me are doomed. But you would have to prove that, and so we come full circle back to a consideration of the historical evidence, which falls flat on its face.

I am disappointed in myself that I didn't investigate this much earlier in life, preferring instead to wallow in the fog of partial information from church life, rarely studying outside my comfort zone. I am staggered by how simple some of this information is. But of course, it's only our personal agendas that make things complicated. When you make the decision to simply look for the truth, instead of always measuring new information against a treasured belief system that you feel you must defend at all costs, things look a lot more straightforward.

THE DEVIL INSIDE

THE opening chapters of the Book of Genesis tell us that God created the first man, Adam, from the dust of the ground and then created the first woman, Eve, by removing a rib from the man and forming her out of it. The man and woman lived together, immortal, in paradise. God placed only one restriction upon them: they were not permitted to eat the fruit of a particular tree: the Tree of the Knowledge of Good and Evil. The consequences would be death. Everything was fine until a talking serpent (originally a limbed creature, it is implied) tempted Eve to eat the forbidden fruit. Both Eve and Adam did so. They realised for the first time that they were naked and sought to cover themselves. When God discovered what they had done, he cursed the serpent by changing its form, so that it would crawl on its belly from then onwards; he cursed the woman so that she would experience pain in childbirth; he cursed the ground so that man would have to work hard to survive. And Adam and Eve lost their immortality; they would now be subject to death.

Some Christians interpret the above story literally, while others view it as myth – not myth in the sense of something that never happened, but myth in the sense of a vague approximation of the beginnings of life on Earth, suitable for ancient readers.

Granted, there are some notable reasons why the passage could be interpreted as literal. For one, the rest of the Book of Genesis is clearly literal in character, telling the stories of Cain and Abel, Noah, Abraham, Isaac, Jacob, Joseph, and making reference to real places from the ancient world. There is no clear dividing line where myth ends and reality begins. Furthermore, the Gospel of Luke quotes the complete genealogy of Jesus (Luke 3:23-38), going right back to Adam – indicating that Adam should be viewed as a literal human being who once lived and breathed as the first man.

Unfortunately, the cost of interpreting the Genesis account of creation literally is the wholesale rejection of the overwhelming consensus of modern science regarding our origins. There are very few scientists who would assert that the world is only about six to ten thousand years old, as the genealogy of Jesus would indicate. Science tells us it is four and a half *billion*. I've heard Christians argue that the Earth was created with the appearance of age and that this accounts for the larger figure. But what kind of God would deliberately insert varying rock layers into the planet's crust to misdirect us into thinking that the Earth is older than it is? Are we dealing with infinite wisdom, or a divine prankster – or simply man, indulging in his usual antics of obstinate dogma-defending in the face of reason?

One way that Christians get around this is by admitting the Earth is indeed four and a half billion years old, but mankind has only been around for the Bible's asserted six to ten thousand years. They do this by interpreting the meaning of *day* in Genesis 1 as aeon; God created the world over several aeons of unspecified duration instead of seven literal days. Even if this were a legitimate interpretation of scripture, the difficulties caused by modern science continue to pile up regardless. The Garden of Eden scenario makes no mention of the dinosaur era, and the idea that man and dinosaur coexisted flies in the face of archaeological research; where we find dinosaur bones, we don't find human bones, and vice versa. Snakes apparently crawl on their bellies as punishment (Genesis 3:14), when in actuality their means of transport is an intricate and wonderful mechanism, no more a curse than any other part of nature's spectacular diversity.

Consider the absurdity of man's original immortality. Imagine he never fell from grace. Picture Adam and Eve retaining their perfection and bearing perfect children. Next, their children bear children, all of whom will live forever. What happens to the world, with its finite landmass, when it's populated by a race of people who keep on breeding and never die? It's cramped enough in the world we do have, where people die every day. Here's another brain-buster: in a world where there is no death, what happens to a person who gets caught in reeds while swimming underwater and runs out of air? To say that one is dependent on oxygen for survival, but one cannot ever die, is a contradiction. Furthermore, in a world without death, what does the lion do with its fearsome claws and fangs, the scorpion with its deadly sting, the crab with its pincers, the hedgehog with its protective spines, the chameleon with its camouflage? These would seem to be useless attributes, since a world without death is necessarily a world without predation.

Some have attempted to explain away this problem by positing the idea that animals may have looked and behaved quite differently before the Fall. I can barely imagine what a lion would look like without its teeth and claws, let alone picture it on friendly terms with a lamb. The notion is also pure invention out of thin air, not backed up one iota by the Bible.

The kindest reaction I can give to the early chapters of Genesis is to interpret them as meaningful myth. As such, the account attempts to present answers to a number of questions that are as relevant today as they ever were. Where did we come from? Why do we die? Why is the world as it is? What is the origin of evil? The ancient people answered these questions and others by approximating the truth as clearly as they were able to reason and intuit it. The construction of myth was an attempt to take something that was vaguely theorised and to present it in a form that made sense in a complete way – like seeing the vague outline of a mysterious object enshrouded in fog, then attempting to draw the complete shape on paper, guessing what's hidden so as to make it meaningful to the viewer.

For instance, human beings are clearly a part of the world's ecosystem. We have a symbiotic relationship with nature and are utterly dependent upon it for our survival. Put simply, we belong here, not on Pluto. It was not known to ancient people in what manner mankind came to be here, but to acknowledge our relationship with nature, the myth states that we were formed out of the dust of the ground (Genesis 2:7). Given what we now know about evolution, we might say that the myth was factually incorrect, but it is more accurate to say that our understanding of evolution fills in the missing details of what was being hinted at, however imperfectly, by the myth.

The theory of evolution remains a major bone of contention to many Christians. They take solace from the notion that evolution is not a proven fact, but a theory. However, this stance shows a failure to understand what is meant in science by the term *theory*. Science works by positing theories based on observation of the Universe. If those theories can be confirmed by repeated tests or mathematical predictions, then they are given credence. This credence does not imply that the theories can never be amended at a later date, or in some cases replaced. Scientists always refer to Einstein's general *theory* of relativity, regardless of its long-held acceptance. When we say that gravity is a fact, we're only stating that our experience of being held to the ground is a fact. But what's behind this experience? That's where *theorising* comes in. And our theories do change – even gravity. One of the great tasks of contemporary science is to come up with a quantum theory of gravity to replace the classical version.

Use of the word *theory* in science does not imply that an assertion is flimsy and lacking in evidence; it implies only that absolute certainty is a hard thing to come by, not just on the fringes of science, but all across it. When an existing theory is shown to have a shortcoming, we modify it to make it right; we don't toss the whole body of research in the trash. Newton's theory of gravity turned out to be wrong, because he didn't know about the curvature of space-time. That doesn't mean everything he wrote about gravity was stupid; his equations still work in a limited context. Similarly, whatever we may discover in the future about the evolution of life, it's pure fantasy to speculate that everything ever written in defence of evolution will eventually be proved wrong. That's simply not realistic, according to how scientific theories work.

So evolution is, and always will be, a theory. It posits that complexity happens as a result of mutation. The more useful the mutation, the more likely it is to survive and propagate. And so, the better mutations remain, while the inferior die off. Later, the surviving mutations will mutate again, and the whole process will repeat itself, eventually generating more complex forms of life. Natural selection: a straightforward principle that offers a rational explanation for the existence of complex organisms.

Religionists often argue against evolution by using the analogy of a tornado blowing through a junkyard and creating a Rolls Royce by sheer chance. This is an unfair comparison, because evolution works by means of *cumulative* selection. Each subsequent change stands on the shoulders of all the previous successful selections. It is never a case of complex organisms springing to life out of a purely random mix-and-match of parts.

Biologists debate the finer points by which evolution occurs, but there is no doubt that evolution itself does occur and that human beings are part of this process. The fossil record attests to this. *Homo sapiens sapiens* (mankind) is the only survivor in a genetic family tree that once included other human subspecies, such as *homo erectus*, whose behaviour patterns were much closer to ours than to any ape's. Genetics also shows us that all animals are cousins of one another, and some, such as man and chimpanzee, are extremely close cousins. The genetic instructions for a creature's physical form are stored in a molecule called deoxyribonucleic acid (DNA). 98.4 percent of the functional portion of human DNA is identical to the chimpanzee. This is precisely what we would expect to see if humans and chimps shared a common ancestor.

The consequences of evolution are also observable in nature as it exists today. Creatures adapt to their environments. When those environments change, the creatures will begin to evolve modifications to compensate. Over a period of time, offspring will be born that are more capable of handling the stresses of the new environment than their parents.

Notice how human beings are not all the same. This is because most of us no longer live in the environment of our ancient ancestors. Our most recent evidence indicates that the human race originated in Africa. The dark colour of Africans is due to an abundance of eumelanin in the skin. This acts as a natural sunscreen by converting the sun's harmful radiation into heat. But this benefit has a downside when living farther from the equator. The body derives Vitamin D from exposure to the sun. In colder climates, where there is not so much solar radiation, dark-skinned people end up deficient in this vitamin (unless they subsidise it with pills). By contrast, my pale Irish flesh produces Vitamin D efficiently from the milder radiation of my homeland, but if I moved to Africa, I would suffer terribly from sunburn and have a higher risk of developing skin cancer.

When our African ancestors migrated to colder locales and had children, any offspring born with a lack of eumelanin stood a better chance of surviving than those born with an abundance. And a better chance of survival means an increased opportunity of reproducing more of the same kind. Given time, this resulted in an entire population shift in favour of the more adapted pale-skinned human organism – evolution in action.

Christians may claim that adaptation and evolution are not the same process. They say that while humans do possess varying characteristics determined by adaptation to environment, they remain forever humans. But surely the very admission that beneficial genetic changes occur at all opens the door to the potential of profound changes accumulating over vast periods of time. To admit that a species may change, but only to the degree that a religious belief system permits, is to impose a false limit based entirely on a personal need to defend an inflexible dogma. If we were all the product of two original parents, Adam and Eve – perfect, unchanging representations of human form – then the differences that we see between Europeans, Africans and Asians are difficult to account for.

Evangelical Christianity has its own brand of pseudoscience, championed by a few Bible-believing scientists. "Scientific" reasons are stated for how man walked with the dinosaurs and how the Earth is only several thousand years old. Suffice it to say, if the claims of this minority are true, there would have to be a conspiracy of almost all the world's scientists intent on global deception. Either that, or the brains of all the secular scientists somehow turned to mush on this one specific issue. Neither position is credible. Tellingly, the rejection of evolution is not asserted on scientific grounds, but is an attempt to force-fit science with a literalist perspective on scripture. The reasoning goes like this: "The Bible is true, word for word, and God cannot lie, therefore any scientific findings that contradict the Bible must be wrong by default." The view that the Bible comes first, science second, is untenable, because science is the very tool that is used to gauge the veracity of the Bible in the first place.

Human beings are not the result of a divine creator forming us out of the dust, but the consequence of aeons of individuated consciousness struggling to explore and adapt, and achieving these goals through increased complexity. Some organisms evolved fearsome teeth and claws with which to survive; others evolved poisons; some evolved protective armour; others evolved complex minds capable of outwitting their opponents. If the world seems miraculously compatible with the human organism, as if it were *designed* exactly with us in mind, that is only because *we* adapted ourselves to the world, by a process of trial and error, over billions of years.

* * *

In a religious debate, nothing is more important than tackling the central ideas around which religion itself is built. Arguments for and against the historicity of Jesus, important as they are, don't really get to the heart of the question: why do people seem to need religion? Even if you demonstrate that evidence for the miraculous deeds of this Christ figure is severely lacking, the Christian will usually not be swayed, because his conviction lies in a deeply held belief: there is something metaphysically wrong with the human race.

Christianity stands or falls on the validity of this assertion. It is not by accident that the opening chapters of the Bible tell a story depicting how mankind fell from a state of grace, for it is this Fall that gives us a potential answer for how "evil" took root within man, and why human existence is filled with suffering.

Note how Christians have pounced upon the theory of evolution more vehemently than any other scientific idea, for they recognise that its acceptance cuts the very heart out of what holds their religion together. Evolution posits an opposing view that says we originated as mere cells which, over great spans of time, mutated into ever more complex forms, eventually composing the human bodies we possess today. Evolution carries a central idea that is in stark contrast to the Christian's most deeply held conviction. It declares: nothing went wrong with the human race in the distant past. Everything is as it ought to be.

Volume of evidence causes the scientific community to agree that evolution occurs in nature. Religion dogmatically clings to its view that man is a special creation of God, not just another animal. Eventually religion is forced to admit defeat and play "If you can't beat 'em, join 'em." We are in a situation today where a percentage of Christians now accept evolution as true. Doing so, however, makes the Fall of Man a non-event and thus renders any need for redemption null and void. Then why did the Son of God die on a cross to save mankind from its sins? The obvious answer is: he didn't. However, Christian evolutionists are unwilling to join the dots and draw the obvious conclusion. But make no mistake, when a Christian accepts the theory of evolution, he presses the self-destruct button on the very basis of his religion.

The Christian evolutionist may attempt to compensate by suggesting that once the evolution of the human form was complete, God then stepped in and imbued it with a soul in his own image. There is no way to prove or disprove that such a supernatural event occurred, but it is a totally superfluous addition to our understanding of ourselves. Furthermore, to assert that any organism is evolutionarily *complete* makes no sense; the current human form is merely optimised for its present environment. At what point does the Christian realise that he is simply pulling imaginary ideas out of thin air so that he doesn't have to face the fundamental error at the heart of his religious beliefs?

Religion's primary assertion and fundamental selling point, that there is something wrong with the human race, relies on the perspective that man is intrinsically different from the rest of the animal kingdom. After all, cats and dogs seem to have no need of Bibles. And so, it must be demonstrated that the mammal classified as *homo sapiens sapiens* (wise, wise man) possesses something that puts him in a class of his own.

In considering our physical attributes first, we find that there's not a lot to differentiate a man from a dog. Certainly there are differences of degree, but not of kind. Both species are mammalian and possess all the same features in differing degrees of complexity: hair, skin, bones, internal organs, sensory apparatus (actually, if we want humans to appear superior to canines, we'd better not mention the sense of smell). Both species have brains, each offering a varying capacity for intelligence. I've heard it argued that dogs are not conscious in the same manner as humans, that their consciousness is entirely limited to stimulus-response activity. This fails to take into account the charming personalities of some dogs, especially when compared to the stimulus-response nature of many dull-witted, herd-following humans. Let's not forget that some dogs have even made it to movie stardom. Persons who argue for the non-consciousness of "lesser" animals should attempt to explain the grief of those people who feel like they've lost a family member when their pet dies. Meanwhile, nobody sheds tears for RoboDog when he lies forgotten in the bottom of the toy cupboard a few months after Christmas. We cannot devalue the consciousness of other animals, just because we're smarter. Note the *er* at the end of smart – a difference of degree, not of kind.

A fabulous example of animal intelligence is what happens when a chimpanzee, having no prior training, is confronted with a transparent tube at the bottom of which lies a nut. The tube has an open top and is fastened vertically to the ground so that it can't be upturned. It is too thin to accommodate the width of the chimp's hand and too tall for a finger to reach the tasty treat at the bottom. What shall he do? Surprisingly, within mere minutes, the chimp has worked out a solution. He goes elsewhere, fetches some water in his mouth, and spits it into the tube. He repeats this over and over until the nut, now floating upon the water, is finally within his grasp. Such ingenuity lies much more in the direction of humanlike intelligence than in the direction of predictable animal instinct. This research is documented by the Max Planck Institute for Evolutionary Anthropology.

Some would argue that the factor which sets man apart is evidenced through behaviour. Animals, it is claimed, are brutal only in respect to their dietary requirements and each species exists in a harmonious balance with nature; mankind, on the other hand, goes to war against his own kind, commits atrocities, strips the world of its natural resources, poisons the planet with pollution, and seeks to expand virally until there's nothing left. Humans, it is asserted, are more than simply predatory; we are, in a nutshell, *evil* – an unnatural aberration in an otherwise balanced world.

Let me pop that balloon. First, animals aren't nearly as nice to their brothers and sisters as you might assume. Chimpanzees have been documented in the wild by anthropologist David P. Watts as possessing a startling capacity for violence. Tribes are territorial, and given the right circumstances, two groups will attack each other in a murderous frenzy. War, it seems, is not a uniquely human behaviour. The chimps will even use objects as weapons, which is a very human form of action. Within tribes of gorillas, the chief occupies a position of authority, keeping all the ladies for himself, while the other males in the tribe live in sex-starved frustration. Now and again someone will challenge the chief's supremacy, and the two will fight to the death for the glory of being number one.

In reality, nature is a killing field, where the privilege of life is not a given, but is earned with tooth and claw. Nature works using strategies that are both collaborative and adversarial, not only as one species preys upon another, but even within the societal structures of species. Man is no different. We might say that he is the greatest killer of them all, but we must acknowledge that his nature is in keeping with *nature* as we find it; it is not something that stands apart from the natural world as evil.

Some may argue that nature, in all its blood-spattered glory, exists in a state of balance, while mankind operates outside of this equation, evidenced by his ability to tip the equilibrium. It should be noted that there is nothing balanced about a plague of locusts sweeping across the country, devouring entire fields of crops, nor a volcano spewing lava and poisonous gas over a landmass, nor the Black Plague sweeping across an entire continent. This balance of nature may be more precarious than we like to imagine.

Nature is kept in a state of *relative* balance due to predation, disease and natural disaster. These are what prevent one species from growing in numbers until it consumes all resources. For every species, there's always something bigger prowling around looking for its lunch. And this is where we spot the *real* difference with mankind. It's not our fundamental nature that is different from the other animals; it's simply the fact that we're at the top of the food chain. By virtue of our highly developed brain, we can outwit every other predator. By the same means, we've got better and better at conquering disease; people now live longer and healthier lives than they ever did. Natural disaster still packs a few punches, but we've grown accustomed to rushing to the aid of victims, rather than standing aloof and watching them die. If you want to blame mankind for ruining the world, it's because we've become too successful for our own good at staying alive.

It's this highly developed brain of ours that allows us a great deal of flexibility in choosing how we behave. In a sense, we possess three brains through our evolutionary inheritance. First came the *reptilian* brain, responsible for our most basic emotions: hunger, fear, excitement, anger. Secondly, in the mammalian phase of our evolution, we developed the *limbic* brain (or paleomammalian complex), which gave us the ability to store memories and employ more complex emotions facilitating the care of offspring and the ability to live with a partner or herd. Thirdly, one hundred million years ago, we developed the *neocortical* brain (or neomammalian complex), granting us the ability to plan our actions, learn more quickly, adapt easily, communicate efficiently, as well as express empathy and altruism. This model of a triune brain is an oversimplification, but for those of us who aren't neuroscientists, it provides a rough description of how successive stages of brain development involve building upon pre-existing structures without replacing them. This is why our basic emotions are still a part of us; their expressions were refined, not destroyed.

Our evolutionary development lumbers us with animal instincts that drive our behaviour, while our higher faculties allow us to examine our natural motivations more closely; we feel the pull of nature while also being able to consider the consequences of our actions and to make more constructive choices.

In an ideal world, there would be a minimum amount of tension between the reptilian, limbic and neocortical levels of the brain. But you won't find this anywhere in the world, except perhaps in some isolated aboriginal tribes. Civilisation came with a price. Prehistoric man, before the rise of agriculture, was a forager. While our information on prehistory is fragmentary, Christopher Ryan and Cacilda Jetha, authors of *Sex at Dawn* (2010), propose a convincing scenario. People lived in tribes and shared everything. If one hunting party had a more successful outing than another, all the food was shared equally. This was a way of minimising risk for the tribe as a whole. Private ownership was a largely unknown idea, including the ownership of another person – which is precisely what marriage is, if we're brutally honest about it. Men and women were sexually free, and when a woman gave birth, she had no idea who the father was. This did not mean that the child would grow up fatherless; it meant that all the men of the tribe took an interest in all the children. This is raw, authentic human nature. Is it horrible or beautiful? You might be thinking, "Those women were sluts." But is that thought coming from your true nature, or from your cultural conditioning? Consider this: ancient man didn't need a police force to hold his community together, because nobody had private possessions and nobody needed to walk over others to get ahead. There was no need for laws governing sexual behaviour, because sex was never in short supply, generating an overall climate of satisfaction. By contrast, we in the modern world have a culture of sexual shaming, scarcity, and frustration. As a result, there is no end to police reports of sex crime.

We've come a long way – a long way from home, maybe. The prevailing opinion is that man is a naturally monogamous animal. Divorce statistics would suggest that this is false. But you need only look within yourself for confirmation. If you're in a monogamous relationship, do you ever fantasise about sex with someone other than your partner? Of course you do (maybe even during sex). This is merely your true nature revealing itself.

Now, I am by no means advocating a return to prehistoric sexual habits, although I say that with a hint of sorrow. If you're interested in becoming a mother or father, monogamy is probably the only practical option today. The nuclear family is the only parental system that our civilisation recognises and supports. So we have to make the best of it. Civilisation currently taking the form that it does, we are forced to live in a manner that is inauthentic. Although I've drawn particular attention to sexuality, this issue affects the whole personality.

Due to the demands of modern civilisation, the triune brain no longer has to cope with tension between the levels, but all-out war, as we strive to suffocate our natural instincts under layers of so-called virtue. This battle between base instinct and cultural conditioning is what forms the basis of the myth of the Fall of Man. Every one of us knows he has a beast within, and none of us wishes to unleash it. Our aspirations towards "virtue" are tainted by an inner animal that wants to be let out of its cage. And so we are led to believe that we possess a sinful nature.

Sometimes our natural instincts make us feel appalled with ourselves. You might be intoxicated with desire for an inappropriate sexual partner, or filled with rage towards someone who has harmed you. This feeling of being at war with oneself can be a source of great guilt, especially when measured against the values of polite society, where most monsters are kept safely out of view in their mental closets. You feel a longing to be rid of what you perceive as your dark side.

Enter religion. The story goes something like this: "You are a sinner with a desperately wicked heart, but God can fix the problem. Jesus sacrificed himself on the cross to pay the price for your sins. Because of this, you are spotless in God's eyes, as though you had never sinned. All you have to do to claim this for yourself is ... devote your life to God" (or rather, devote your life to God's alleged representatives on Earth, who will tell you what to do).

Bliss – all your sins forgiven. Even though your sinful nature remains for the duration of your earthly existence, ongoing forgiveness is a simple matter of ongoing repentance each time you fail. Furthermore, you have God's promise to perfect you when you get to heaven. The cost, in the present, is the total enslavement of your mind and body to an external authority. Believe what you are told to believe and do what you are instructed to do.

When I engage in debate with a Christian, I almost always fail. When I make points that are straightforward, I say to myself, "*Surely* he will see it now." But every time, he retreats behind a veneer of quasi-logic. I understand now why I can't succeed. It's because Christianity is meeting the deepest of his needs. Without Christ, he cannot accept the kind of person that he is, whereas with Christ, he is a new creation, forgiven of all his sins, restored to a state of grace, and on the road to perfection.

In one word, the civilised man's malady is *self-hate*. And religion is the commonly offered solution to this. No amount of rational debate about the falsehood of Christianity will ever de-convert a wholehearted Christian. He is not participating in the discussion with any willingness to be affected by what he might hear; his mind is made up, his need satisfied, and he will not allow anything to upset that, because to lose his religion means to return to the self-hate that was once his daily portion. And that is unthinkable.

But religion is not the only solution to self-hate. For anyone willing to strive for a high degree of self-realisation, the answer is to learn to love yourself just as you are. And you can do that by *understanding* yourself. Your mind is the product of aeons of evolutionary development and your base instincts are its most ancient parts: the powerful drives of self-preservation and propagation. Today, nature has bestowed upon you the gift of a complex brain that is capable of transcending the stimulus-response nature of its basic mould. You have the ability to decide for yourself when to indulge a desire and when to hold it in check. So play the game of civilisation, but crucially, *know* that it's only a game.

Your base instincts, when understood, are no cause for self-hatred. They should be recognised as mere reflections of the less complicated creature that you used to be, once upon a time. Rejoice in the fact that you have become an intelligence that can govern its own basic nature, deciding when and where the animal gets to come out and play. Feel the continual inner struggle, not as a dysfunction, but simply as the way things are meant to be. You are imperfect only in that you are an unfinished product of evolution, still on a journey forward. Instead of hating yourself, strive to understand yourself, and in so doing love all parts of the glorious being that you are. Respect the needs of your inner beast while guiding him with pragmatic advice.

With religion out of the picture, you might think that guilt would no longer play a role in your life. This is true only insofar as your intelligence agrees with your actions. Thanks to our neocortical brain, we are perfectly capable of condemning ourselves without God's, or society's, help. This faculty is actually quite useful, as the guilt we feel urges us to change our behaviour.

For anyone who is able to see themselves in this light, the Fall of Man becomes a faulty myth based on an outdated assessment of human nature. And religion loses its primary sales pitch. This understanding is the escape hatch for the countless numbers of nominal Christians who begin their spiritual lives with the best of intentions, only to discover later that religion doesn't live up to its promises. Old vices continue to poison lives, despite the alleged power of the Holy Spirit. As you strive for a completely artificial standard of purity, your life becomes an unending torturous cycle of sin, guilt, sorrow, repentance, forgiveness, joy, and back to sin – rinse and repeat. God seems distant, after hundreds of unanswered prayers. Church sermons become an uninspiring drudgery to sit through, because they don't reflect the reality of your life. And the Bible is rarely picked up and read in the home. All of this happens for one simple reason: *you have been conned.* And deep down, you know it to be so; it is revealed by the quality of your spiritual life. When you started out, your social conditioning and your lack of self-understanding fostered your self-hate, then religion offered you a convincing lie as the solution. In time, that lie becomes apparent to everyone whose religion lets them down, but few will admit it to themselves, for fear that there is no alternative except to return to the old pattern of unrelieved self-hate.

Religionists see man as special, as uniquely made in the image of God above all other biological life. *That* is the error at the root of a whole succession of erroneous deductions, the end result of which is a poisoned life. What we truly observe is that man is just another animal, possessing all the characteristics of mammalian life. And as your dog has no need of salvation from sin, neither have you. If man is unique among the animals, it is only in this regard: he's the only one that tortures himself silly about his own natural instincts.

* * *

The belief in a fall from grace is rooted in our desire to find a reason behind the "sin" and suffering of creaturely existence. Science has now given us a better answer for this predicament than the one provided by religion. There is a fundamental reason why nature, with all its beauty and horror, is as it is.

On the largest visible level of the Universe, we see colossal forces spanning the entire diameter of galaxies. Matter collides and forms stars. Older stars explode as supernovas. Asteroids crash into unsuspecting planets, wreaking havoc. Were it not for our sun's expenditure of energy across the blackness of space, there would be no life whatsoever on Earth.

And while the sun's radiation warms the Earth, it burns our neighbour Venus. Here on the ground, volcanoes provide further warmth to the planet, but their lava destroys animals and vegetation without mercy. And in the animal kingdom, everything is eating everything, in the clash of predator and prey. Look into a microscope and we see a whole other world engaged in warfare, as microorganisms battle for supremacy.

What is the nature of this game? In a nutshell: energy conversion. All matter is energy, and that energy is in a continual process of change on every fractal level of the entire Universe. What makes us think this should not apply on the creature-to-creature level? And indeed it does apply. We might like to imagine a heavenly paradise where no being harms another, but this is contrary to the very nature of energy itself, which is always moving and changing. No organism survives on the biological level without becoming an energy thief. If you wish to live, something else must give. Thus we have the predator and the prey. It cannot be any other way, unless you think there is some way to reconfigure the operation of the entire Universe.

When you understand the nature of energy, it becomes the final deathblow to the myth of the Fall, because you are forced to see that the plight of Earth's inhabitants is a perfect reflection of what is happening across the entire Universe, not a localised divine punishment against one species on one planet. This is a *hostile* Universe, and the creature's experience of adversity is nothing more than the natural, inevitable outworking of energy conversion in the arena of biological life.

Myth only goes so far. Try to make it real and it fails you. The problem we have today with Judeo-Christian mythology is that there are people who are still trying to cling to the notion that the Bible is the word of God, truth handed to us on a platter by the divine architect of the Universe. Not only is the Garden of Eden account *literally* untrue, it's also *figuratively* untrue. We are not fallen, in any sense of the word; we are perfect in our imperfection, just like every other animal. When we compare ancient approximations of truth in the Bible to our more complex approximations of truth in modern science, the former is shown to be exactly what it is: a limited myth containing a mixture of insight and guesswork, now well past its use-by date.

Many in Western society today continue to take literally the story of a man who rose up into the sky and vanished into a cloud (Acts 1:9-11), as if the location of heaven were just beyond the edge of the Earth's atmosphere. I don't see what possible relevance the mode of Jesus' departure had, other than as a device for a writer constructing a myth for his time – a story for people who could accept the idea of heaven as physically positioned above the Earth. In reality, if Jesus ascended into the upper atmosphere of the planet, all he got for his trouble was a dose of ultraviolet radiation, lowered body temperature, shortness of breath, and eventual asphyxiation.

Of course, ancient man couldn't know this. But we do, and therein lies the problem for the Bible's credibility.

A myth serves the culture it was created for as a means of comprehending the world relative to that culture's level of understanding. When a culture develops beyond the limits of its own myths, then those myths have outlived their usefulness and must be modified or removed. The central myth of Christianity, the Fall of Man, can now be clearly seen, in the light of science, as the great error at the foundation of this whole edifice of belief.

SURVIVAL ETHICS

RELIGIONISTS argue that God is necessary because man left to his own devices has no objective standard by which to measure right and wrong. A word like *good* has no value unless there is a God who can define it for you. Without God, why is helping someone preferable to harming him? A rapist believes it is fine to sexually assault women; who am I to say that he's wrong, since we are both merely men with differing personal opinions? It's a good line, until you realise that the religionists who use it don't even believe it. And this can be tested quite easily.

Imagine a man, who happens to be an atheist, faced with the opportunity of placing an unusual bet with even fifty-fifty odds; a simple coin-toss. If the result comes up heads, he will receive a huge cash prize of, say, one million pounds. But if it's tails, then he must allow his wife to be viciously raped and tortured to within an inch of her life. According to the religionist's view of unbelievers, the man should have no worries about the potential outcome of the bet, because all actions and consequences are equally amoral. But in reality, no sane person, religious or otherwise, could look at the scenario in that light. This instinctive rejection of amorality has nothing to do with what is printed in the Bible. Why do we feel this way? Because choices have real-world consequences, and those consequences are either desirable or undesirable, in relation to our *nature* as creatures.

The Christian claims to obtain his ethics from the Bible. He hails this as the source for his objective, unchanging definitions of good and evil, because the laws come from the perfect mind of an eternal God rather than the variable opinions of man. Here's one example of these values: "If a man happens to meet a virgin who is not pledged to be married and rapes her and they are discovered, he shall pay her father fifty shekels of silver. He must marry the young woman, for he has violated her. He can never divorce her as long as he lives" (Deuteronomy 22:28-29). Let's be objective about this Bible passage and place it in its historical context. In ancient Israel, the virginity of a young woman was highly prized. If this was violated, the woman's chances of obtaining a husband and raising a family became zero; she was forever tarnished. And to Israelites, a successful life was largely measured by how many children you produced. Odd as it may sound to modern ears, the passage above was actually trying to do rape victims a favour. Israelite women would probably have been grateful for the regulation, because without it, the lives of rape victims were essentially over.

Our culture is vastly different. People live meaningful lives without bearing children; virginity is not considered an essential attribute of a potential mate. Imagine a rape victim being told by the authorities: "You have to marry this man now. It's the law." I think we would be hard-pressed to find a Christian in the present day that would support this regulation for women.

The sensible Christian realises that we're not supposed to transpose Old Testament laws word-for-word into the twenty-first century, because of the massive cultural differences. But the problem with taking this position is that we believe our modern civilisation is ethically superior to Old Testament Israel. The culture of the people of Israel is the culture that the Judeo-Christian God put together in his wisdom, and it is a culture that defends the genital mutilation of children (Genesis 17:9-14), animal sacrifice (Leviticus 1:3-9), slavery (Exodus 21:20-21), executing adulterers (Leviticus 20:10), executing witches (Exodus 22:18), and genocide (1 Samuel 15:1-3) – practices that no sane Christian would wish to reintroduce. In fact, if we're dealing with infinite wisdom, it's a disturbing mystery why God's early dealings with man took the form they did.

So the modern Christian does not get his values from the Bible. He cherry-picks his rules and regulations, instead of accepting them all at face value as wisdom beyond human understanding. But what is the objective basis of this selectivity? That's an interesting question. It seems the Christian, like the atheist, is measuring the Bible against values he inherited from somewhere else – values that seem to be more important. This is a subtle admission of his own personal autonomy – that he doesn't truly need divine revelation to formulate meaningful ethics. But is he ready to admit this to himself?

Christians also talk about the judgement of God in relation to ethics – as if our actions should be guided by our desire to escape punishment. This is the most infantile basis for ethics imaginable. Clearly, the reason why we do what we do is because we recognise that actions have consequences. If a man rapes a woman, the woman has to live with that permanently. The rapist might later go boo-hooing to God about what a terrible person he has become and how he needs forgiveness. But this totally misses the point of why ethics are important – not because of future judgement by an offended deity (or indeed future reward for being obedient), but because your actions matter in the here and now. The consequences of your behaviour, upon yourself and others, are permanent. Whatever it is you do, you can't take it back. Forgiveness of sin is a total irrelevance – taking our eyes off the importance of acting responsibly in the first place. Don't screw up, because there are no second chances where it really counts: in the world that you make with your actions.

Culturally inherited values are not necessarily any better than religious principles. They may reflect our natural humanity, or they may not, depending on when and where we are born. Culture can function as yet another false external authority imposed upon our lives, sustained by the unquestioning minds of those that abide by it. To get to the heart of the matter, we must distinguish what is *cultural* from what is *human*. There is a scene in the movie *Terminator II* where the boy John Connor argues with the Terminator robot that had been programmed to protect him. Crucially, it was not programmed to protect anyone else. John argues, "You just can't go around killing people!" The Terminator asks, without sentiment, "Why?" John responds, "What do you mean 'why'? Because you can't!" Again: "Why?" John can't get through. The robot lacks humanity – human programming, if you prefer. Humans, even in the absence of religion and culture, are not blank slates. We have our *humanity*. Defining precisely what humanity is can be difficult, given that we all suffer cultural influence, but it is certainly not an illusion. This becomes clear when we look at ourselves in relation to the other animals.

Notice how the rest of the animal kingdom gets along just fine without a Bible (or a cultural value system). Consider the lion: fierce predator, social animal and devoted parent, all without any need of stone tablets from a divine lawgiver. Don't make the mistake of assuming that the lion's behaviour operates purely on instinct. According to the documentary *The Truth About Lions* (2011), these cats are intelligent, demonstrating the ability to count and strategise when hunting. They possess a rich experience of consciousness, just like man. When a Christian accuses an atheist of having no basis for his ethical behaviour, it's essentially the same as facing a lion and saying, "Why aren't you tearing each other to pieces? You have no objective moral grounds for getting along so well with your own kind." That would be ridiculous, wouldn't it? The underlying principle at work is this: social animals create societies for themselves because that urge is in their nature. And it's in their nature because evolution favoured it. And evolution favoured it because survival is more assured when a species collaborates. Why would man the animal be any different? We are civilised because it works for our benefit.

We also possess a capacity for aggression, but that is no contradiction. Like other animals, we need to defend our territory against attack, so our instincts equip us to fight. Alongside this, we have the ability to love. When an adult kisses a child with affection, it is not because he was instructed to perform this action by God, but because he feels affection on an instinctual level.

Children develop ethics naturally, with or without the influence of religion. What we call the terrible twos is the period when a child goes through a process of realisation that the world does not revolve around him and his needs. Gradually and painfully, under his parents' discipline, he learns to see himself as an aspect of his environment, rather than as the centre of the Universe. He comes to understand that life is better when he obeys his parents' instructions instead of simply yelling in frustration. Whether God declared a particular action good or evil is irrelevant to a young child. If the parents are irresponsible, caving in to their child's every wish for the sake of a quiet life, they will pay the price in later years. They denied their child the valuable lesson of how to successfully integrate his individuality into a wider world of experience, and the terrible twos will become the terrible sixes or the terrible tens. There are tragic children who end up practically friendless at school; no one desires their companionship, because they are all take and no give. As adults, we balance our individuality with the responsibilities of civilisation every day, because we learned a meaningful basis for ethical behaviour as children, not because God wrote the Ten Commandments.

The religionist's stance is based on a faulty analysis of man as separate from the animals, possessing an evil nature that needs to be cured by an outside agency. Sadly, the Christian, steeped in grossly inaccurate propaganda about human nature, might picture independent thinking as bringing about only barbaric chaos. If that were true, those who call themselves atheists should be the most brutal tribe in the world. But I don't see many atheists getting together to organise church burnings. Conversely, history shows that the widespread acquiescence to an externally imposed morality is a major rallying point on which the worst atrocities are committed, whether it is a heretic or witch burned at the stake for the crime of thinking different, or Christians and Muslims slaughtering each other for the glory of their respective gods.

Yet perhaps my view of the essential goodness of the natural man is too romantic. What does man truly become when the constraints of law and order are removed? Let's do a little role-play.

Imagine a plague that wipes out the entire population of the planet, save for roughly one in every thousand persons. You are one of these survivors. Scared and alone, your first natural impulse is to find companionship. Others are thinking in the same fashion. Soon you become a group of fifteen, including men, women and children. Co-dependency ensues as each member uses his individual strengths for the mutual benefit of the whole. One of the members has strong leadership abilities. He suggests stocking up on supplies from a local supermarket then heading for the countryside. The aim is to find an isolated house, well away from the inevitable disease of the decaying corpses and the potential threat of encountering a gang of unfriendly survivors.

Once your new home is established, the group turns its attention away from immediate survival to long-term survival. Canned goods will not last indefinitely, so you all get busy learning how to farm the land and hunt game.

After a great deal of effort, the future looks relatively bright and safe. Then one day, two strangers stumble upon your property. The men seem friendly, but you are cautious. They quickly charm their way into the group's confidence. Finally, they make their move, sensing your civilised friends to be easy pickings. But they haven't counted on your lingering suspicions. You get the drop on them before they can do any serious harm. Keeping them at gunpoint, you escort them beyond the boundary of your property, well away from the eyes of the others.

In a civilised society, such men would now be put in prison. But that world is gone. And it's simply not practical to imprison them yourself. Resources are already strained without the added burden of two unproductive mouths to feed, not to mention living with the potential of the villains breaking free and killing you in your sleep.

You are faced with a clear choice: release them, or kill them. You weigh the potential consequences of letting them go. They might be grateful for being spared and thus never return. Or they might be angry at being thwarted and return with a vengeance. They could be lone wanderers, or scouts from a larger group of like-minded parasites. The worst case scenario is a whole gang showing up on your doorstep, to steal your food supplies, rape your women, and destroy your home. You realise that if you let the men go, the only safe option is to uproot your whole group, move to another location, and start over, leaving behind all of the crops you have planted. If you choose this option, how will you get through the coming winter without starving? And what's to stop this same circumstance from happening all over again?

All of this worry goes away if you just pull the trigger. Could you do it? In this situation, the most dangerous person to the wellbeing of your group is the one who is too compassionate to do what needs to be done to keep everyone safe.

Post-apocalyptic fiction often provides a rich canvas for exploring morality. A notable fictional character is the convicted murderer Tom Price from the TV series *Survivors* (2008). While the other members of his group are clinging to the morals of a civilisation that was recently obliterated due to plague, Tom is the guy who is willing to simply do what needs to be done to keep his group alive. When the others cannot face stealing from another clan of survivors, Tom will do it. When the others haven't got the stomach to kill an enemy who would surely return in greater numbers, Tom will do it. The others hypocritically wash their hands of such dirty jobs, but secretly they know that if it weren't for Tom, they would all be dead by now. While this is merely fiction, it illustrates a powerful message: any ethical system that defines conflict as evil is destined to fail. When our definitions of good fail to make room for the necessity of aggressive action, we become the prey. Animals know this instinctively, whereas many humans are melodramatically preaching, "All you need is love." Some may react to this assessment by saying, "I would rather die than become a thief and a killer." Unfortunately, anyone who promotes such a "noble" thought is not only ensuring his own demise, but sowing the seeds of destruction for *all* who would cling to such an ideal, thereby destroying the ideal itself. An ethical system built upon a foundation of pacifism is untenable simply because the practice of such a stance leads to its own doom. Any workable system must, of necessity, embrace conflict, for the simple reason that life brings adversity.

Of course, I am by no means advocating looting and killing as acceptable behaviour for us in the present day. In a fully functioning society, we recognise the benefits of law and order and support them accordingly. But moral absolutism for all circumstances is impossible. If you doubt that, then simply tell me where this objective standard of morality is to be found. The Christian will say, "In the Bible." But would that be the Bible interpreted by a medieval Christian (embarking on a crusade or beheading a heretic), or the Bible interpreted by a Christian from the early part of the twentieth century (for whom dancing and cinema were sins), or a contemporary Christian from any number of denominations, strict and liberal? Everywhere we look, so-called objective morality is engaged in an unending process of change. There is no place where we can find the absolute standard for all time. In the general run of life, most of us will gladly subject ourselves to becoming law-abiding citizens and reap the benefits. But imagine a government that decides to steal children from loving parents and turn them into soldiers. How many of us would remain law-abiding citizens then? Morality has always been, and always will be, a matter of personal pragmatism. Even those who deny that observation will find themselves unavoidably using it when a dreadful situation can be avoided by simply telling a lie. As circumstances change, so do the rules we make for ourselves.

When you understand that man is qualitatively no different from the rest of the animals, then observation of the animal kingdom yields much wisdom. We learn that what works for the lion is not what works for the lamb. Each species acts in accordance with its own unique evolutionary development. There is no *one* standard for all, but a multiplicity of choice based on a universally desired outcome: *survival.*

Post-apocalyptic fiction has its bad guys, often portrayed as men who would rape and pillage without conscience, spending their days scavenging on the decaying corpse of the old world rather than working to build a new civilisation. Would we all regress to such an appalling level, if given the opportunity? No doubt some would. More importantly, what would be the ratio of cooperative, forward-thinking individuals to destructive parasites? We can bypass all speculation, because the bottom line is this: despite countless wars and genocides, despite thousands of conflicting ideologies, no matter where we look, *civilisation exists*. It needs no other justification than the observable evidence of its own success. In the grand scheme of nature's stratification, the civilised have beaten the uncivilised in the game of life. Even a villain will see the benefit of strength in numbers. For any street gang or criminal organisation to survive, there must be adherence to a code of conduct, or the group disintegrates due to anarchy. The need to civilise ourselves is an inescapable practical necessity, even amongst the lowest of us.

People are capable of taking responsibility for their own actions without any guidance from a higher power, because such responsibility is a natural fact of life across the entire animal kingdom. The limbic brain of mammals empowers them to take an interest in the survival needs of their family or tribe, instead of engaging only in reptilian selfish concern for individual survival. Survival is, after all, made easier through collaboration. Man's neocortical brain allows him to go one step further. Life is not so fraught with danger for many of us as it is for our cousins in the animal kingdom. When there is safety and abundance, our urge to survive is given the opportunity to flower into an interest in mutual prosperity.

There is no double standard concerning a man who, in a life filled with plenty, would be a kind-hearted sharer and, in a life filled with lack, a cold-blooded killer. It must be understood that personal survival is the necessary first step on a path that has the potential of reaching altruism at its end. Just as water transforms itself into ice or steam depending on the temperature, so our behaviour must change in relation to our circumstances. This is a far cry from flimsy moral relativism, where one standard is no better or worse than any other. This is nothing less than a scientific stance on morality, based on realism about human behaviour. We may not always agree on precisely what moral judgements to make in individual cases, but we have identified the core principle on which meaningful ethics are based: individual and group survival. We must be good to ourselves before we can be good to others. And why is it that we feel happy when we do something altruistic? Not because we are "spiritual," but because our evolutionary development has imbued us with the type of brain that makes such behaviour desirable.

I suspect this was all a lot clearer to our hunter-gatherer ancestors, who lived in small tribes and moved from place to place. The survival of the individual and the survival of the group were one and the same. Man could not survive alone and the group could not survive without the collaboration of its members. Although life would have been much harsher than it is today, I can't help but think that a hunter-gatherer would have felt much more self-worth than a typical modern human. The tribe was made stronger through each individual's contribution. By contrast, modern man lives in a world that tells him he is unnecessary; he must compete against all his fellows for gainful employment. If he never gets a job, the great machine of civilisation is no worse off, because somebody else will fill the position. A great deal of crime happens, not because man is evil, but because modern man has been forced into a state of alienation from his neighbours. Modern man is tribeless and we instinctively feel the wrongness of that. I have a pet theory that our fascination with post-apocalyptic fiction comes from our feelings of dissatisfaction with modern civilisation; we secretly long for a more authentic human experience of tribalism – of belonging. But we have to deal with the world as it is, where we are forced to play dog-eat-dog with our neighbours or perish. Meanwhile, we utter a subtle cry for help as we compulsively litter social media with anecdotes from our lives, craving validation that we matter to someone other than ourselves. We walk all over people to stay alive then beg them to love us because we feel so alone. And it's not our fault. Here we are in the great melting pot of modern civilisation, struggling to be authentically human in an overcrowded world that doesn't fit our true nature.

No one is good or evil. These terms become obsolete when we understand the workings of our own brains. We see that we are both good *and* evil. Ethics provide a spectrum of behaviour rather than a strict polarity of opposites. I am in some ways a responsible adult and in other ways a rascal. I enjoy a high degree of moral stability, but there are also moments of relaxing decadence. I have helped someone in need and felt the joy of altruism; I have also done things that later filled me with self-loathing. I make this confession without embarrassment because I know there is nothing particularly good or particularly evil about me – just like you.

A more descriptive word for evil is criminality, and the essence of criminality is the taking of a shortcut. For example, a band brings out a new album and a percentage of fans download the music illegally from the Internet instead of buying it from a retailer. An unemployed man wants to experience the thrill of driving a sports car; instead of getting a job and saving sufficient money to buy a car, he breaks into one and takes it for a joyride. A woman in an adulterous relationship persuades her lover to murder her rich husband so that she can inherit his wealth prematurely. A sexually frustrated man doesn't want the lengthy task of seducing a woman, so when he spies a naïve girl walking home late at night, alone and vulnerable, he rapes her. If we're brutally honest, we're all at least a little bit criminal; we all take shortcuts, even if they are only minor ones (some of you may be reading this in the form of an illegally downloaded ebook, you rascals). The human drama exists because everyone individually decides which shortcuts are worth the risk – not only risk of prosecution, but also risk to the human psyche. You have to be able to live with the psychological consequences of your choices, because you will be judged by your own *humanity*.

Sometimes we attempt to justify an action that we feel is wrong, to make the action feel right and thus eliminate guilt. This is all well and good if the negativity has been externally imposed from culture or religion. For instance, I would once have felt guilty for working on a Sunday, but no longer. Personal experience has also taught me that this tactic never works when you attempt to strive against your humanity. Hours after committing a questionable act that I've tried to justify, I might find myself suddenly flying off the handle because of a minor irritation, such as struggling to unscrew the lid from a jar of peanut butter. One minute earlier, I wasn't even aware that I was angry; now I'm ready to throw the jar across the kitchen. When a tiny frustration triggers such a massive overreaction, something big is clearly going on internally. I'm angry with myself, of course. Despite my rationalisation of the original act, there's no fooling myself; my humanity is a quality that runs deeper than thought and I would be wise to listen to it.

A memorable example of this (whether true or legendary) is Judas Iscariot betraying Jesus to the chief priests for thirty pieces of silver (Matthew 26:14-16). Afterwards, he discovered that he couldn't live with the consequences of his actions, so he hanged himself (Matthew 27:1-5). His humanity wouldn't let him get away with his criminality. It strikes me that the criminal mind must be a deeply unhappy place. Ironically, the criminal wishes to deepen his enjoyment of life using ill-gotten gains, only to find his happiness tainted by the nagging inner voice of his humanity. Catch-22.

The greatest hurdle I face in maintaining my own personal ethical aspirations is the fact that I'm striving to overcome a lifetime of bad habits – habits that have formed as a result of unwise choices and decades of confusion about what it means to be human. When a person finds it easy to do good, that's not a sign he's particularly special; it's just a result of having nurtured positive habits. For instance, if I find someone's wallet on the street, it comes naturally to me to return it, intact, to the owner. Someone else discovering the wallet might choose to pocket the cash. Now, I could give myself a big pat on the back and congratulate myself on what a fine human being I am. But the truth is there are also parts of me that I don't like – behaviour patterns that I know are detrimental to me, but I find extremely hard to overcome.

What we think of as our identity is largely the crystallisation of our repeated behaviours into something that now comes habitually to us. What's ironic is that if a person acts in a way that is not in keeping with his established identity, we call him a phoney. But the only way to change who you are is to act in that non-habitual way until, by a process of repetition, a new habit is crystallised and the old one erodes.

Crystal is a good metaphor, because bad habits can be hard to break. Some of mine are so ingrained that they might haunt me till the day I die. It helps to recognise that identity itself is something fluid; there is no *true you* defined by fixed and immovable characteristics, except perhaps some foundational aspects of your behaviour that are due to your own particular genetics. The larger part of you is down to the choices you have made – choices that grew into habits, and habits that grew into an identity.

The use of ethics is basically the use of the neocortical region of the brain to govern the limbic and reptilian regions. It's worth noting that there is a vast difference in meaning between *govern* and *suppress*. The latter is like a government that rules with an iron fist, refusing to concern itself with the needs of the people. In the end, it has a bloody revolution on its hands. Similarly, your natural instincts will not be restrained and denied. Those who attempt this may end up in a psychological mess. Governing our animal passions involves expressing them responsibly and sublimating them when necessary – *never* suppressing them.

Everything I have just explained about ethics may still seem erroneous to Christians, because they have a different idea about the function of ethics. To them, an action is wrong principally because it offends God. They are not accustomed to the entirely practical notion of an action being considered wrong simply because it adversely affects civilisation. I sense that a great deal of debate between religionists and secularists could be simplified if both sides recognised this fundamental difference in approach.

Ethics do not require a divine lawgiver; they are a natural consequence of brain development. In this realistic context, ethics could be defined, not as the *overcoming* of natural instinct through supernatural guidance, but as the *fine-tuning* of natural instinct in the interests of individual and group survival and prosperity. If you want to live a life that is satisfying, strive to live in harmony with your humanity.

THE ENLIGHTENMENT HOAX

I T's not only Christianity that attempts to persuade mankind into accepting a solution for the "problem" of our supposedly fallen nature. The same mistake is made in subtle ways by some modern spiritual teachers who are not associated with any religions, even by those who encourage people to think for themselves.

Consider an author who is by no means a man devoid of insight and whose work is worth studying, despite what I'm about to say. Eckhart Tolle, author of *The Power of Now* (1999), classifies human beings into two categories: the enlightened (those who view themselves as the formless essence of Being) and the unenlightened (those who see themselves as individual egos). It's the haves and the have-nots, the saved and the lost. In essence, he is saying, "There is something wrong with the human race and I have the fix."

What Tolle fails to see is that conflict is a natural fact of life. Thus, pain and suffering of one kind or another are unavoidable. If we are lucky, we may minimise these factors, but we have no ability to extinguish them, for the simple reason that we are not in control of everything that life throws at us. Tolle's worldview is essentially an attempt to make heaven on earth through insulating oneself from pain and suffering. He achieves this by suggesting that we identify our true self, not as the individual mind, but as Being: the collective essence of everything. So, while all manner of unpleasantness is occurring in the mind, it is not happening to *the real you* that is observing the mind. Admittedly, he's on to something. But then he mischaracterises the value of this insight by asserting that the attainment of it is enlightenment or salvation. Tolle, like Christianity, is preaching that mankind is fallen (or, in his terms, the mind in its natural state is *insane*) and he claims to provide humanity with the esoteric teachings that can rescue us from that unfortunate state. Frankly, Tolle's "enlightenment" can easily be dispelled by holding your hand in a flame or smashing your finger with a hammer. Then notice how difficult it is to remain an unaffected passive observer of your individual ego. To be fair, Tolle is not talking about suffering caused by the influence of the world upon our sensitive bodies, but self-created suffering – the mind running amok, generating undesirable emotional states. But we cannot really separate the sources of suffering so cleanly, because the only consciousness we know is consciousness at the mercy of both the mental state and the world beyond it. The emotions we experience (including negative ones) have been tailored to serve our survival interests over millions of years of evolution.

In *A New Earth* (2005), Tolle writes, "Fear, anxiety, expectation, regret, guilt, anger are the dysfunctions of the time-bound state of consciousness." Tell that to the gazelle as it runs away from the lion. Fear, far from being a dysfunction, is the emotion that is keeping the gazelle alive. Fear floods the bloodstream with adrenaline, unlocking much needed additional energy for the desperate sprint to safety. Fear is an essential living reality for animals. Anger is an equally useful emotion. When a wild animal draws back its teeth and snarls at an aggressive opponent, this is an effort at intimidation. If the enemy backs off, as is intended, further conflict is avoided.

If you think humans are some kind of special case, exempt from the trials that "lesser" animals face, then just imagine a zookeeper who carelessly lets a lion out of its cage during public visiting hours. A marvellously "enlightened" public apparently wouldn't feel the urge to scream or run. They would be living entirely in the present moment, not looking ahead with fearful expectation, not trapped in the "time-bound state of consciousness." Perhaps they would choose to run out of pure pragmatism, without feeling any of that pesky dysfunctional fear. But here's the most important observation: the person who is so terrified out of his wits that he manages to scale a seven-foot wall on pure adrenaline is the one least likely to end up as the lion's lunch. All thanks to fear.

The time-bound state of consciousness is a rich state of consciousness and the emotions that it provokes are entirely practical. We are able to reach back into a vast store of memories and put them to use in the present moment; we are also able to look ahead, visualise possible futures, and tailor our present behaviour to cause or avoid particular outcomes. To give Tolle some credit, he is speaking about the unfortunate human habit of wallowing in the past and future while ignoring the present – the place where life is actually lived. By all means, break that habit. Meanwhile, there is still value in devoting some of your attention to the future. If I'm driving to a bank with the intention of committing armed robbery and I imagine a possible future where I'm staring out through the bars of a prison cell, the anxiety I feel is a powerful motivator for me to stop the car before I ruin my life. On the pleasurable side of the emotional spectrum, the anticipation one feels in looking forward to a special event infuses the present moment with delight. Recall how you felt as a child on Christmas Eve.

Sometimes spiritual teachers, even those with large followings, can be profoundly naïve about life and short-sighted about ordinary avenues of knowledge that would inform them of so much – in this case biology. Tolle has little or no awareness of man's place in the animal kingdom, or the predicament that all life faces. He speaks from the false perspective that most religions speak from: man is not just an animal, man is special, and man needs saved from something that has gone wrong with him.

I know what it's like to experience "insane" emotional states, as much as anyone. I once found myself unable to sleep because someone in my life was taking liberties that I was not happy about. The matter was trivial and in the beginning I was only slightly irritated about it. This feeling was urging me to take action in the form of a confrontation. And it would have been a mild, well-mannered confrontation, designed to get the person to change his behaviour towards me. But I wouldn't allow myself to do this, because the social situation was complicated. So I bottled the emotion up. The end result, after a period of time, was me lying awake at night obsessively thinking about the person and feeling enraged over something that was relatively unimportant. The problem here is not that the ego is insane; the problem is that we've been culturally conditioned to deny our emotions their proper expression. We're expected to live politically correct lives and never do anything to risk offending anyone. So we suppress our true nature and the frustrated emotion mutates out of all proportion. This is why we're so obsessed with sex – particularly Christians, because they're the ones who make the biggest fuss about suppressing that side of human nature. Suppression fuels obsession. The root of the problem is not the mind itself, as Tolle thinks; the mind behaves insanely as a reaction to our misguided attempts to force it to conform to unnatural ideals of behaviour.

Much as I have benefited from some of Tolle's legitimate insights, the foundation of his message is merely a repackaging of salvation. He is playing the same game (perhaps unconsciously) that religions have played for millennia – convincing the human race that there is something inherently wrong with it then offering a unique fix. The reality is that nothing went wrong with the human race. Everything is as it's supposed to be. You were given individual consciousness for the purpose of experiencing individual consciousness, not to spend your days attempting to reconnect with an all-encompassing blissful oneness. Individuality was dispensed to you so that individuality might be experienced, or else it would not be. The whole Universe appears to us individuated, one object divided from another, given substance in space and time. Why seek to escape from this? Why would I want to insulate myself from my individual mind, when that mind is capable of experiencing so much pleasure as well as pain? And if I subdue the latter, do I not also lose the former?

The need to be free from pain, suffering, hunger, adversity, conflict, "sin" – this is the ultimate itch that can never be scratched. Understand that it is this very wishful thinking that can form the basis of a spiritual teacher's sales pitch to you. But you can't build a successful worldview on ideas that don't accurately reflect the nature of the world as it reveals itself to us.

When you see through the false claims of authoritarian religion and make your exit from it, this is only the first step on a difficult path fraught with pitfalls. Abandoning one religion can leave behind a void that begs fulfilment elsewhere. Some spiritual teachers play the role of recapturing such wandering souls with a fresher smelling pack of half-truths. Only when you reach the point where you understand the depth of the statement "There is nothing wrong with the human race just as it is" will you finally be free from the snake oil salesmen.

What about me and my claims? Am I yet another of these spiritual teachers trying to tap into your need and sell you a solution? No. Unlike many others, I do not claim to possess an ideological endpoint. I have not attained a special state of enlightenment, nor am I free from suffering, nor am I content all the time, nor am I even ethical all the time – even by my own standards. What I am offering you is more akin to an experience of *initiation* – to borrow a term from magical orders and secret societies. The words enlightenment, awakening, liberation, salvation, all imply a singular, once-for-all-time change that occurs within you at a particular moment in your life, splitting you into *you before* and *you after*, and separating you from the ordinary herd of the unenlightened, asleep, enslaved and lost. But initiation is something that happens by degrees. Gaining understanding of a mystery forms a stepping stone to the probing of further mysteries. And the philosophy I propose in this book is probably not a meal you will be able to eat in one sitting. It certainly wasn't for me; it took years to digest.

When you learned to read in school, you were essentially being initiated into a new way of interacting with the world. We take this ability for granted, but pause for a moment and imagine the difficulties experienced by an adult who has been denied this skill. Not only is the general administration of life made much more problematic, but a massive avenue of further education is walled off. Learning to read is a first initiatory step that can lead in all kinds of directions. Many initiatory experiences later (including basic arithmetic, algebra, calculus, just to get the ball rolling), one might end up as a theoretical physicist, possessing an ability to understand the Universe in a vastly different manner from the layperson, for the simple reason that he has been initiated into mysteries that are beyond the comprehension of most of us.

Becoming initiated enriches life and opens new avenues for further enrichment, but at the same time, there is nothing particularly wrong with you as a human being if you remain uninitiated. It is like the choice of being stranded on a desert island, with or without the prior knowledge of how to make fire. You'll survive, either way, but in the former scenario you'll be much better off during the experience.

So, if you would rather close this book and devote your time and energy to becoming, say, a skilled guitar player, that is an entirely valid choice.

Nobody *needs* the insights provided in this volume. They are there to enhance your life, but you will have a life with or without them. And you may end up doing exciting things with your life that I'll wish I had done with mine. I am not here to offer a secret that will save you from all the difficulties of material existence, or relieve the incessant itch to become "awakened." All I offer is an improvement to the quality of your consciousness.

Similarly, if you study Eckhart Tolle's teachings with a view to improving your consciousness, you will benefit from them. But they can't turn this mundane life into everlasting, uninterrupted bliss. Profound eureka experiences are available, and I've had my share of them. But the long-term integration of an esoteric truth into one's life experience is never as exciting as the initial moment of discovery. And once we have sufficiently mined the many avenues of human knowledge for treasures, fresh insights tend to become less frequent. The subtle danger is that one can become a spirituality addict, always lusting for the big insight that will blow his mind to such a degree that he will feel like he is floating on air forever. Instead of viewing knowledge as a means of improving consciousness, he is simply interested in getting high without drugs. He misses the initial high that he experienced, so he wants it again and again, and if possible he wants it permanently.

David Icke, a spiritual teacher and conspiracy theorist, has written around twenty books in just over two decades, catering to this sort of addict. The early volumes, such as *The Truth Vibrations* (1991) and *Heal the World* (1993), were concerned with spiritual awakening and saving the world from our own destructiveness. Then, with *The Robots' Rebellion* (1994), he introduced a conspiratorial element: a shadow government, the Brotherhood, that had been shaping the destiny of the world for millennia, suppressing the knowledge of who we truly are and planning global enslavement in a New World Order. In *The Biggest Secret* (1999), Icke proposed that the Brotherhood (now called the Illuminati) was actually a race of inter-dimensional reptilian entities in human guise. In *Tales from the Time-Loop* (2003), he used the holographic Universe theory to provide a pseudoscientific explanation for human-reptilian shapeshifting. In *Human Race Get Off Your Knees* (2010), he claimed that the moon was not a natural satellite, but an artificial construction that was being used to project a false reality to Earth.

Each new book attempts to blow the reader's mind in a manner that exceeds the previous release. And they are published year after year with alarming speed. The average lay reader can easily fall prey to the author's poorly researched claims. The reader comes to view himself as part of a special minority of "awakened" individuals. One's ordinary life of "slavery" to the system is viewed as part of an ancient war that stretches into other dimensions of reality. We are Infinite Consciousness, and the Illuminati will fail, because there's a global awakening coming for all humanity! Inspiring stuff – except much of it is totally disconnected from reality. But no doubt the spirituality and conspiracy addicts are salivating over what David Icke's next book will reveal. I'm sure they will get their fix in due course.

I watched the tail end of Icke's lecture at Wembley Arena in 2012 and was shocked by how much it resembled a Pentecostal church service. There was music and dancing; Icke spoke with the passion of a religious preacher. The crowd was in a state of bliss. I even spotted a young woman in the audience with her face tilted upwards, eyes closed, and one hand raised – just like church. But the problem with every high is that you have to come down from it. All those people at Wembley eventually went home, got up for work the next day, and their lives returned to normal. The glow of this seemingly spiritual experience faded. Ah, but for the addict there is always the *next* book, or the *next* lecture.

You may have heard the Christian saying: "There's a God-shaped hole in your heart that only Christ can fill." While I don't accept the solution, this statement does identify the very real sense of restlessness that permeates our lives. We rarely seem to be content with what's right here, right now. This gnawing dissatisfaction places our focus on the future; we feel that we always have to be getting somewhere. Desires mutate into cravings, and the void is never filled, no matter what we invest our time in. Some would define enlightenment as the conquering of that restlessness. I agree that it's good to overcome excessive restlessness; we suffer less when we learn to desire less. But in my experience, too little restlessness is as troublesome as too much.

The most profound peace I ever experienced was in the wake of a small medical operation that I underwent in my mid-twenties. I lay on the hospital bed for hours, doped on painkillers, staring at the opposite wall. The skin around my wound was horribly swollen, but oddly I didn't feel the slightest anxiety about that. The TV was on, but I didn't feel any desire to turn my head to look at it. And I didn't feel the remotest trace of boredom, either. Although this was a chemically induced state of serenity, that doesn't invalidate it as a means of revealing the relationship between desire and suffering. I was privy to the direct experience of what so many spiritual seekers are striving to attain without drugs. All restlessness of the mind had ceased, leaving me in complete peace. Life felt absolutely perfect just as it was, with me merely gazing at a wall. Imagine this state of mind had continued indefinitely. My life would have amounted to little more than eating, drinking, urinating, defecating and sleeping. Totally satisfied with every waking moment, I would have lacked all motivation to create change. The book you're reading only exists because I felt restless enough to write it. Clearly, there is a balance to be found between too much restlessness and too little; it doesn't have to be all or nothing. If enlightenment means permanent uninterrupted serenity, it serves only to destroy your potential as a human being. The desire to attain a renewed state of being is entirely dependent on the conviction that there is something intrinsically wrong with human nature in the first place. No insight is ever going to flip that imaginary switch inside you that will illuminate your whole being and insulate you from all suffering.

The search for enlightenment ends not with the seeker becoming enlightened, but with the realisation that enlightenment is a hoax. Consider: what would a dog have to do to become enlightened? The question is absurd, of course. Enlightenment, for a dog, consists of being a dog. "But I'm not a dog," you may object. "I'm a human being." In such a sentiment, I sense the lingering ghost of Christianity's outdated anthropology, where man is God's special creation, fallen from grace and now attempting to claw his way out of that hole. But if we understand that we are animals, then enlightenment for a human consists of being a human. Be on your guard for anyone claiming they're here to fix the human race. It's merely the message of the cross in another guise. But it's the message that's broken, not us.

On the other hand, I can understand why some have a particular attachment to terms like enlightenment, awakening and liberation. Sometimes the process of grasping an elusive secret about life can be so sudden and dramatic that it really does seem as if there was *you before* and *you after*, especially if you've spent a large part of your life suffering under false beliefs. The inner change that took place in my own life at age thirty-five was striking, but I also understood that I hadn't solved all my problems, freed myself from suffering, or reached any sort of finish line. Use the terms enlightenment, awakening, or liberation to describe your own transition, if you must, but don't fall for the trap of thinking of it as salvation. There is no new you, only an improved you – which is really a continually improving you, as long as you keep learning.

In the quest for truth, insights are but stepping stones on a journey with no conceivable terminus. When you look for truth in this fashion, then the never-ending pursuit of it becomes an enjoyable and life-enhancing activity. But if you think of it as a quest with a definite ending called enlightenment, you will be increasingly frustrated as you fail to find it, or you will settle for an illusion and pretend that it works. The truth is we don't need fixing; we were never broken in any fundamental sense. We should stop judging ourselves against an idealised picture of human nature that exists only in the imagination. Imperfection is reality, and we're perfect in our imperfection.

How ironic that the real reason you need to go on a spiritual journey is to realise that you didn't need to go on a spiritual journey. But remember: the value of undertaking that journey is the value of that realisation. The liberation that I experience is liberation from the burden of believing there's a special message somewhere out there that can save me, if only I can find it.

PART TWO
DEEP DIVE

The more we look into what we think we know, the more hitherto undetected things we shall find lurking in our assumptions.

H.G. Wells, *The New World Order*

Man suffers only because he takes seriously what the gods made for fun.

Alan Watts

FOREVER FORWARD

S EVERAL millennia ago, a man stood on an open plain and gazed afar. To him, the Earth and the sky were the entire Universe. He understood perfectly well that the Earth was flat, because he saw this truth with his own eyes. Any other idea would have seemed absurd.

Around 340 BC, a Greek philosopher called Aristotle thought, like those before him, that the sun and moon moved around the Earth. This was, after all, exactly what he witnessed these heavenly bodies doing each day. In these endless revolutions, occasionally the Earth would stray precisely between the sun and moon. He knew this because the Earth's shadow fell upon the moon (in what we now call a lunar eclipse). Curiously, the shadow was always a perfect circle. This, Aristotle reasoned, could only be possible if the Earth was a sphere. Had the Earth been a flat disc, the shadow would have been elliptical.

In the second century AD, the Roman astronomer Claudius Ptolemy (90-168) made further logical inductions about the Universe. The Earth was indeed spherical and it was enclosed like a Russian doll by eight invisible spheres, upon which moved the sun, moon, and five known planets, all rotating on orbits around the Earth. The outermost sphere housed the fixed stars, which were not understood to be anything more than mysterious pinpricks of light.

The orbits of the five planets, however, were quite complex, not at all like the straight paths of the sun and moon across the sky. At times the planets moved back upon themselves in curious zigzags. It wasn't until 1514 that a Polish priest, Nicolaus Copernicus (1473-1543), proposed a different model of the Universe – one that simplified this anomaly beautifully. Up until that point, everyone believed that the Earth was the centre of the Universe (geocentrism). Copernicus proposed that the sun was the true centre (heliocentrism). The Earth, like the five other planets, orbited the sun. This theory was resisted by both the Church (with its belief that man was made in the image of God) and by the scientific orthodoxy of the time.

In 1609, the Italian astronomer Galileo Galilei (1564-1642), after hearing about a new invention, the telescope, built his own. He began observing the night sky and became the first man in history to see that a planetary body other than Earth (Jupiter, in this case) had its own moons. It was now conclusively proved that the Universe contained bodies which did not revolve around the Earth. And so, the Copernican model of the Universe gained support and Ptolemy's model became obsolete, but unfortunately not before Galileo was put under house arrest for the remainder of his life on the charge of heresy. The lesser known Giordano Bruno (1548-1600) proposed the existence of many worlds similar to Earth. This heresy, among others, cost him his life at the hands of the Church; he was burned at the stake.

These heretics paved the way to our modern cosmology of the Universe. We went from viewing Earth as God's special object of attention at the centre of a smallish Cosmos, to seeing our planet as a miniscule dot occupying an insignificant spot on the spiral arm of a random galaxy – just one of some two hundred billion galaxies, some of which contain perhaps two hundred billion stars. The statement "God created mankind in his own image" (Genesis 1:27) starts to sound a little arrogant when you understand that the presence of mankind is less than a speck of dust in a Universe that is far grander in scale than we ever previously imagined.

Did Copernicus finally uncover the *real* truth, where many before him tried and failed? Not quite. He corrected one vital mistake in our understanding, but still had the erroneous impression of a small Cosmos with the sun at its centre. The pursuit of knowledge is not a matter of being right or wrong; it is a matter of ever sharper approximation gained over great spans of time. As soon as we think we know something with finality, that knowledge becomes a stepping stone to a wider context of enquiry that we never dreamed of. This often ends up casting new light on our existing assumptions.

After Copernicus came Isaac Newton's laws of motion, Albert Einstein's general theory of relativity, and notable inventions like the Hubble Space Telescope. Aristotle, Ptolemy, Copernicus, Newton, Einstein: all of them offered something better than what was understood beforehand, but none saw the Universe so clearly that his own assertions avoided the ordeal of future modification. How could Ptolemy's Earth-centred cosmology survive indefinitely, when he didn't possess the understanding that our planet revolves around the sun? How could Newton's laws speak with finality about the Universe, when he didn't know about the curvature of space and the elasticity of time? And today, Einstein's relativity feels the pinch of quantum theory.

Many people, in their desire to *know*, seem to need an ideological endpoint – to be able to say "I'm an atheist" or "I'm a Christian," as if those statements represent the harnessing of an ultimate, unchangeable truth. In practice, being an atheist generally means that you look at life through a materialistic lens. The Universe is a machine that runs on unconscious clockwork principles, and human consciousness is a largely insignificant product of evolution. These presuppositions could be entirely wrong, but atheists are often unaware that they are making any presuppositions.

The assumed position then functions as a restrictor of thought. Similarly, Christianity asserts that God has, in times past, communicated absolute reliable truth to mankind. When that "truth" inevitably comes into conflict with scientific discovery, it reveals the folly of such a mentality. Human history, taken as a whole, is silently screaming at us that there is no ideological endpoint to discover, by the simple fact that nowhere do we see it. Even if it were possible to find such a thing, how would we know we've grasped it, since the future always tantalises us with undiscovered knowledge?

The harnessing of truth has always been progressive, never absolute – more a matter of fine-tuning our theories over time than of knowing something with total objectivity. It is perfectly sane, and even logical, for a man to believe that the Earth is flat when he is not in possession of any information to indicate otherwise. Likewise, Ptolemy's idea of spheres within spheres was a good theory for its time and lasted for over a millennium. Today, we could be harbouring a thousand false assumptions about reality that we are simply failing to notice because we aren't advanced enough in our thinking. We can never tell how unknown information will affect what we already "know."

Perhaps the most unexpected can of worms ever to spring open was what happened when we starting looking inside the atom. We identified components that we termed protons, neutrons and electrons. Electrons, whatever they were, did not behave themselves at all. In the everyday world of objects, we had come to understand that nothing can travel faster than the speed of light, but in the quantum world of very small things, a single particle can exist in several places at the same time or travel from place to place by exploring the entire Universe. That's what the mathematics told us, and the mathematics was giving us very accurate results. I personally don't pretend to understand the equations, but I must bow to what has now become firmly established science. The classical model of reality was nice and tidy, but it didn't apply inside the atom. And since the world of form around us was really made of this subatomic strangeness, we had to concede that classical physics was a mere approximation of reality, limited to the context of everyday objects. We needed a new model of reality to account for everything. And so, quantum theory was born. We had opened up a sphere of enquiry so complex and unusual that physicists today are still struggling to get to the bottom of it in the quest for an elusive Theory of Everything.

Sadly, the typical human herd animal will search for a package deal truth – a ready-made belief system that he hopes will transform him from unenlightened to enlightened, filling a perceived void in his life, allowing him to feel that he has found the answer and can now stop searching. But the wheel of progress will keep turning, regardless. This forward motion is not usually the work of the masses, but the obscure activity of individuals, often working against the tide of popular opinion, sometimes in the face of ridicule, and occasionally at great peril.

The two greatest hindrances to progress are: (1) those who say, "It's true because my God said so," and (2) those who think that what they "know" will never suffer change. Religious dogmatism and scientism are the chief enemies of progress, for they are both claims that we already possess absolute truth that will never become outdated.

Do you need to identify yourself with an existing ideology? That is fine. Benefit from whatever truth you see within its dogma, but know that you haven't reached the end of your learning – or your correction.

If you cannot attach yourself to an ideology, even better. By refusing to join, you are undoubtedly closer to the truth. For across the great expanse of history, there is not one ideology that hasn't become outdated. What makes the present batch on offer any different?

WHEN TWO "TRUTHS" GO TO WAR

A UFO investigator handed copies of a photograph to his associates David and Peter, who were both experienced photographers. The photo showed an odd looking flying saucer. It was silver, about thirty feet in diameter, and could best be described as resembling a wedding cake. The craft hovered a few feet above a parked van, right next to a tall leafy tree that rose even higher. The picture had been taken in the countryside of Säckler, Dürstelen, on 26 March 1981, by a Swiss man named Billy Meier, who was allegedly in regular contact with extraterrestrial beings from the Pleiades.

"Boys, I need a thorough analysis of this photo from the both of you," the ufologist said. "Work solo on this; no comparing notes. Two opinions are better than one. I want you to put aside any personal prejudice and give me the facts about this picture."

The following day, the investigator met with David first. "What have you got for me?"

"Well," David said, "when I first looked at the photo, I knew something wasn't right. I think most people would get the same gut feeling, without really knowing why. It's because our brain processes a lot of things for us that we take for granted. We've been looking at objects all our lives, basing our opinions on distance and size, without really –"

"Give it to me in plain English, Davey-boy."

"Basically, the saucer is slightly out of focus, and it shouldn't be. If you look at the van directly underneath, that's in perfect focus. The two things are supposed to be about the same distance from the camera, so they should both be in focus, or both out of focus. This can only mean that the saucer and the van are not even remotely the same distance from the camera. The saucer is probably no bigger than a dustbin lid – actually, it probably *is* a dustbin lid – and it's being suspended close to the camera. There's no escaping the facts: it's fake."

"All right, David. Thanks for your insight. All that remains is to see whether Peter confirms your analysis."

The investigator promptly visited the other photographer. "Well, Pete, is it real or fake?"

Peter was visibly excited. "It's definitely real."

The investigator raised a sceptical eyebrow. "And you can prove this?"

"I can. At first, I thought this was a bit silly. I mean, what sort of alien drives a vehicle that looks like a wedding cake? But I went the extra mile, anyway. I scanned the photo into the computer and fiddled with the brightness, contrast, gamma level, and so on. Look what showed up – right there in the shadows where the left side of the saucer meets the tree."

The ufologist peered at the monitor. His eyes widened in surprise. "The leaves on the tree ..."

"You spotted it: the branch is poking out ever-so-slightly in front of the ship – which is impossible if this is a dressed-up hubcap dangling right in front of the camera. As it is, there's no way that this thing is anywhere other than *right there* beside the tree. There's no escaping the facts: it's the real deal."

Furrows of frustration appeared on the investigator's brow.

"What's the matter?" Peter said. "Didn't David back up my assessment?"

"No, he didn't."

Peter spread his hands. "Well, what can I say? The facts speak for themselves."

"Yes, they do," the investigator replied. "Yours and David's!"

It's all well and good for Sherlock Holmes to say, "When you have eliminated the impossible, whatever remains, however improbable, must be the truth" (Arthur Conan Doyle, *The Sign of the Four*). But our intrepid ufologist is in a predicament where one perspective says it's impossible for this photo to be authentic and the other says it's impossible for it to be fraudulent. In both cases, logic is being used to determine the truth. In both cases, the evidence seems conclusive. But due to the differing factors of what goes noticed and unnoticed, two investigators draw entirely different conclusions. And only one of those conclusions can be true.

Now we begin to see how slippery this concept called truth is, and subsequently how flimsy our determinations of possibility and impossibility. Clearly, one of the examiners made a wrong assessment of the evidence somewhere, an error that would have gone entirely unnoticed if not for having two heads in the game. This shows how easy it is to latch on to one or two fragments of information that seem to be unquestionably, objectively true. The trouble is, the information has to be passed through a piece of machinery called the human brain, which is vastly limited and all too prone to making bad decisions due to simply not having the whole story.

Human beings have a fragmentary relationship to truth. In proving an argument, how do we know there isn't some missing piece of the puzzle that we've failed to spot – something that will reshape our deductions. We're creatures with limited minds, always operating with partial sightedness. That is our relationship to truth, always and forever. We cannot *know*. We can only do our best to think clearly and to iron out the contradictions and paradoxes in the puzzles we attempt to solve, never knowing what new mysteries lie around the corner. If we can make several puzzle pieces line up snugly, we allow ourselves to feel a measure of confidence and we label such ideas true. And so we should. But we must also understand that what we assert today as truth remains forever open to reassessment by other minds who will tackle the same problems from new angles. We need to appreciate reality as an immensely deep and mysterious arena that we are attempting to map using only five senses and a primate brain.

The term agnosticism is derived from the Greek word *gnosis*: to know. With the letter *a* placed in front, the opposite meaning is intended. An agnostic is one who freely admits he does not know. This is a healthy mental attitude, where one is humble enough to recognise his own limits and shortcomings. There is, however, a pitfall to be avoided here. Agnostics sometimes fall prey to an eternally non-committal attitude, where there is an unreasonable expectancy that we ought to be given absolute certainties about the Universe before we allow ourselves to flirt with any ideas about it. This leads only to an impotent life, devoid of any convictions about truth.

Is there *anything* we can know with absolute certainty? Well, yes: two plus two equals four, for instance. We can have one hundred percent confidence that this is a true statement, because it is based on pure logic. Similarly, the question "Is it possible to throw a seven on a six-sided die?" should be answered absolutely with a negative. However, outside of mathematics, such certainty is rare, and the more complicated a hypothesis, the greater the danger of error.

When seeking the truth, it is imperative that we identify the correct premises on which to build an argument. A premise is a foundational statement that is demonstrably true without exception. Let's apply this to our UFO case study. I will suggest two premises that occur to me as a suitable starting point: (1) Stationary objects that are the same distance from a camera will exhibit an identical focus on the resulting photograph; (2) if object A obscures object B, then object A must be closer to the observer than object B.

Those two premises can be shown by everyday experience to be true without exception. Unfortunately, look where the purity of this kind of logic takes us – to the contradictory conclusion that the UFO must be both close to the camera and far away.

What is now required is not deductive logic, but creative thinking. There must be a missing observation that allows the two contradictory findings to mesh, but deduction from the premise will not provide it. We are forced into *imagining* what that observation might be. Progress must involve *inductive* as well as deductive thinking. If all science were purely deductive, then the entire scientific enterprise would have been completed long ago, because it would have consisted purely of following a logical trail of breadcrumbs from the beginning to the end of the course. Hey presto: the Theory of Everything. But real science is messy; sometimes logical deduction brings us to a standstill, or presents us with a bewildering paradox. In those circumstances, we use induction to move forward. That means we creatively imagine answers that are fully supported by the original premises, but not deductively provable from them.

In considering premise 1, it occurs to me to ask: what if the UFO is not a stationary object? What if the technology behind this alien craft causes it to vibrate when hovering? That could account for the object's fuzzy focus, while the van remains in sharp focus.

In considering premise 2, the branch that's protruding in front of the craft appears to belong to the tree behind it, but is that really the case? What if the branch is actually much, much closer to the camera than it appears at first glance? What if it's not even part of the tree? I would expect the leaves on the close-up branch and the leaves on the distant tree to be drastically different in size, but the type of tree, the overcast weather, and the focal setting on the camera all make this extremely hard to spot. This crafty piece of misdirection provides the very means of secretly holding the *miniature* UFO aloft: the left side of the craft is actually attached to the branch. The branch could even be a metal pole decorated like a branch.

I now have two hypotheses, neither of which I can prove beyond a shadow of a doubt. Both suggest different solutions to the original problem, one providing a reason why premise 1 might not apply, and the other providing a reason why premise 2 might not apply; one positing that the object is a genuine UFO, the other positing that it is a deliberate hoax. Which do we choose as the truth?

Where there are two or more competing hypotheses, the one that makes the fewest assumptions is more likely to be the right one. This principle is called Occam's Razor. Assumptions in favour of the view that this is a genuine UFO are: (1) Earth is being visited by aliens; (2) alien craft vibrate when hovering. Assumptions in favour of the view that the photo is a hoax are: (1) Billy Meier is a liar.

Now, the belief in alien life is certainly not a laughing matter (it's a big Universe), but making the assumption that ETs are visiting us requires a leap of faith about which we have no persuasive data – especially in an age where almost everyone walks around with a phone, and a great many phones have built-in cameras. We would reasonably expect there to be a lot more convincing photographic evidence today than in the 1980s. But there isn't. Furthermore, assuming that alien spaceships vibrate when hovering is pure invention out of thin air, imagined for convenience. What we do know for sure is that some people tell lies for personal glamour. Taking all this into account, the safer bet with Occam's Razor is the conclusion that Billy Meier's UFO is a hoax.

Occam's Razor can, of course, sometimes lead you to the wrong conclusion. It deals only in likelihoods. Notice how we have now moved from pure deductive logic to probability. We've lost the absolutism we were originally aiming for. But in order to make any progress, we had to move in this direction, because deduction without induction took us to a dead end. In the arena of deductive logic, any solution you arrive at is always already in the premise. Reaching it simply involves careful step-by-step deduction. But in this example, the solution was not in the premise. It required imagination.

When searching for truth, it's also important to take care that the premises upon which you rely are correct to begin with. It's possible to build massive belief structures upon faulty premises. I've done this myself in the past. When I was a Christian, my mind was filled with all sorts of intricate and interwoven theological principles. The whole picture seemed profound. I could see its validity because I could logically join all the dots. But *valid* doesn't necessarily mean *true*; it only means logically consistent within the constraints of the original premise. If the premise upon which the whole edifice of belief relies is shown to be wrong, then everything you build on top of it ultimately fails to stand. And my faulty premise was: the Bible is the inerrant word of God.

The same criticism can be made in the arena of science. As recently as the late nineteenth century, we relied upon the premise that space consisted of something called *ether*. Later, we found out that there was no ether, and any science that relied upon its existence needed revision. There have been many such moments in the history of science. The main difference in approach between religion and science is that scientists actively try to prove themselves wrong, while religionists tend to cling to their own rightness in the face of all evidence to the contrary. A scientist looks upon being wrong as a step towards being right, by virtue of elimination, while a religionist says, "The answers have been handed to us long ago by divine revelation. They're perfect and not to be questioned."

Here's a little thought experiment that illustrates the importance of creative thinking. Take three matchsticks and place them on the table, end to end, in the shape of a triangle. Now take three more matchsticks. Add the new ones to the original triangle so that you end up with a total of four triangles the same size and shape as the first. There is a path to this solution, but it will not be arrived at through logical deduction. What is required here is imagination, an ability to think outside the box of conventional assumption. If you like, take a break from reading for a few minutes and try to solve this puzzle.

The failure to solve it rests on a faulty assumption that almost all of us make when first tackling the problem. We assume that the solution must be two-dimensional, because the first three matches were laid down on a flat surface. But no one enforced this rule; *you* unconsciously presupposed it. With this realisation made, have another think about the puzzle.

Did you get it? The simple and elegant solution is to place your three additional matches on top of the first three in the shape of a pyramid. The four faces of the pyramid (including its base) are made up of four equivalent triangles.

You would never see this with deductive logic. It requires guesswork, creativity, intuition, imagination. When a solution to a problem is not apparent deductively from a premise, there is absolutely nothing unscientific about thinking outside the box. In fact, it's essential.

When an atheist debates with a theist, it's common for the atheist to ask, "Where's your evidence for God?" This could also be phrased, "How do I logically deduce the existence of God from the available evidence?" A smart theist will not be fazed by such a question, because he knows there are more roads to truth than examining physical evidence. The fact is, we are confronted with a Universe that requires explanation. So we ask: "What idea provides the best explanation for why there is a Universe?" The God hypothesis is one explanation. It's not the only one, it may not be the best one, but it's worth considering nonetheless. And if it provides an elegant solution to the problem of why there is a Universe, it should not be dismissed on the grounds that it relies upon creative thinking. If that's your grounds for dismissal, you would have to throw away a great deal of science, too. Remember, in our triangle puzzle, we could only solve it by adding an extra dimension. In the same manner, perhaps the puzzle of the Universe itself can only be solved by imagining a dimension of existence beyond space-time itself – an unfathomable dimension where cause and effect are transcended in a manner that a mere creature could not possibly comprehend. The imaginative thought, "God may be real, but who or what is God?" holds far more creative potential for modelling reality than the boxed-in, materialistic thought, "There is no God."

There's nothing wrong with taking your best shot at the truth. If you realise somewhere down the line that you got it wrong, it's no big deal. Simply change your mind and keep right on going, rejoicing in your newfound clarity. Is this not the very process that all human knowledge has undergone from the very beginning? We get some ideas, we run with them for a while, then we figure out some new things, and replace the old ideas with better ones. Later, those superior ideas get replaced by further insights that are better still. Knowledge evolves. It was never static in the past, nor is it static in our present day. But for knowledge to progress, we need to do two things: (1) stop defending the notion that what we "know" will never change, and (2) be willing to take the puzzle pieces we've got and try to put them together, rather than stare forever at the unfinished jigsaw and refuse to play. When we dig for truth, we might strike gold, or we might strike something that merely looks like gold until carefully examined by eyes more perceptive than ours. Either way, nothing gets done unless you're willing to get your hands dirty.

Look up Billy Meier's photo on Google and have fun confirming my analysis. You'll have no trouble locating the picture; how many wedding cake UFOs are there likely to be, really? You will also come across commentary in favour of the photo's authenticity. Remember the moral of the story: don't get overly cocky about truth when you're in possession of a few fragments of evidence in your favour. Sometimes the truth lies in what you've failed to see. So if you believe in something with confidence, get out of your comfort zone and study something that potentially contradicts it.

The tight constraints of deduction and the fluid guesswork of induction are both required in the task of furthering our understanding. I notice an unfortunate trend among those interested in science to abandon creative thinking and to rely exclusively upon deduction from empirical observation; they're very accurate people, but they will never be pioneers, because they've got themselves stuck in a very limited mode of thinking. Mystics seem to suffer the opposite tendency, relying too much upon creative thinking and too little upon logical deduction; they can end up on irrational flights of fancy that are far removed from reality. The key is to understand that the two ways of thinking are not mutually exclusive; they complement each other.

MAN THE MYTHMAKER

LIGHTNING flashes across the sky followed by a deafening boom of thunder. The ancient Germanic pagans, knowing nothing about atmospheric pressure and electricity, knowing only that there must be a hidden cause of this awesome phenomenon, declare that this is the handiwork of the god Thor with his mighty hammer Mjöllnir.

I used to consider the ancient world, with its many religions and its dizzying array of gods and goddesses, as utterly backward. It was hard to imagine how the human race could fall for these wild stories so obviously created in the imaginations of men. But in this assessment, I failed to recognise that these people did not possess anything remotely comparable to the knowledge we take for granted in the modern world. On closer reflection, the ancient people were doing something that was quite understandable and even progressive; they were articulating things unknown by composing labels that were based upon their current level of understanding about the Universe. Here's an illustration of the probable reasoning processes that went on in the ancient world: The name Thor was selected, not because a god had spoken and identified himself, but simply because language is a tool for differentiating one thing from another; in other words, they had to call him *something*. Identifying the source of lightning as a god deserving of reverence is perfectly understandable, since man regularly saw himself at the mercy of forces greater than himself, forces that possessed an order suggesting an underlying intelligence.

The belief in many gods is known as polytheism. Monotheism, which is what we have in Christianity, Judaism and Islam, simply chooses to identify a singular all-powerful source responsible for all phenomena, rather than outsourcing various responsibilities to a pantheon of lesser gods.

Ancient cultures created elaborate myths about their gods as a means of explaining the Universe. Science is commonly thought to be the means of uncovering the true reality behind faulty myths, but when we look closely, we will see this is not quite so; science actually brings to light a more detailed and accurate *mythology*.

Consider how the pagans sought to explain the force behind lightning. They did not know what this was, but in order to discuss it, they had to name it; man is a communicating creature, and if we are to communicate successfully we must invent a matching vocabulary for ourselves. On this occasion, Thor is what rolled off the tongue.

The tendency to see gods in the forces of nature is not exclusive to paganism, but is even reflected in Christianity. On 2 July 1505, Martin Luther (who would later become the founder of Protestantism) was travelling on horseback during a thunderstorm. Suddenly a lightning bolt struck the ground close to him. Fearing the judgement of God, he cried out, "Help! Saint Anna, I will become a monk!"

If we define the term *reality* as the true nature of the Universe beyond all appearances, we then understand science as a means of creating a *model* of reality. Well, this is precisely what the ancient pagans were doing when they invented gods behind the outward appearance of the world. The difference is only that they had not developed a rigorous set of rules (what we call the scientific method) to help them separate good answers from bad ones, and so their answers where highly inaccurate by today's standards. But if we're inclined to assume that the use of the scientific method puts us in a position of complete accuracy, think again. Is reality made of particles or waves? If we look at it from one angle, it's made of particles; from another, waves. It cannot be both, and yet if we didn't have two conflicting models to work with, we would make the mistake of thinking we had a complete and accurate model. We are playing essentially the same game as ancient man: modelling reality by approximation. We differ only in that we are playing with a much greater scale of detail.

From our more enlightened perspective, we've seen into the belly of Thor and we know a little more about what makes him tick. At some point in recent history, we came to understand that thunder and lightning occurred due to entirely natural processes of electricity and atmospheric pressure; there was no need to see sentience in the storm. And so, the pagan myth of Thor (or the Christian myth of the monotheistic Yahweh expressing his displeasure via weather) became obsolete. In its place we now have the myths of electricity and atmospheric pressure, and the stories of how they relate to each other.

The *myth* of electricity? Did I really say that? Well, consider what the word electricity is. It's a label appropriate to our level of understanding, just as Thor was a label appropriate to a past level of understanding. It might be tempting to say that Thor was the myth and electricity is the reality, but it's important to realise that we don't actually know what electricity is. We can describe electricity by experimenting with it, observing the results, and labelling everything we discover. Notice that we are still stuck in a pattern of observation and labelling, just like the ancient mythmakers. The difference is only that we are using a more intricate scale of detail. Ultimately, we understand that all phenomena are composed of energy, but no one really knows what energy is. If we say energy is the stuff that everything is made of, it looks like we've defined what energy is. But if the question we wanted an answer to was "What is everything made of?" then the answer "Energy" isn't really telling us anything. We've merely doubled back on ourselves.

A good example of how science is myth-in-disguise is Isaac Newton's theory that planetary orbits were due to the gravitational pull of the sun. Newton was able to come up with mathematical equations relating to gravity that could predict the positions of planets with some limited accuracy. This lent credibility to his theory. Much later, it was discovered that space and time were nothing like we assumed; they were not fixed and absolute, but curved in relation to the masses of stars. In terms of our solar system, this meant that the planets were not moving in an arc around the sun but in a straight line. Gravity was not the culprit, after all, at least not in the way we had assumed. Einstein came up with his general theory of relativity, which took all this into account, and his mathematical predictions about the orbits of planets proved more accurate than Newton's. In short, Newton's theory about planetary orbits was wrong; his approximation of truth was replaced by a better approximation of truth. Put another way, Newton's myth had outlived its usefulness.

Today, we have a mesmerising amount of detail to play with, right down to molecules, atoms, and subatomic particles, and this is what causes the modern thinker to assume that he's holding the essence of reality in his hands, when he's really only holding *symbols* that attempt to approximate reality. Likewise, ancient myths are symbols, only not so intricate and accurate. When people assume that contemporary science represents the unshakable truth, this gives rise to the notion that we have now reached a pinnacle; we have found that which is true and thus irreplaceable. That's the very same game that religion has played for thousands of years, and it gives rise to the same old unproductive dogmatism. The claim that one has achieved *objective knowledge*, whether from a religious or scientific standpoint, results only in the desire to hold knowledge at a standstill against any new discovery that calls present assertions into question, resulting in the failure to carry knowledge forward to heights unexplored. This attitude describes many atheists and sceptics, who enforce contemporary science as the singular tool in forming their worldview.

My personal area of interest is the clash between the scientific and the occult, specifically the effect of consciousness upon the physical world in a manner that could be described as psychic or magical. To most atheists and sceptics, such a fascination is laughable. In my experience, atheists are generally smart, rational people, but their knowledge tends to be restricted to specific disciplines that they have elevated above all others, and this unfortunately causes them to suffer a degree of tunnel vision.

Three thousand years ago, nobody knew the truth about life, the Universe, and everything. That much is clear from a study of history. Does living in the twenty-first century give me a special advantage in finding that elusive total worldview? No. Our present is just an arbitrary point on the great journey of the evolution of the Universe. When I think about how much more advanced our understanding is today, compared to the ancient world, I like to imagine a hypothetical 5000 AD. I picture someone flicking through the history books and saying, "The twenty-first century – oh yeah, that was when people thought everything was just molecules and atoms. How backward!" Yet those future people, with their ultra-advanced knowledge, may have modern myths of their own to overcome, the likes of which we can't even imagine.

When you understand that science is the modern myth unrealised, your entire focus changes from keeping that myth intact to seeking whatever holds the potential of moving the myth to a deeper level and of taking your understanding forward. The choice is whether you want to align your thinking with the mass of humanity in the present day, as most do. You can join the herd of any of the major world religions; you can even join the herd of materialistic atheism. But the track record of all past herds is that none ever possessed a true and complete worldview that stood the test of time. So there is no reason to assume that the present offers you such a gift by virtue of it being *your* present. It is only our own collective hubris that causes us to dogmatise the present. When we become aware of that failing, it enables us to choose a route not often taken: the path of the pioneer.

H🕯W G🕯DS ARE MADE

WHO or what is God? The Oxford Dictionary states: "creator and ruler of Universe in Christian and other monotheistic religions." Webster's Dictionary says: "the Supreme Being." Christianity defines God as all-powerful (omnipotent), all-knowing (omniscient), and present everywhere (omnipresent). He is eternal, having no beginning and no end; he is the uncaused, self-sufficient source of everything that is; he created the Universe and sustains it by his infinite power.

Notice I said "he." Is God a man? If he is, then we have a problem, because man is a limited being, certainly not omniscient. Then is God, shall we say, *male*? Again we have a problem, for maleness and femaleness are purely aspects of biological life, and God is far more than a biological creature.

This is where I have the task of introducing an ugly but essential word to your vocabulary: *anthropomorphism*. It sounds more complicated than it is. Anthropomorphism is simply the use of human terms to describe God. We anthropomorphise God when we call him *he*, or when we read, "Has the LORD's *arm* been shortened?" (Numbers 11:23). We know intuitively that the use of arm is metaphorical. You've likely heard someone refer to a set of fortuitous circumstances by saying, "That was the *hand* of God."

We know that God is not a man, but we use anthropomorphisms to describe him, and this is done for more than merely poetic reasons. When we conceive of God, we are attempting to wrap our heads around something that is transcendent of space and time. You can't capture the infinite within the finite. The best we can hope for is to approximate the essence of God in terms that we can understand.

For instance, our language allows us three designations when referring to nouns: he, she and it. Which of these fits God best? The very term God carries the idea of consciousness; God is an intelligent being, not a lifeless object. Everyone has heard of the view of God as a bearded old man looking down on us from the clouds. This is, of course, merely a crude anthropomorphism that doesn't do justice to the concept of a divine mind. Notice how we tend to think of God as having a mind. After all, mind is what makes creativity possible, and if we want to conceptualise God as a creative intelligence, he needs a mind. However, it's all too easy to miss the subtle anthropomorphism in what I'm asserting. The reason we describe God as having a mind is because man has a mind. Mind is an anthropomorphism, just like hand or arm. Each time we attempt to describe God in human terms, what we inevitably do is limit him.

Consider what mind actually is. We use mind to interact with the physical world around us. It gives us the ability to process information, store memories, make decisions. Mind is, in essence, a tool for biological creatures to survive and propagate within a linear time-based existence. A goldfish has a type of mind appropriate to its limited needs, just as a human has a more advanced mind appropriate to his. Now, when you consider the eternal nature of God, that he transcends space and time, knows every aspect of past, present and future all at once, what use has God for something as crude as a mind? Since he knows the future, it's not like he can ever change his *mind*, so to speak. We see that mind is what the human uses to engage in creativity, so we posit that God must have a mind, but in doing so we fail to realise that mind is only the creative mechanism in relation to *creatures* that are localised in space and propelled through time. The essence of God transcends the need for such limitations. The lesson here is this: when dealing with the infinite, don't mistake the metaphor for the reality. You'll only put God in a box he doesn't fit inside.

At this point, it's becoming increasingly hard for me to continue using the word God, because it's a loaded term in the ears of most hearers, carrying ideas about a personal being who listens to prayers, accepts worship, declares laws, and executes justice. Thinking purely at a philosophical level, before coming to the matter of religion, I must admit that I have no idea whether any of those qualities apply to God. A better term than God might be the Source, the Whole, the Infinite, or the Transcendent. Frankly, until I deal with religion, I have no idea whether God cares one bit about whether I live or die.

Has the Source interacted with mankind in history? That is perhaps the pivotal question. Let's see what conclusions we can draw from a brief overview of God's alleged dealings with mankind in the Bible. The book of Exodus tells of how the people of Israel were slaves in Egypt until God rescued them using Moses, promising to give them the land of Canaan. God visited ten plagues upon Egypt, including the death of every firstborn Egyptian child in the country, until finally the Pharaoh (king of Egypt) agreed to release the Israelites. Israel then became a nomadic nation for many years, wandering in the wilderness, before finally conquering the land of Canaan. There were many battles in the history of Israel. Genocide, involving the mass slaughter of men, women, children, infants and animals, was not only tolerated but commanded by God (1 Samuel 15).

The activity of God in the Old Testament is that of a tribal deity. His actions were consistent with the establishment and advancement of Israel. This nationalism was most clearly visible in the attitude of God to other nations, where even innocent children of those nations were mercilessly killed. In modern times, this makes for uncomfortable reading, but the Bible presents it without apology. No excuse was needed at the time of writing, because such brutality was common to the era.

Life is drastically different within contemporary Christianity. The kingdom of God is no longer a particular nation, but is scattered throughout the world as disciples within all nations. Nationalism is no longer the aim of the game. God is a God for all peoples of the world. He is a God of love, with a plan to rescue man from the penalty of sin.

There is simply no way to reconcile the God of the Old Testament with the God of the New. They are different in character. The New Testament presents a God who cares intimately about people as individuals, whereas in the Old Testament he was like a steamroller, flattening any innocent women and children who were unlucky enough to be non-Israelites. Is the Bible an account of a *real* God who had real dealings with mankind? On the grounds of the changing character of this deity, I would dare to answer that with a confident no.

There is a clear reason why the God of the Bible is so mercurial: man is a mythmaker. And so, it stands to reason that he conceives of a God (or gods) that serves his particular needs relative to his culture. Consider: after men constructed the Tower of Babel, as the story goes, God took notice and said, "If as one people speaking the same language they have begun to do this, then nothing they plan to do will be impossible for them. Come, let us go down and confuse their language so they will not understand each other" (see Genesis 11:1-9). Was this the action of an eternal being who knows the future from the past? Why was he opposed to people being unified and progressive, as if such behaviour constituted a threat? And if God was so unhappy about a simple tower, what does he think about all our modern science? The passage states, quite clearly, that the Old Testament God was not in favour of mankind educating itself too much. This style of god may have served the needs of a people that had little interest in progress of a scientific nature, but what possible relevance this has for today's culture is beyond me. And it does paint God's motivations to be, let's face it, rather human.

Ancient Israel's goals were nationalistic, and so they had a nationalistic god, whose character approved of the brutality they sought to inflict upon other nations for their own advancement. The modern Church's goals are global, and so the character of God now reflects all-inclusiveness and control: the invitation to everlasting life and the penalty of eternal damnation for rejecting the invitation. Man furnishes the character of his God (or gods) to serve his particular cultural needs.

When I open the Bible, I don't see a real God interacting with mankind; I see the elaborate myth of a poorly realised underlying truth. I see the

Infinite reduced to fit inside a crude box of man's making, told in tales of human imagination. The Book of Genesis states: "God created mankind in his own image" (Genesis 1:27). The truth is the reverse of that statement. If we are prepared to be honest with ourselves, we will see that our ideas about God are actually based on an idealised image of man. We say God is a humanlike consciousness, because that is what we are; we say God has ethics, because humans have ethics; we say God is a monarch, because this mimics the political system of man. All this is merely human egotism at work. We attach these attributes to God because we put such importance on ourselves; the Universe revolves around man, we assume; the whole show is about *homo sapiens sapiens*. And although many Christians will rightly dismiss the crude depiction of God as the white-haired grandfather figure who lives in the sky, they will never fully escape this image because of their need to personalise that which is unfathomable. In the place of a divine old man, they end up relating to something like a blinding light with a human personality – which isn't so different.

We've imagined God in our own image, an anthropomorphic being that is now an outdated myth, kept alive only by our tendency to mistake the metaphor for the reality. When an atheist says to a Christian, "There is no God," he tends to mean, "There is no grandfather in the sky." That is certainly true. But I prefer to put it this way: "Whoever or whatever God is, he/she/it is not what you think."

THE IMPENETRABLE MYSTERY

THEISM is the belief in deity (defined as God or Supreme Being), while atheism is the lack of belief in deity. On the surface, both stances seem as different from each other as black is from white. But beneath all the baggage that we attach to both theism and atheism, these seemingly conflicting paradigms are more alike than you might realise.

Both the theist and the atheist appreciate the concept of cause and effect. For every effect, there is a cause. The proof of this lies in every aspect of the Universe around us. For instance, ripples on a pond tell us that an object previously disturbed the surface. When we say "*Something* created the Universe," we are immediately faced with the need to invent another thing to create the first thing, and so on into infinity. This is termed the problem of infinite regression.

The mythmaking machinery of the brain goes to work to solve this, seeking a logical way to break an infinite chain of causes. We might reason: "Since we exist, we know that *something* has existed forever – something which has permanent existence outside of the known realm of cause and effect, transcending what we call space-time – an Uncaused Cause that is fundamentally *other*, formless and eternal."

This answer satisfies many, especially theists, who use it as an argument for the existence of God. But an important question must be raised: is this Uncaused Cause separate from the Universe, or is the Uncaused Cause the Universe itself?

Am I seriously suggesting that the Universe has always existed? The ancient Greeks could embrace that notion, because they observed a night sky that was largely unchanging. We can no longer entertain that view, because modern science has informed us that the galaxies are moving away from each other. This suggests a unified origin point – what we term the Big Bang, which happened roughly 13.8 billion years ago, according to present calculations.

The Big Bang theory is one of the most misunderstood pieces of science, particularly by theists. They tend to picture an infinite expanse of vacuum into which something popped into existence from nowhere. This is why they insist on a supernatural creator. And I agree. Such a premise would indeed require a supernatural creator of some sort. But the premise is entirely wrong.

Picture, if you will, the "creation" of the Universe in reverse. Imagine all the energy going backwards in time towards that original explosion. It gets smaller and smaller until – poof! It's gone. Or so it seems. It's certainly gone from the point of view of an imaginary observer floating in space, waiting for something to happen. This is a subtle error in perspective that usually goes unnoticed. You see, not only is the observer imaginary, so is *space* itself. The Big Bang was not just the expansion of energy, but the expansion of space.

The real nature of space and time are nothing like what common sense dictates. If you look at a two-dimensional map of the solar system, you will likely imagine that the space between the planets conforms to ordinary geometric assumptions. You might think that drawing a straight line between Mars and Venus would give you an accurate measurement of the distance between these planets at a given moment. In actuality, space is bent and warped all over the place, due to the masses of astronomical bodies. A moon that orbits a planet appears to be moving in a circle, but it is actually *falling*. The reason it doesn't fall directly downward and collide is due to the unusual curvature of space itself around the planet.

We make a similar incorrect assumption when we think of time. We imagine it to be composed of fixed units of measurement, such as the seconds on a clock. But time actually runs at different rates depending on our speed (strictly speaking, a physicist would say that the distance an object travels in space-time changes with respect to its velocity). Amazing as it sounds, time appears to move faster on board a moving train than it does on a nearby platform. According to the mathematics, spending 100 years on board a train moving at 300 kilometres per hour would extend your lifetime by 0.0000000000039 years. Not very practical, but still amazing for being a form of time travel that is real. Time also runs at different rates depending on the strength of a gravitational field, such as that of a planet. If you could somehow spend a year living in deep space, far from any planet, you would discover, upon returning to Earth, that the population has aged more than you have in the time you've been away. Since space and time are linked in this way, they must be thought of as two aspects of a single phenomenon: space-time.

The bizarre idea of space being non-existent prior to the Big Bang is impossible to visualise. Videogames provide a rough analogy. I can take part in a "physical" arena of objects that gives the appearance of three-dimensional space on my television screen. But where do the spatial dimensions of the game arena exist before I switch on the console and after I turn it off? Nowhere. The objects in the arena don't disappear and leave behind an empty arena; the arena itself vanishes. Similarly, without a Universe, there is no space.

When we imagine the Big Bang in reverse, we are conceiving of the Universe shrinking into what we call a *singularity* – a point at which the space-time curvature is infinite. That's a phrase that will take some explaining, but the key factor is that the energy of the Universe does not vanish. It only appears to vanish, if you insist on picturing yourself in space before space existed. I realise this is a somewhat mind-bending scenario, but bear with me. A better way to understand the origin of the Universe is to again imagine time flowing in reverse, but don't look upon the Big Bang as an outside observer. Instead, place your point of observation *within* the energy that makes up the Universe and let it suck you right through the eye of the singularity. Now you're not hanging around in an imaginary blackness, waiting for something to happen; you're in a whole other dimension, immersed in the indescribable "light" of the unmanifest Universe. And if that sounds more poetic than scientific, that's because science cannot transcend space-time.

The singularity at the beginning of the Universe is all the energy of the Universe compressed to infinite density and zero volume. Notice that a singularity refers to *infinity*. The Big Bang is not something out of nothing, as theists commonly misrepresent it. The "creation" of the Universe was more like the bursting of an infinitely big balloon, or the poking of a hole into an infinite *completeness*. This is not something that the mind can fully comprehend.

If we understand the word Universe as a catch-all term for the energy that makes up the Universe, we are justified in saying there never was a time when there was no Universe. In the moment before the Big Bang, the energy of the Universe is still present, only in a formless state. This is the Uncaused Cause, but it isn't something aloof from the Universe, creating the Universe as a thing separate from itself; the Uncaused Cause *is* the Universe.

This understanding is further reinforced by looking at the laws of thermodynamics. The law of conservation of energy states that energy cannot be created or destroyed, only converted from one form to another. It has long been established that matter and energy are not separate; matter is merely a form of energy. Energy is essentially what *everything* in the Universe consists of. For instance, when a predator kills its prey, the physical body of the unfortunate animal is consumed by the attacker and converted into nutrients, which will later be expended as physical activity. When wood is burned, it doesn't vanish, but is converted into heat. Even light is energy. When light strikes a bright surface, it does not disappear, but bounces off and travels elsewhere. When it hits a dark surface, instead of rebounding, it is absorbed. But even then it doesn't cease to exist. It is converted into heat (this is why your body stays cooler if you wear bright clothes on a sunny day). The indestructible nature of energy is an observation of massive metaphysical importance, because we see that energy is imbued with *permanence* – a quality that removes it from the chains of cause and effect.

In other words, if energy is permanent, without end or beginning, then it never had a cause; it simply *is*.

Energy is a term that is used so frequently in science that familiarity breeds contempt; we mistakenly think of energy as something mundane that we have a comprehensive understanding of. In reality, nobody knows what energy is, and our attempts to define it only cause us to double back on ourselves. We ask, "What is energy?" and we answer: "Energy is what everything is made of." But if we should ask, "What is everything made of?" we then answer: "Everything is made of energy." And we pretend we've actually explained something. The question "What is energy?" is one of the great unanswered questions. It may even be unanswerable. After all, explaining something requires contrasting it with something that it is not, and since everything *is* energy, then there is nothing left with which to make a comparison.

The nature of cause and effect is easily misunderstood. When we look at causes of effects, we are always moving backwards in time to things that already existed. At no point in the chain do we ever witness the creation of something out of nothing, only of energy continually changing in form. In positing a separate Uncaused Cause, we are misinterpreting the underlying principle behind causality. In a fundamental sense, there is never any "creation," never anything truly new. When a cause produces an effect, this is merely the recycling of energy that has always existed and will always exist. That observation is both scientifically sound and utterly mind-blowing.

The monotheist should be feeling the hairs stand up on the back of his neck, because the attribute of eternal existence, without beginning or end, is supposed to belong exclusively to God. He is the great *I Am*. And yet science has already proved that the same attribute applies to energy. It is impossible to separate the creator from the creation. The creation never had a beginning and will never have an end, therefore it is *uncreated*. The Universe is not a creation at all, in the strictest sense of the word. What need is there, then, for a creator?

If I believed in God as a deity, I would have to be a panentheist rather than a monotheist. Panentheism views the Universe as an extension of God, not something separate. Not only is panentheism much more in keeping with the scientific evidence, it is much more logical in a very basic sense. If God is the source of everything that exists, then he must have made everything out of his own being. And this is precisely what the law of conservation of energy shows. Once it is understood that the energy of the Universe is *permanent* (uncaused, indestructible, eternal), then the Universe itself is inseparable from the Uncaused Cause, or to the theist, God.

However, I question the necessity of representing God as a divine personality. Human beings are a rather late addition to the Universe; our concept of God as humanlike is really just a reflection of our own feelings of self-importance. It is much more rational to simply bask in the mystery, without striving to put it in a box suitable to the categories of our limited minds. If I absolutely had to embrace a label centred around the Greek word *theos* (god), I would call myself a pantheist, *pan* meaning all: God is the Universe (defined as the totality of everything seen and unseen).

Monotheism should give way to pantheism. This is a bitter pill for religionists to swallow, because they are emotionally attached to the invented human personality of their God, so some are only prepared to go as far as panentheism, which is an attempt at keeping the best of both worlds. It is an admission that the Universe is not separate from God, but God is still viewed as a humanlike overseer with whom creatures can communicate. I cannot disprove that, but there is simply no reason to add it to the existing picture of reality. A religionist cannot explain why an eternal deity should exist any more than a scientist can explain why an eternal Universe should exist. Occam's Razor encourages us to opt for the simplest explanation that makes the fewest assumptions. What we know, beyond a shadow of a doubt, is that energy exists and energy is eternal. Panentheism provides no additional explanatory power whatsoever. One can believe in it on the grounds of religious revelation, if one wishes, but there is no philosophical or scientific necessity for it. Don't get me wrong: there is a colossal mystery behind the visible aspect of energy. But the monotheist (and the panentheist) poisons this mystery by insisting that his own personal caricature of the divine is the reality. If you want to view God as an idealised human, then you might as well view him as an idealised goldfish, because both are merely creatures that evolved from a common ancestor, and this ancestor was not remotely humanlike.

One of the monotheist's chief objections to taking God out of the picture is the problem of infinite regression. Did time begin at a certain point in history, as Christianity would assert, or is there a chain of cause and effect that extends backwards infinitely, Universe after Universe? I favour the latter position, because I don't see infinite regression as a problem. If anything, it's more problematic to explain how time could begin if there's no time to begin with. It's as much of a problem to explain an infinite chain of thoughts in the mind of God as it is to explain an infinite chain of events in time. When did God start making decisions? Presumably since forever.

Infinite regression is only thought to be a problem because we cannot wrap our limited minds around infinity. But we can actually demonstrate the tangible existence of an infinite regress using mathematics. Consider the number pi (π), which is the ratio of a circle's circumference to its diameter. It can be approximated as the decimal value 3.14. A better approximation would be 3.1415926535897932384. But even that is far from close to the *actual* number. It would take all of eternity to write out the numerical value of pi, because the number of digits is infinite. The record number of digits unearthed as of September 2011 was five trillion. Pi can also be expressed as the fraction $^{22}/_7$, but even this is inaccurate. Unlike fractions such as ⅓, the true fractional value of pi cannot be written as a ratio of two integers; 22 and 7 are only close approximations. Pi is what is known as a *transcendental* number. Think of a measuring tape marked out in inches. Pi is an actual number that exists between 3 and 4, but its absolute value cannot be pinned down. You would need to place the tape under a microscope and set the lens to infinite magnification – impossible, and yet the number is real.

Some argue that there is no deep mystery here: the value of pi cannot be stated in full because a perfect circle does not exist in nature. While that is true, it misses the point. The mystery lies in the fact that we can engage ourselves in the task of perfecting the circle for more hours than exist in eternity. The digits of pi just keep coming, and they don't come from nowhere. That should evoke a sense of the transcendent.

And the main lesson from pi: since an infinite regress of ever changing digits can be shown to exist in mathematics, on what grounds do we insist that an infinite regress cannot exist in the wider context of cosmology?

From our understanding of energy, we know that the Universe had no origin in the sense of *creatio ex nihilo* (creation from nothing). As limited beings, we will never grasp the full essence of what lies on the other side of the Big Bang singularity, but we are in a position to appreciate that it is the *transcendent* essence of the Universe itself.

Transcendent of space-time, the singularity is therefore formless and eternal, an all-encompassing One, subject to neither birth nor death. Transcending time, all knowledge is in its grasp (omniscience), and transcending space, all the Universe is in its power (omnipotence). The careful thinker realises at this point that even in making these deductions we are anthropomorphising, for to say that something *knows* is to say that it has a mind, and to say that it has a mind is to limit it in the manner of a creature. We realise that we can't wrap our heads around *It*, but we intuit Its existence (whatever It is) by virtue of the simple fact that *we* are here.

The labels *singularity* and *God* are mythic references to the same underlying reality that I choose to call the Infinite. Underneath all the trappings, the atheist myth and the theist myth are one and the same. The disagreements that arise are not due to a fundamental difference between atheism and theism. It's only the vector of approach that varies. Each side is looking at the same reality from a different angle and so dresses up its myth in a different fashion.

The atheist, with his focus on science, has a natural tendency to view the cause of the manifest Universe in mechanistic terms. The theist, with his focus on spirituality, has a natural tendency to view the cause as a humanlike mind. Neither mythic outlook suffices, because both seek to conceptualise the infinite and unknown in terms that are relative to the finite and known, and in doing so they impose false limits. The Infinite is neither conscious nor unconscious; being formless and eternal, it is not subject to any of our limited categories. It is the Mystery of Mysteries. We can't comprehend it any more than a sparrow could understand algebra.

The strictly scientific approach has always rendered the Infinite as non-conscious, which has caused a failure of modern man to derive meaning from his myth, rendering him sorrowful over his insignificant place in a cold, clockwork Universe devoid of meaning. This is one small advantage of the spiritual approach to the Infinite. While religionists have often reduced the Infinite to an anthropomorphic shell of its true profundity, they have still been able to derive meaning from a sense of personal connection to something greater than their individual selves. This meaning is, unfortunately, poisoned by our tendency to go too far in anthropomorphising God, such as when he is portrayed as hot-tempered, tyrannical and genocidal in the Old Testament – traits that are projected onto God simply because they are seen in man.

Even the term the Infinite is inadequate, because it sounds so cold and mathematical. We don't have an accurate term for this, because language acts as a box, confining our ability to express our thoughts within a limited set of existing categories. If I refer to the Infinite as *he*, I've limited it as a personal deity; if I refer to the Infinite as *it*, I've turned it into a lifeless object. I could call it Raxxla, which sounds mysterious, hinting at secret lore from an ancient forgotten culture. Truth be told, it doesn't mean a thing, and that's the point. If I could understand it in finite terms, then it wouldn't be what I'm referring to. Whatever terminology we employ, it's vital not to lose the awareness that we are foolishly attempting to define *that which cannot be imagined.*

Recognising the false limits imposed by both theism and atheism, I am able to extract meaning from the understanding that the Infinite represents the fundamental reality beyond space-time. All that is here comes from there. The finite components of the Universe (of which you are one) are manifestations of their infinite source, because without the infinite there is no finite. Monotheistic religions have viewed the Infinite as something aloof from us – something that formed the Universe as a creation separate from itself. But science has shown us that the Universe *is* the Infinite exploding into time and space, the One given expression in a realm where individuality is made possible through physical form and temporal duration.

I am convinced that the pursuit of a Theory of Everything is a fool's errand. We will never fully comprehend the Universe by examining the components of the Universe. Certainly, we can understand the behaviour of one component as it relates to the other components; when Einstein paid enough attention to light, he came up with the theory of relativity, and that's just one example out of thousands. But to fully comprehend something, we need to look at where it came from. For instance, our understanding of what it means to be a human being is informed by our knowledge of the evolution of organic matter. But to gain a complete perspective, we need to look back even further – as far as we possibly can. And here's what we find: everything in the Universe, including you, originated as a singularity. Form is an outgrowth of formlessness, and formlessness is completely baffling to the mind. How do you categorise something that transcends categories? It can't be done. Science gives you a lot of useful data and then it confronts you with a brick wall. The realistic goal of science is *practical* knowledge, not conquering infinity. No matter how much you learn, you will always be left with an infinite mystery that science cannot penetrate. The philosopher Socrates said, "The only true wisdom is knowing you know nothing." You can either let that predicament frustrate you, or you can bask in its glow.

What does this mean in relation to me as a creature? It means I am the Infinite expressed within the finite. I am the Singularity flung into the physical and temporal. I am the Transcendent reduced to fit inside a limited body and brain. I am the One manifesting itself as one of many.

So, in answer to the question "Are you a theist or an atheist?" I can only reply, "Neither. I believe in the Infinite." And when asked to define that term, though I am acutely aware that this twenty-first century ape is only in a position to scratch the surface of infinity, I reply, "The impenetrable mystery behind everything that is."

Put simply, this is a return to the sense of wonder that we naturally experience as children, before dogmatic religion dictates man-made lies as truth, or materialistic science blinds us with nihilism.

SPACE: THE PERCEPTION DECEPTION

A BOY was walking through the neighbourhood with his dad, when the man made a critical remark about some graffiti that had been painted on a wall across the road.

The boy looked at the wall. "What graffiti?" he asked.

"*That* graffiti," his dad said, pointing.

"What are you talking about? There's nothing there."

The man didn't find this game particularly funny. "What are you – blind?"

As it turned out, the boy was colour blind. From the beginning of his life until that event, no one had known, because nobody had been able to look out through his eyes except him. And he had no idea that he was viewing the world differently from others.

To be severely red-green colour blind is to stop at a road junction and watch the traffic light change from red to amber to red again – or from green to amber green. Take your pick, because both colours look the same to a person experiencing colour blindness. What does this weird mix of red and green look like – brown? Not quite. To be red-green colour blind is to play a game of snooker and not be able to tell the red balls from the green ball. The brown ball is still brown. Actually, that's not quite right, either. A colour blind person would see brown as something different from the way we see it. Colours are perceived by cone cells in the retina which activate a pigment when they absorb light. A correctly functioning human eye has three such cones. With these we perceive every possible colour from black to white. A form of colour blindness occurs when only two of the cones are functioning.

This is similar in principle to computer printers that have separate cartridges for cyan, magenta and yellow. If you've ever printed a page without realising that one of your cartridges is faulty, the resulting image will look a little trippy. It's not just green grass or red lips that are affected; it's *everything*, because everything on the page is made up of combinations of just three colours. This will give you some idea of how the world looks to a colour blind person. Just bear in mind that it looks perfectly normal to him, because it's all he has ever known. Imagine red lipstick and green grass appearing to you as almost the same colour. In the example of the graffiti, the wall must have been a particular shade of red brick and the paint a particular shade of green. A lucky balance on the colour spectrum rendered the whole message invisible to the boy, while it stood out starkly to his father.

Before you think "The poor guy never gets to see what the world really looks like," are you certain that what you're seeing is what it really looks like? Consider the bee. Its eyes are able to see ultraviolet light, which is invisible to humans. Flowers look vastly different to bees and other insects, compared to how people perceive them. So, never mind having a faulty human eye. Who sees the world as it truly is – the human or the bee?

Or how about the bat? Bats have extremely poor eyesight and navigate by a form of radar called echolocation. Have you ever wondered what sort of picture of reality a bat has in its little brain? Something quite different from what we humans have, and yet I'm sure the bat feels it's "seeing" the world as it really is.

In 1897, George Stratton, a psychologist from California, designed an experiment involving a pair of goggles that made the wearer see the world upside down. The goggles were worn all day, every day, for a period of several weeks. First of all, the observer had trouble coordinating himself, as you would expect. But after a period of time, an interesting effect occurred: he started to see the world the right way up again, while wearing the glasses. What really happened was that his mind had learned to adjust itself to the new way that the world was being presented to him. As a result of uninterrupted habit, the mind decided that this was how things should look. It got so comfortable with upside-down vision that upside-down vision became the norm. Even more interesting was what happened when the observer finally took the glasses off, returning his eyes to their normal operation: the whole world suddenly flipped upside down. And it stayed upside down until the brain went through yet another period of adjustment.

Interestingly, our perceptions of the world around us are not fixed. When we deliberately distort those perceptions, our minds will grow accustomed to the new way of seeing the environment and we will feel that it looks perfectly normal. Whether it's upside down or right side up matters not. Either way, it's just an interpretation. We can't get our hands on the *actuality* of the physical world.

It's not even true to say that we see with our eyes. Light enters the eyes. It is then converted into electrical impulses and sent to an area at the very back of the brain called the visual cortex. It's *here* that we do our seeing, deep inside the darkness of our own skulls, which no actual light can penetrate. Light stopped being light the moment it struck the retina of the eye. None of us has ever actually seen light, strange as that sounds. What we see is a product of light, a second-hand pictorial representation inside our heads of a world outside our heads.

But I have to wonder, since I can't reach that world beyond my eyes, what can I say with certainty about it? If I've never seen light, is light really light? Or is it something else? If all I've got is the interpretation that my brain presents to me, what can I really say about the source? What can I say about the *actuality* of light? Nothing.

Can I claim with certainty that the Universe around me has any more substance than a dream? "Of course! Don't be silly," someone will say, slapping their hand against the table. "Look. I can feel this. It's solid. It's real." But let's look closely. Do you really feel the table with your hand? Isn't it more true to say that your hand transmits a message to your brain via your nerves, and your brain then says to you, "You felt that in your hand." Notice it's not your hand telling you that; it's your brain. The solid feel of the table is no more an indicator of the solidity of the world around you than what your eyes are telling you. All of the information your mind receives about the world comes second-hand, via your senses, therefore there is no means of determining the essential nature of the source of that information.

"Shouldn't we just have a little faith?" you might ask. "It seems a bit obvious that the world is more than a dream." Well, this journey is all about questioning our assumptions, so before we jump hook, line and sinker back into conditioned thinking, consider the following factors.

Firstly, when we dream, we experience an interactive world of sight, hearing, smell, taste and touch. For the duration of the dream, our consciousness is usually convinced that it is awake and experiencing the real world. Take note that during this experience, at no time do we see with an actual pair of eyes, hear with an actual pair of ears, or touch with actual skin. Certainly, the laws of physics in a dream-world tend to be a little free and changeable, and in this respect dreams and the external world are clearly different. The only point I'm making is that a "real" external world is not necessary in order to have a five-sense experience. You appear to be in the dream, but the dream is really in you. So, my question is this: is your physical body, and the Universe it inhabits, truly physical in its fundamental nature? Or is physicality just a perception, as it is in dreams? We really have no way of knowing, since the answer lies on the other end of our perceptions.

Our common sense tells us that the five distinct means we have of perceiving the world correspond to five separate aspects of the world: lights, sounds, scents, tastes and material objects. But this is not the case at all. One of our senses is called touch, but all five senses are really variations of a single sense that can best be described as touch. When we smell, this is due to airborne particles *touching* our nostrils; when we see, this is due to particles of light (photons) travelling through space and *touching* our retinas; when we hear, it is because subtle movements of the air around us *touch* our eardrums.

We exist in an arena of sense-perception called the electromagnetic spectrum. Visible light (that which humans perceive) is only a tiny part of the whole spectrum. Adjacent to visible light, on one side, we have ultraviolet light, then X-rays, and gamma rays. On the other side of visible light we have infrared light, microwaves, and radio waves. When we look across the room, we see what appear to be solid objects and solid walls, but if our bodies possessed organs that could emit and perceive X-rays, we would be able to see/touch beyond the walls in a remarkable way. There would be little point in children playing hide-and-seek in such a world.

We feel as if the radio waves around us don't exist, until we switch on our radios and televisions and a whole world of sound and vision suddenly springs to life out of thin air. We think of the objects around us as solid and impenetrable, because our bodies, being made of the same kind of energy, cannot pass through them. But that doesn't deter radio waves, which will pass through the atoms of the walls of your house and touch the aerial on top of your radio. Your suitcase, as it passes through the X-ray scanner at the airport, is anything but solid on the monitor. Sound will pass through solid matter to an extent (noisy neighbours, anyone?), but when sound waves meet a vacuum, they stop as if striking a brick wall. This is why we have double-glazed windows – two panes of glass separated by a slice of vacuum. Imagine a powerful sound wave travelling upwards through the atmosphere. As the air thins, the wave's progress is impeded until finally it reaches the vacuum of space and ceases altogether. To sound, a vacuum is an impenetrable barrier, whereas a solid wall merely dampens its progress. For visible light, the opposite holds true; light travels through the vacuum of space unimpeded, whereas it stops dead when a physical object gets in its way. Taking this into account, we come to the remarkable understanding that what we call solidity is entirely relative; matter is only solid in relation to a creature's optic nerve and the molecules of its body.

Quantum physics has established that matter itself isn't truly made of particles, but waves, just like the electromagnetic spectrum. The famous double slit experiment, pioneered in 1803 by Thomas Young, showed experimentally that photons behave like waves rather than particles. The experiment consisted of a device that would fire photons at a barrier. The barrier featured two thin vertical gaps, side by side. Any photons that made it through the gaps would continue their journey. After a short distance, the finish line was a photographic plate that the photons would strike and leave their mark. Common sense dictated that when enough particles were fired, the image on the plate should have consisted of two parallel vertical lines. But in an act of extreme weirdness, the result was an interference pattern of many vertical lines, consistent with wavelike behaviour – like the intersecting of two sets of ripples, caused by two pebbles tossed into a pond.

We could understand this if two distinct photons entered the two slits at the same time, creating two separate waves that then interfered with each other. But the really mind-blowing aspect of this experiment is what happened when the photons were fired one at a time. According to Newtonian mechanics and plain old common sense, a single photon ought to pass through only one of the two slits, or none. When enough photons were fired, we should have ended up with two lines on the photographic plate, as some photons entered via the left slit, others entered via the right, and still others struck the barrier and stopped. But amazingly, we still ended up with an interference pattern of many lines, an interference pattern that gradually built up *one* photon at a time. If that doesn't strike you as utterly mind-boggling, then you're not thinking carefully about what the word interference means. One pebble dropped in a pond will create waves of perfect circles expanding from the centre. There can't be interference in the waves unless there are two pebbles dropped. So how does *one* photon create interference? Each photon seemed to begin as a particle, become a wave of potentiality while travelling, turn into two waves that interfere after passing through the slits, then turn back into a single particle as it struck the plate. Whatever this implies about reality, it's clear that we are not living in a material world that consists only of Newtonian mechanics.

The original experiment was concerned with light, but in 1999 a team of physicists in Austria replicated the experiment successfully using a series of football-shaped molecules made of carbon atoms. This is documented by Stephen Hawking and Leonard Mlodinow in *The Grand Design* (2010). We now know conclusively that matter can and does behave in a manner that is supposed to be impossible according to Newton's laws. What exactly is the Universe made of?

At school, we are taught that atoms are like the LEGO blocks of the Universe – the fundamental units stacked together in three-dimensional space. Once you dig a little deeper, you discover that atoms are made of protons, neutrons and electrons. Don't worry too much about what those are, other than tiny bits that make up the material Universe. These bits actually constitute the minutest fraction of the atom itself. Atoms are more like tiny forcefields than blocks; they mostly consist of empty space. This is what allows some parts of the electromagnetic spectrum to pass through "solid" matter. But keep digging and the forcefield analogy doesn't hold true, either, as quantum theory reveals electrons jumping around the Universe in a manner that defies all common sense.

Since I am not a physicist, nor do I even remotely comprehend the mathematics behind quantum theory, I will quote directly from those who know what they are talking about: "Quantum theory is perhaps the prime example of the infinitely esoteric becoming the profoundly useful. Esoteric, because it describes a world in which a particle really can be in several places at once and moves from one place to another by exploring the entire Universe simultaneously. Useful, because understanding the behaviour of the smallest building blocks of the Universe underpins our understanding of everything else." That's from the opening chapter of *The Quantum Universe* (2011) by Brian Cox and Jeff Forshaw.

If I called this subatomic teleportation, that doesn't come close to explaining the strange behaviour of the electron. Einstein, who established that nothing can travel faster than the speed of light, called it "spooky action at a distance." His context was the classical level of reality. But we know that the classical level is ultimately constructed from the fuzzier, weirder subatomic arena. The world you see with your eyes is not reality itself, but the product of a more fundamental reality that is almost incomprehensible to the mind – and I'm not sure I'm justified in including the word *almost*.

The atomist philosophers of ancient Greece originally employed the term *atom* to represent the theoretical fundamental particles of reality; *a* in front of *tom* means non-divisible. But atoms, as it turned out, weren't so fundamental. Inside the atom, we uncovered the electron. And the electron, instead of behaving like a nice tidy Lego block bound by the laws of physics, was simply going bananas. It was as if the Universe said, "Ah-ha, you thought you had me all figured out. Now, watch *this*."

Our failure to arrive at a complete and coherent classical view of the Universe tells us that the Universe's fundamental nature is not classical; it is *non-local*, not bound by the laws of space-time that apply to everyday objects. We needed a whole new theoretical science, along with strange terms like entanglement and superposition, just to deal with the misbehaviour of the electron – a science so complicated that a popular saying (widely attributed to the physicist Richard Feynman) is: "If you think you understand quantum mechanics, you don't understand quantum mechanics." There are various competing quantum theories on offer, but what is certain is that commonsense materialism no longer works. The entire Universe is better modelled as a *unified field* – an interconnected unity where nothing is separate, including the fundamental particles. When a particle can exist in several places at once, that's telling us the idea of a localised particle is an inadequate symbol for modelling reality. The Universe seems to appear to us as particles when we're observing or measuring it. But when we're not looking, it behaves as waves.

It's not as if the Universe actually flips between two states, depending upon observation. We simply need to differentiate between the *appearance* of reality and reality itself. Colour, for instance, is an aspect of the appearance of reality. But any physicist will tell you that colour is not real in nature. Nature contains frequency and wavelength; colour is only how those *appear* to human consciousness. The fact that we can *observe* fundamental particles and waves makes them both aspects of the *appearance* of reality. Wave and particle are both inadequate terms, because they are symbolic representations of reality, not reality itself. That is why they appear to conflict. The term *unified field* is one that allows us to transcend the limitations of our current symbols. Unified field points to reality itself, beyond appearances. Crucially, reality is never anything but a unified field, despite how it appears when measured by humans.

Try to visualise an incomprehensible mass of interpenetrating waves. Within this sea of energy, some waves interfere with each other, creating patterns. The persistent illusion of seemingly solid matter is the pattern that arises in our experience. But let's ignore this mirage, in an effort to get in touch with whatever else is going on. Try thinking of the world around you as invisible; see only the edges of objects and walls. Visualise the various electromagnetic waves flowing through the structure as an array of colours. This crude approximation is closer to the true essence of reality than the world in front of your eyes, which is really the world seen through a pinhole.

It's hard for our common sense to embrace the idea that solidity isn't truly solid, regardless of what the science says, but modern videogames provide a useful analogy to help us make the transition. In a game, we can take part in adventures across city-sized maps, with amazingly detailed roads, buildings, and countless nooks and crannies for exploration. We can make our game character turn his head in any direction and watch the real-world laws of geometry playing out in two-dimensional space on the flatness of our television screens, beaming out texture, light and shadow. Once, while playing a videogame, I had a moment of clarity. I was standing on a virtual hillside, gazing down through the trees at a lake and a castle on the opposite side. It was a picturesque scene, and in the real world it might have made me reach for my camera. I thought, "No one else has stood on this precise spot and looked down the hill at this exact angle. Not even the game's creators. The game arena is just too vast." It struck me as profound that something so aesthetically pleasing – something that was just for me in this moment and no one else – could spring to life from nothing more than a rapid series of mathematical equations being processed inside my computer. In videogames, we experience an interactive world of sight, sound and touch – a limited but spectacularly detailed facsimile of the physical world. The big question, then, is this: since we are able to create this 3D experience inside a computer, should we assume that our Universe is truly 3D in its deepest essence, in its actuality? The three-dimensionality of a videogame is nothing more than a river of binary ones and zeroes flowing through electrical circuits, and yet the laws of physics in a game are as solid and dependable as the laws of physics in the real world.

Where does all the mathematics in a videogame come from? It comes from observing the physical Universe, understanding how it consists of geometry, light and shadow, then recreating it elsewhere. Using today's powerful computers, the mathematical computations can be so extensive as to produce photorealism almost indistinguishable from the real world, such as the special effects in big-budget movies. The reason why we can create an approximation of the physical Universe on a two-dimensional television screen using nothing more than mathematics is because *the Universe has no more actual substance than its mathematics*. We are so used to thinking of atoms as the building blocks of reality, but in an even deeper sense, it's mathematics that's holding everything together, and the atoms are nothing more than bits of information being organised by mathematical principles. We tend to think of the physical world as being the fundamental reality – what's really real – but from a mathematical perspective, the world doesn't need actual solidity in order to be experienced. It only needs mathematical organisation. Solidity is the interpretation that your consciousness places on the information it receives.

"But the Universe is so big!" you object. Well, when I hold a disc in my hand containing a videogame that allows me to explore an entire city, does the magnitude of that city have any bearing whatsoever on the tiny object I'm holding? No. Likewise the physical size of the Universe has no bearing on its fundamental essence.

A group of people can exist in various places across the world and can take part as players in a single three-dimensional videogame arena via the Internet. By the same principle, consciousness can experience the Universe without the need for an actual physical Universe in the classical sense. Life conditions us to automatically make the assumption that the mathematics is an expression of a fundamentally real physical world, but when you dig deep and really think about it, you realise it's the other way around: the apparent solidity of the world is an expression of the mathematics. Solid matter is only the mathematical organisation of data.

If you've never witnessed a hologram in real life, I recommend the experience. There are many cheap holograms on sale, which feature only two flat levels of depth, one on top of the other. A proper hologram is a much more startling image to behold. I have one in my possession: a holographic photo of a panther facing the camera with its jaws open (presumably a *stuffed* panther). Some people have asked me, "Why do you have a black picture on your wall?" The hologram is invisible in normal lighting conditions, but when you dim the lights and shine a light onto it at a certain angle – wham! The panther's snout is poking right out of the glass at you, while its forehead is somewhere inside the glass, fully 3D. You can even change the viewing angle of the photo and watch the head tilt slightly from left to right, allowing you to literally see around corners. If you look inside its mouth, you can peek behind its fangs to parts of the tongue that were previously hidden from view. It all looks completely solid to your mind, and yet it's not. Reach out and touch the end of its nose and your finger passes through air. The appearance of three-dimensionality does not require actual three-dimensionality, and if we are able to demonstrate such a principle with our own human inventiveness, it should not be so great a leap to comprehend that the Universe itself acts on a similar principle.

When we gravitate towards our established understanding that the Universe is solid, we're not necessarily gravitating to the truth, only to the familiar. And that familiarity is based on nothing more concrete than the assumptions of our heavily conditioned life.

Someone may say, "I switched on my camcorder, pressed record, and left the room. When I came back and checked the tape, it had recorded the room successfully. Clearly the physical world exists apart from my perceptions of it, since I've managed to capture a part of it on video when I wasn't looking." This is a misunderstanding of the holographic perspective. All the mathematical computations that keep the Universe running are quite real, including the computations of a holographic camera recording a holographic room. I once played a videogame where one of my character's gadgets was a camera that I could stick to a wall, enabling me to wander elsewhere in the game arena and check on the camera remotely any time I wished. Here is the same principle, existing in a completely virtual world. In the real world, when you look at a recording, you are proving nothing about the nature of reality, because once again, you can only see the recording as a perception through your eyes and brain.

To call the Universe a hologram is not to make assumptions about it, but to strip the existing assumptions away – assumptions that have festered there simply by the conditioning of your life experience and education. It is to say, simply, that the Universe is *information*. The Universe according to Newton is officially dead. The realm of separate objects stacked in three-dimensional space is merely an appearance of a much deeper and stranger reality where everything is interconnected as a unity.

Some people simply will not enter into this manner of thinking, because it seems repugnant that the Universe should be telling us fibs about itself. But consider: we thought the Earth was flat, because that's how we saw it, but it was spherical. We thought the Earth was stationary at the centre of the Universe, because that's how we experienced it, but it was actually orbiting the sun. We thought space was fixed and absolute, because that's how it appeared, but it was bent and warped. We thought time existed in discrete units, because that's how we experienced it, but it was elastic. When a kitten sees its reflection in a mirror for the first time, it thinks it's looking at another kitten, one that mimics its every move; its interpretation of the world is wrong until it eventually learns its mistake. We are no different. The key question is whether you want to trust your perceptions or try to see the bigger picture. To assert "There is no deeper truth than what my eyes tell me" is to lock yourself into the outdated classical paradigm.

The Universe lies until you figure out the lies. Its purpose is not to tell you its innermost secrets. Its purpose, at least in relation to creatures, is to facilitate conscious experience. It is up to us to probe its true nature.

MIND: A CASE OF MISTAKEN IDENTITY

THE common model of consciousness here in the West is that man consists of a body and a mind. The former is seen as physical, while the latter is regarded as metaphysical – at least within spiritual traditions. The modern psychologist, seeking to define everything in the Universe in materialistic terms, has attempted to view consciousness as a purely physical phenomenon, but he has been confounded by the fact that he cannot locate it in the brain.

Some clarification is required. It is true that the mind is utterly dependent upon the physical brain. A person with Down's syndrome will suffer a compromised personality. Alzheimer's disease hinders one from thinking straight. A head injury can result in memory loss; a knock sufficient to induce a coma will cause consciousness to cease altogether for a spell, as will an injection of anaesthetic. Chemical substances, such as caffeine, alcohol and psychoactive drugs, bring about temporary personality changes. The masculinity in a man's nature and the femininity in a woman's are due to a hormonal balance. The same is true of the differences between adult and child personalities. Furthermore, in the very early stages of our evolutionary history, we didn't even possess anything that you would realistically call a mind. We were nothing more than clumps of cells, mutating and replicating. The brain is a material thing that took billions of years to evolve into what it is today, and mind and brain are inseparable.

Clearly, consciousness requires the brain in order to function. We've even been able to identify the specific roles of various sections of the brain. An understandable assumption, then, is that consciousness is a component of the brain. Interestingly, it hasn't been found. The reality of subjective experience remains a profoundly weird phenomenon to explain, so tricky that science refers to it as *the hard problem* of consciousness.

If we take what we know about the mind and seek to reproduce one artificially, we get a clearer sense of the difficulty facing the materialist in his attempt to find the core of himself. Consider the robotics toy LEGO Mindstorms. We can create a body from blocks, implant a computer processor which can receive information from the physical world using a sensor – the same principle as our eyes. The processor interprets that information into a usable form that makes sense, just like our brain does with what our eyes see. The robot would even be able to perceive itself as an aspect of that environment, enabling it to move about and determine where it's going from where it has been. But it's not real consciousness. It's mere mimicry – a feedback loop with nothing at the centre. The robot does not experience what you know so intimately as an I-feeling. The robot's mind is merely blind, predictable electricity flowing through electronic logic gates. To say that this is the same in principle as consciousness is to say that consciousness doesn't exist. But you feel your own existence very keenly, don't you? And who or what is this mysterious *you*?

The scientifically oriented Westerner does not like the fact that he cannot seem to locate, measure and disassemble consciousness, so he has an unfortunate tendency to throw the baby out with the bathwater – essentially declaring himself to be an automaton. "Consciousness is a brain-generated illusion," he claims. Fortunately for me, this is not a position I need to waste much time refuting, because I don't believe in arguing with other illusions, and I don't know why illusions would want to argue with me. So, if we are going to argue, at least admit that the conscious activity of arguing is *real* – or disappear. If we say consciousness is an illusion, it can only be an illusion in the sense that we might refer to the material Universe as illusory, meaning that the seemingly solid classical Universe is more fundamentally a non-local Universe. This does not mean that matter isn't real; it just means that the fundamental nature of matter isn't what sense perception informs us. Similarly, we should not claim that consciousness is unreal, for we will make liars out of ourselves every waking moment as we depend upon it. Declaring consciousness an illusion preserves a materialistic worldview, with all the I's dotted and the T's crossed, but the conclusion simply doesn't match experience: you *feel* conscious – whatever it is we mean by *you*.

Something profoundly strange is peering out from behind your eyes – something that doesn't exist inside a robot, or inside any artificial intelligence. I suspect it's the feeling part of this predicament that's hard, because the one-dimensional thinking of the material minimalist won't allow for anything that refuses to be neatly catalogued in rational language. Nevertheless, there it is: *you* are here.

A less extreme conclusion than declaring consciousness an illusion is the anticipation that one day we *will* locate it within the brain. Experience tells us that consciousness is real, only currently not understood. This view may be accompanied by speculation that we will one day be able to create an artificial intelligence that is genuinely self-aware. But I'm confident we're never going to locate consciousness in the brain. Why not? Because the direction of this endeavour stems from a faulty model of the human organism – one that we unwittingly imbibed from our culture's Christian heritage: mind-body dualism. The quest to make a computer conscious begins with the subtle presupposition that consciousness is a tangible entity made out of parts. But it's not, as I aim to show.

In the Christian tradition – as well as many other spiritual traditions and especially the philosophy of René Descartes (1596-1650) – the mind is viewed as an entity. Even if we call it a soul and consider it immaterial, it is still conceived of as an identifiable *thing* distinct from other things, just as much a component of the body as the heart or lungs. While on Earth, this soul pilots the body, and when the body dies, the soul possibly continues. Although the modern rationalist is much more realistic about the nature of the mind, the subtle influence of our religious heritage often weighs in as a silent partner. We buy into mind-body dualism without realising it, by continuing to look for the pilot of the vehicle. Surely the reason we can't find it is obvious: the model itself is wrong.

Look at what happens to this hypothetical pilot when a person is struck over the head and goes into a coma. The pilot does not continue to exist in a dark room, consciously waiting for the body to recover. The pilot is simply not there; it has stopped existing entirely. And when sufficient physical healing has taken place, the pilot appears to pop back into existence. How odd. If you believe in an afterlife, you really must face up to how absent your hypothetical soul is at times during *this* life, never mind the next one. When you are in a coma, your soul's lack of presence is every bit as profound as it was before you were born. In fact, the phrase "when you are in a coma" is nonsensical. There is no *you* having an experience called *coma*. A coma is pure non-experience. When you wake up, there is no memory of having gone somewhere. You were simply not there, and now you are there again. Let's imagine that your assailant looks at your unconscious body, checks your pulse, and says, "Oh, he's still alive. I can fix that." So he whacks you on the head a second time, dealing a fatal blow. At this point, does it seem likely that the pilot, which had already been rendered non-existent, would suddenly pop back into existence outside of the body? Why would a soul be immortal when it can both be and not be during this life?

Someone might object: "It's quite a leap to say that souls don't exist just because they sleep and wake up." Notice that they "sleep" when the physical brain is injured. By the same reasoning, they would sleep permanently when the brain is terminally injured. I propose that whatever consciousness is, we should not view it as an entity, because entities do not flip in and out of existence. We're not a mind or soul piloting a vehicle, nor are we a pilotless vehicle. The solution does not have to be one or the other, because the whole foundation of the dilemma is in error, creating false alternatives.

A much more rationally satisfying understanding of consciousness will become apparent once we dispense with the existing dualistic model. When the Universe is understood as a unified field, we come to appreciate the world in front of our eyes as a vast sea of energy where nothing is separate from anything. Objects appear to be separate to our senses, but their fundamental essence is not so. Even when this esoteric perspective is grasped, there is still a tendency to view oneself as a separate observer of the Universe. But if the Universe is unified, there cannot be *you* and the Universe; the unified field isn't unified if there's an entity called *you* separate from it. The only possible conclusion is either (1) there is no you after all, or (2) you are the Universe itself – not a *part* of it; you're IT. We naturally resist both options. The first denies the reality of our experience as conscious creatures; the second looks like egomania. Nevertheless, let option two simmer for a moment, and see how it sits with you when augmented with the following considerations.

Consciousness is not a tangible entity made of physical bits, because any arrangement of pieces is never anything more than an arrangement of pieces, each of which can be examined and its function identified. For instance, if I put various metals and plastics together in a particular way, I end up with a combustion engine. And if I build other metals and plastics around it in a certain manner, I have a car. But there are no actual *entities* called car and engine. There is only a functional arrangement of metals and plastics, which in turn are made of molecules, which in turn are made of subatomic particles. The only result you ever achieve from construction is utility, the performance of a function.

In recognising this, it suddenly becomes clear that consciousness is not a physical component of the brain, but the *function* of the brain – just as turning fossil fuel into motion is the function of a combustion engine. You would never say, "Where can I find the component called 'turning fossil fuel into motion' within the engine?"

So consciousness is what the brain *does*, not what it *is* – not even a component of what it is. The function of anything is what occurs when its components work in harmony. The question "Where do I find consciousness in the brain?" is actually a nonsense question. It doesn't immediately look like nonsense because of a subtle trick that language plays upon us. Nouns are words referring to persons, places or things. Note that consciousness is a noun. This unfortunately causes us to instinctively think of consciousness as a tangible entity separate from all other entities, requiring explanation as an entity. But what we really mean by consciousness is the feeling of being aware.

A significant roadblock to a correct understanding of ourselves is the feeling that we ought to formulate our sense of self as a noun – an entity, a thing. "I am a *being*," we think. But there really is nothing stopping you from viewing yourself as a verb, and it's much more rational: "I am a *doing*." It sounds odd, but it's true. Nothing about you is stationary and unchanging. Physically, you age from moment to moment. Imagine an entire life, from birth to death, sped up so that you see the body age in ten seconds flat. Is that a being? It looks more like a doing. The mind is similarly changing over the course of a life; it's also a doing. We mistakenly believe we are beings because the process of change happens so slowly that we become attached to immediate experience. But nothing is truly being; it's all doing. Every "lasting" entity that you identify with a noun is really a *process* that is verbing away: the galaxy, the sun, the pyramids, life, awareness – all verbs masquerading as nouns. So let go of the need to define yourself as an entity. There are none!

Many people think they possess an individual soul only because they inherited this particular idea through their culture and were never made aware of any alternative model of the mind-body relationship. Terms like mind, consciousness and soul are so convenient to use in communication, and for most purposes they serve us effectively. But if we are to understand the nature of reality to a greater extent, we need to be aware of the subtle trap that language puts in our path, even though we must continue to use inaccurate words in communication.

All nouns are, in a sense, problematic, because they identify *things* in a Universe where nothing is a thing-in-itself. What a noun really identifies is an object-environment contrast, a pattern standing out within a larger pattern. *Things* only make sense when perceived in relation to each other. This is true of *everything* in the Universe. Can you have solids without space? No, because everything would be solid and thus formless. A solid is really a solid-space contrast. We don't notice this, because we have a tendency to ignore the background.

Can you have a single colour without a colour spectrum? No, because everything would be one colour and thus indistinguishable. It's not even strictly true to say that red and orange are different colours. My computer is capable of displaying millions of different shades of colour across the whole spectrum from white to black. When I identify red, this isn't just *one* out of several million. Red is part of a vaguely defined range of shades. If I move the slider on my photo editing software halfway between red and orange, then ask several individuals to identify the colour, some might say red and others orange. Is it a reddish orange or an orangey red? There's really no distinct entity that I can label red. There is only the single spectrum of colour and the labels we attach in order to quantify it. The more we try to isolate individual units of colour, the more names we require for the different tones: amaranth, byzantium, periwinkle, viridian, to name just a few. How many *real* colours are there? Well, even the sixteen million shades of colour in my computer are due to the digital limitations of the microchip. We would need an infinite number of words in order to name every colour tone, because underneath our subjective divisions, there are no individual units; it's *one* spectrum.

The same is true of the measurement of distance and time. The millimetre and the nanosecond can be divided into even smaller units, and those can be divided again, *ad infinitum.* All our attempts at defining the Universe in terms of bits are foiled, because the Universe is not ultimately made of *units* of stuff. Not even when you get right down to fundamental particles, because those particles are also waves, depending on how you look at them.

Let's now attempt to see the Universe, not as a vast collection of separate entities, but as a *field* where nothing is separate from anything, not even the division of mind from matter, nor the division of living matter from dead matter. Since life and consciousness both exist, we could refer to the Universe as a super-organism engaged in a vast array of *relationships* with itself.

First, understand that the human body is not a thing-in-itself; it is a series of relationships between bones, muscles, blood, and so forth. But notice how these relationships extend outward from the body into the environment. We tend to make the distinction between self and other at the point where our skin encloses our internal organs, but the body is just as dependent on the air entering it from "outside" as it is on the blood circulating "inside." There is no fundamental separation. When I jump on my motorbike, in a very real sense I become an organism that you might call the man-bike, for the duration of the ride. The nerves and sinews of my body interface with the cogs and wheels of the machine, and it all works together as a unity. It makes no difference that the rubber of the bike's seat is a separate substance from the denim of my jeans and the flesh of my legs. It all acts as one. Everything is inseparably interfaced with everything.

Defining the self as the body is merely a commonsense observation that falls away when we think a little deeper about what's really going on. If we define ourselves as our bodies, then we must define ourselves, not as an organism, but as an organism-environment. The two go together inseparably. And how far does this series of relationships extend? Well, the parts of my body are all dependent on each other; the body itself is dependent on the environment of the Earth; the Earth depends on the sun; the sun depends on the galaxy; the galaxy depends on the Universe. Nothing truly exists in isolation from anything else. Our acts of labelling are merely a means of distinguishing aspects of a vast organism-environment field. This is the same, in principle, as the established understanding of time and space as inseparable. We may discuss space and time separately, but in each case we're unavoidably referring to what we know as space-time. Similarly, electricity and magnetism eventually had to be brought together and understood as two aspects of one force: electromagnetism. Practically speaking, your body cannot be separated from its environment, in the same way that it makes no sense to think of a red blood cell as distinct from the body it inhabits. So, if you wish to define the real you as your body, there is actually no *you* separate from *everything.*

Consider bees and flowers. The flower produces nectar, which the bee needs. While collecting it, the bee accidentally covers itself in the flower's pollen. When it moves on to another flower, some of this pollen is deposited, enabling the flower to reproduce. So, without bees, there would be no flowers, and without flowers, there would be no bees. We think of them as separate organisms, but there is no one without the other. The fact that there is atmosphere between them is quite arbitrary. An organism is really a series of interwoven relationships far more spread out than a tightly packed arrangement of internal organs, so a bee and a flower could actually be thought of as a single organism called the bee-flower. The bee did not cause the flower, nor did the flower cause the bee. They evolved together and they remain co-dependent.

The Universe is not made of separate entities; it is *one essence* consisting of a multitude of relationships wherein it experiences itself. Our common sense may resist perceiving the Universe in this fashion, because we're so accustomed to thinking in terms of separate entities as a result of our Newtonian education. But even our understanding of atoms and molecules supports the non-dual perspective, if we think deeply enough about it. A human body can be reduced to a complex series of relationships between molecules, and the body's relationship with its environment is also a relationship of molecules to molecules. Air might be gaseous and invisible, but it's still there, and it's made of molecules, just like your body. It's easy to point at your body and say, "Here I am; this enclosed bag of meat and bones is me." Then you point at the woods and say, "That's not me; I'm over here, see?" But there is no you apart from the trees that give your body its oxygen.

As we have already discussed, the function of the brain is to enable conscious experience. But since the brain is not a thing-in-itself, it is more accurate to state: a function of the *Universe* is to enable conscious experience. The real mystery is how ordinary "dead" matter can give rise to awareness. Those who think they can dismiss this profound puzzle with a wave of the hand are seriously kidding themselves. Maybe matter isn't quite as dead as it appears.

Historically, there are two opposing philosophical positions regarding the question of what constitutes the prime reality, the foundational *stuff* of which the Universe is made. These are called materialism and idealism. Materialists believe that matter is the prime reality and consciousness is a product of matter. Idealists believe that consciousness is the prime reality and matter is purely an experience of consciousness. There is, however, a third option, called neutral monism. This is the idea that consciousness and matter should both be understood as manifestations of a singular essence.

Materialists underplay consciousness as an emergent phenomenon within a fixed and solid Universe, while idealists dismiss the material

Universe as an insubstantial illusion of the mind. In trying to discover which one caused the other, we are failing to see that they actually go together inseparably. It's the old chicken and egg conundrum. Which came first? Neither, of course. They are really a single organism whose parts evolved together. Similarly, consciousness and the material Universe are both manifestations of the mysterious stuff we call *energy* and, as such, they are inseparably one.

There is no doubt, obviously, that stars and planets existed before human brains, therefore they must exist independently of human minds. But I don't intend to make the argument that *humanlike* consciousness is as fundamental as physical matter. I propose that the energy of the Universe is invested with a kind of non-localised primordial awareness – a basic drive to experience itself. In this model, the brain is not the generator of consciousness, but an *aperture* for it. A useful analogy is how a television set works. Pretend for a moment that you have no prior knowledge of the concept of broadcasting. You might mistakenly conclude that the TV set *creates* the programme. It certainly appears that way to basic observation; you switch the set on, select the desired channel, and the set makes an episode of *Breaking Bad* for you. But is the programme a component of the TV? No. The programme exists as an invisible signal that is flowing through the world all around you, even passing through solid matter. The TV, connected to an aerial on top of your house, merely acts as an aperture, funnelling the signal into itself and converting it into moving pictures and sounds. Similarly, there is a field of consciousness-in-potential that permeates the whole Universe, and this field is focused into subject-object awareness by the brain.

When we contemplate the enormity of a galaxy, a human brain seems extremely insignificant by comparison. This is certainly true if your measure of significance is *size*. But it's not true at all if your measure of significance is *complexity*. Our brain is the most complex structure that we have yet observed in the Universe. Stars and planets, by comparison, are relatively simple in composition and behaviour. A similar simplicity is observed in the microscopic realm, where we discover that all of the diverse forms of matter/energy in the Universe are made from combinations of only twelve fundamental particles, acted on by four fundamental forces. In between the microscopic and the cosmic is the grand spectacle of life on a terrestrial world. The complexity of life on Earth, and of humans in particular, gives us good reason to speculate that the function of the Universe is to produce complex forms of consciousness, on this world and others. This is not quite the same as saying, "God made mankind in his own image," but it looks as if the whole show might be for our benefit, after all.

Billions of years ago, the field of primordial awareness focused itself inside tiny clumps of cells. It was able to touch the world only in a very simplistic way. It could not yet do anything remotely comparable to what we call thinking. After numerous replications and mutations, some happy accidents allowed it to try out new interactions with the world. Mutations continued to happen, sometimes making life better, sometimes making it worse. And so began the evolutionary process. Eventually, after a staggering amount of trial and error, the primordial awareness ended up with a human brain and body around itself. And even though it now feels very advanced, all of the complexities of its elaborate awareness are merely outgrowths of that base urge of the Universe to experience itself.

Brain-centred consciousness is only one manifestation of the Universe experiencing itself. Plants, for instance, have a consciousness of sorts, in that they are capable of perception and action. They are alive, just as we are, and when you look back far enough on the evolutionary family tree, animal and plant were one. We are essentially the same stuff. And when you get right down to it, we are all made of star-stuff. There was a time in the Universe's history when planets had not yet formed. The particles that later made up the stars are the same particles that formed your living body. With that in mind, who knows what strange forms of consciousness are evolving out there in distant galaxies.

Is there any evidence for this non-localised primordial awareness? There is some, but unfortunately it is off the beaten track, in that oft maligned area called parapsychology. Phenomena such as extrasensory perception and psychokinesis can best be explained by positing the existence of what we might call *field consciousness* – an interconnected field of awareness that permeates everything. I realise that is too large a leap for many readers to make at the moment. Psychic phenomena will be discussed at length in part 3. Until then, hold that thought. Aside from the perceived lack of evidence, the best reason to embrace this view is the long-term lack of a solution to the hard problem. Non-local primordial awareness, as part of the fabric of space-time, provides an elegant theoretical answer.

At its most basic level, consciousness is a phenomenon that arises when there is a perceptual relationship between I and not-I. One cannot be conscious unless there is something to be conscious of; it takes *two*. The I-feeling is not a physical or metaphysical mind or soul that can be located within the brain. It is not a thing-in-itself at all. What we experience as *I* is the Universe focusing itself to an area of limited awareness through a lens. That lens is the human organism. The only real you is the Universe as a whole. The only real *anything* is the Universe as a whole. We can't find the self in the brain, because it isn't there. Consciousness is simply the Universe experiencing itself through the perception of separate forms.

Examine the following two related statements carefully: (1) You are a focused area of limited awareness for the Universe; (2) you are the Universe focused to an area of limited awareness. The difference in the two statements is subtle, but vastly important. The first makes the mistake of defining *you* as an entity separate from the whole. The second clarifies that the only fundamentally real you *is* the whole. Truly grasping this requires a profound shift in your sense of self that is alien to the Western mind and thus hard to integrate. Nevertheless, this model of consciousness provides an explanation for why we can't find it in the brain. It also fits perfectly with our deepest understanding about the nature of reality. Why is everyone still looking for a Newtonian explanation of consciousness when it has long been established that we're living in a quantum Universe?

When the Universe is understood in this fashion, where nothing whatsoever is a thing-in-itself, then there is only one possible conclusion: you are IT. Unfortunately, there is a lingering materialistic monism in the West. The Universe according to Newton has been successfully replaced by a non-local quantum-entangled Universe. The key question to ask oneself at this point is: "Am *I* fundamentally real?" If you answer with a yes, then you *must* conclude that you are the Universe. Monism does not do parts. The fundamental reality is the unified whole. So if you're real, then you're the whole. No clauses, no exceptions. Any reference to parts is a return to outdated classical thinking.

This conclusion generally seems to be unpalatable to those who insist on a materialistic view of the Universe, and so they opt for the conclusion that consciousness is a brain-generated illusion. For the materialistic monist, this really is the only option left, but it's an absurdity, as we've already discussed.

Monism is monism. It can't be thought of as materialistic at the expense of consciousness, or conscious at the expense of material. Since mind and matter are both real, then monism must include them both as one. While it is certainly true that the Universe existed long before there were biological organisms wiggling around on suitable planets, the potential for conscious life had to already exist as a property of the Universe from the beginning. Speculation is not necessary, for consciousness *is*, and like all else that is, we trace its origin to the singularity from which everything springs.

In many respects, this is an automatic, deterministic Universe, since science has identified laws that operate on strict mathematical principles. But that's only half the story. It is also true that this is an unpredictable conscious Universe, and *you are it*.

TIME: THE IMAGINARY COSMIC MOVIE

G OD is standing at an ice-cream counter, in human form, deciding whether to choose vanilla or chocolate.

"Quit stalling," the vendor objects. "You know everything, past, present and future, so you already know what choice you're going to make."

"Indeed," God replies. "I knew I was going to choose vanilla, so now I'm going to thwart my foreknowledge by choosing chocolate."

"But wouldn't you already have known that you were going to thwart your foreknowledge?"

"Ah."

Clearly, there is something wrong with our ideas about God as a humanlike consciousness, bound within the passage of time as we are. Such a being, by virtue of his ability to see the whole of eternity at every moment, would be incapable of a single act of free will. God would be more chained by his infinite knowledge than any creature.

A more philosophically mature idea of God is that he/she/it is an impenetrable mystery that is unbound by time and space. If God is to be thought of as conscious, then clearly that consciousness is nothing remotely like a living entity's, so much so that perhaps the word consciousness is not even appropriate. Theists tend to think of God as a mind, but when you really consider the position their God occupies, what use would God have for something as crude and limiting as a mind?

I could indulge in the speculation that God created the Universe so that he could experience freedom of choice, by hiding himself in all the creatures and playing their roles. We're all God-in-disguise, only we don't know it. The Infinite fragments itself, creating finity: duality, incompleteness, separation, space-time. In relation to creatures, the Infinite places itself into a situation where it cannot access the fullness of its own being. Beyond my limited awareness is the Infinite holding itself in this body/mind. Likewise, beyond your limited awareness is the Infinite holding itself in another body/mind. We are one and the same "being" forced into a state of apparent alienation. To be a creature is to leave eternity and enter time – to deliberately forget your totality and undergo a period of learning filled with thrills and spills, joys and sorrows.

This view makes sense to me, but I also see that it's unnecessarily complicated. There is an unfortunate tendency to view the Infinite as a vast collector of experiences, a divine Mind that presides over space-time, seeing everything as an eternal present. We view ourselves as departing from this Mind at birth and being absorbed back into it at death. I used to think in this fashion, until I realised that my thoughts were coming from the lingering influence of monotheism. There was really no need to invent an overseeing entity in any shape or form, and doing so only created an unnecessary duality: little me down here separate from Big Me upstairs. Pure consciousness, or godlike consciousness, is a meaningless abstraction, because consciousness requires subject and object, observer and observed. Consciousness is a phenomenon that happens *within* space-time, and any attempt to conceptualise it outside of that context turns it into formlessness. The mythical gods of Mount Olympus could be thought of as conscious because they were really just ideas about a higher order of creature, bearing more resemblance to modern comic-book superheroes (and supervillains) than to a transcendent essence. But once you start conceiving of God as the mystery of mysteries, unbound by time and space, then it becomes impossible to think of him/her/it as a conscious person. Ah, but then the revelation hits you: God is indeed a conscious person: *you*. Limitation is the very means that the Infinite uses to experience consciousness. We really don't need to overcomplicate it by inventing higher orders of consciousness that make no sense and serve no purpose. Superfluous ideas should be trimmed mercilessly with Occam's Razor.

As conscious creatures, we experience limited perception in space and something that we call the passage of time. We tend to think of time as a sort of filmstrip. This is because our brain functions as a recording device. We can scan through our memories of yesterday's daily activities, isolate something interesting, and replay it mentally. This little filmstrip is a tiny piece of a much vaster reel that we call our life.

We have a feeling that the events of our lives exist somewhere, or some-*when*, in a compartment of reality called the past. We see the past as real, just inaccessible as direct experience. Visualise, if you will, a horizontal line, subdivided into years. Start at the left-hand side with the year you were born, put the present year somewhere in the middle, and extend the timeline into your future. Mentally pin some images from your past along the line, such as being born, your first day at school, a memorable birthday party, your first kiss, a favourite holiday – you decide. On the present year, place an image of you sitting here right now reading this book. And on future years, pin some images of what you hope to be doing at particular times in your life to come. For our purposes, it's not important whether your chosen events come to pass or not. What matters is that you can visualise, in general terms, your whole life stretched out across time.

Now imagine a little marker positioned at the time of your birth. Push the marker gradually to the right, along the line. This motion, as you can guess, represents the progression of time. And what does the marker itself symbolise? The present. We think of time as a kind of fabric through which a thing called the present moves. And we feel that the present exists at only one specific point on the entire fabric. Currently, that point is the date and time displayed by your watch, and no other (for convenience, we can forget the man-made convention of timezones, since it's only the numbers that change, not time itself). But this view of the present is entirely subjective, caused by the brain's ability to store recordings and make predictions. Objectively, the present does not move; it is completely and utterly still. This, however, will take some explaining.

Select one of your memories and replay it mentally; I'll do the same. I see myself on my ninth birthday. I'm in my back yard playing with a *Star Wars* toy that was a gift from my parents. I may say to myself, "I am gazing upon the past," but what I'm really looking at are images that my brain is generating in the present – a mental reproduction of something that I call the past because of my vantage point in so-called time. But look carefully. This vantage point is the present. The playback device of my brain that gives me access to images of the boy exists in the present. The recording itself exists in the present-day flow of information through that brain. Furthermore, if I take my present awareness and my memories out of the equation altogether, I can also understand that when the boy experienced his birthday party, it was a present-moment experience for him. At every turn, I am confronted with the inescapable reality of the present.

If you're still struggling, think of it like this: right now, we are in the present. As you read these words, time appears to be moving forward. Pause from reading for a moment and count to five aloud. Where are we now? Oh, look, we're in the *present*. The numbers that you spoke exist as a memory that you call the *past*. But look carefully at this memory. When you said, "One," you said it in the present; when you said, "Two," you said it in the present. All memories are mental recordings of experiences of the present that you can only access in the present. You have never known, nor will you ever know, anything except the present. Even if you spend a great deal of time absorbed in thoughts about the future, that is simply the activity you are choosing to do in the present. And if any of your future predictions come to pass, they will happen to you as experiences of the present. Thousands of readers are paying attention to these words, each person at a different calendar and clock position from all the others, each one feeling that they are hearing this *now*, no matter when it is.

Ordinarily, as you observe the motion of an analogue clock, you get a sense of time as a tangible thing that is moving forward. Now let's alter our sense of time a little, without actually changing anything that's happening. All we have to do is look at the clock in a weird fashion. We need to use an imaginary clock, for reasons that will become apparent. Focus on the seconds hand. As it comes back around to zero, mentally restrain it in the vertical position, as if it's nailed to an invisible point in space. But don't stop time. Instead, see the clock itself rotate around the seconds hand. Assuming the clock is hanging on a wall, picture the entire room rotating around the seconds hand. This hand (which represents the present) is always entirely stationary. Instead of viewing the present as a fleeting moment that is always racing forward, you can come to appreciate it as a fixed and immovable moment that you are forever immersed in. This is counterintuitive to the brain's natural appreciation of time as a real structure containing a past and future. But past and future are only conventions that we use when we insist on turning a sequence of events into a story. This is not a dysfunction of the brain. The ability to turn an ever-changing present into a meaningful narrative provides a rich experience of consciousness that is not possible for much smaller organisms. Crucially, when each moment of our personal story happens, it happens as the present.

Right now, in the present, I can gaze internally at an image of myself as a teenager kissing my first girlfriend. I can jump to a picture of myself getting baptised in a tank of water as a Christian. I can see my mother taking her last breath. I can visualise myself riding a motorcycle for the first time. It appears as if there are multiple vantage points in time, but the only vantage point I've ever experienced is the present. The present-that-once-was has no tangible existence. As the present undergoes change, its prior shape ceases to be real. The image of that prior shape only continues to exist as activity that the brain is doing in the present. When we remember something, we're not reaching into an actual past and pulling it into the present; we're merely consulting a mental storage compartment that exists *now*. Everything that happens happens as the present.

Consider the wind. Picture it as you see it on the television weather forecast. You're looking down from the sky at churning masses of clouds and the empty spaces in between. You can turn it into a story, if you wish. In fact, that's what a weather forecast is. Where is the wind blowing next? Will we have rain tomorrow? Will the hurricane continue heading east? But if we set aside our human interest in the wind and just look at it for what it is, we might gain an elusive insight about the nature of time. All of that motion is happening in a sequence, but is there really any value in thinking of it as a stored recording? Does our concept of reality require that all of these changing patterns are retained in a dimension called time? The wind certainly doesn't care about its own story. It just blows where it blows. And no moment in its history or future has any more or less importance than any other. Instead of understanding time as past-present-future, we can view it as a single moment in continual flux, without preservation.

Our ability to retain memories is just a consequence of evolution, nothing more. Much simpler organisms don't need memories in order to function, and so they don't possess them. They just live in the now, reacting to what's directly happening. In an organism as large and complex as a human, memory is essential to survival. Unfortunately, the ability to move one's awareness internally through a sequence of events prompts us to make the unwarranted assumption that "time" exists outside of the brain, as part of the fabric of reality.

Reality is commonly modelled as a four-dimensional structure, with the first three dimensions relating to space (length, breadth and height) and a fourth dimension for time. Einstein discovered that time is affected by the velocity of an object. We had to start using the term space-time, because we could no longer think of space and time as separate concepts. Doesn't this make time a real dimension of the Universe? Not quite. I have no doubt that the mathematics behind Einstein's theory of relativity is sound, but this in no way changes the observation that reality consists solely of what is happening right now, including the present curvature of every twist and turn in space-time. Relativity does not require the memory of what went before, or the shape of things to come, as an actual dimension of existence; we invent time in order to reconstruct a filmstrip in our minds that has no substance outside our minds. Time is a useful mental abstraction that allows us to chart the previous and successive shapes of the present with great accuracy.

This insight about the illusory nature of time was one of the most difficult ideas for me to grasp. But when I did, my mind was blown. The flash of clarity came like a bolt from the blue when I was out cycling one evening, travelling along a route that I had rode since childhood. I was reminiscing about what it had felt like to be here doing this when I was a teenager. I playfully imagined I could ride through a time-warp and suddenly be that young person again, reliving those memorable school days from the 1980s. And it suddenly hit me that time itself wasn't real. Our ability to construct a sequence of events in our brain didn't mean that time was a real "place." The past only happened as the present. It didn't matter that the past was only accessible as memory; when any event happened, it happened as *this moment*. I had seen through the illusion of the marker moving forward through time. I understood that every seemingly separate moment of my life was this moment. And wherever my life was heading, the destination would always be this moment.

I had once believed in a God who existed in an eternal present and I had regarded his perspective as aloof from my present. Now I understood that the eternal present was *this very moment* and no other, because there was no other. Not only was eternity right here under my nose, it was something

I couldn't ever escape from and something I had always been immersed in without noticing. Grasping the unreality of the past and future made me feel amazingly grounded; I was standing still in the unshakable reality of the present, as so-called time continued to flow.

When we believe in time as a real structure containing all the moments of our existence, we feel less *here*. The present that we're experiencing feels arbitrary – just one moment in a vast collection, each one as real as all the others. Obsessed with our story, we wallow in nostalgia, pining for past pleasures, or we indulge in wish-fulfilment fantasies based on regret or foolish imagination, or we worry over events that are likely never to happen. All the while, the present moment is staring us in the face, being completely ignored. It's true that you can't truly escape the present; you're in it, even if you choose to live with your head in the past or the future. But ignoring the present is a very low-quality way to experience the present.

That moment when I first saw the nature of "time" clearly was one of the most amazing transitions of my life. My reaction was joyous laughter (fortunately I was alone). I wish I could re-experience it just as deeply right now, but that's me talking like a spirituality addict. More importantly, I've integrated this insight rather than forgotten it. In studying mind, space and time, time has definitely been the hardest nut to crack, but the most rewarding.

When the pieces of the jigsaw spontaneously clicked into place, I suddenly got a new perspective on the question: "What happens to my consciousness when I die?" Or as Christians would say: "Where will you spend eternity?" I'm not heading for anywhere, heaven or hell. I'm standing still in eternity right now. We tend to think of the future as something that we are moving towards, but we never meet it; we only encounter it as the present. The centre of eternity is *this* moment and every moment, and each moment is the *same* moment. If I am belabouring the point, that is only because I am keenly aware of how difficult this is to truly comprehend in a meaningful way.

When I was a Christian, the focus of my life was on the anticipation of a future beyond death. The present was only meaningful as a temporary training ground. I couldn't get it out of the way fast enough, as I coped with a "sinful" nature that regularly made existence miserable. I longed for the next life with its promise of perfection. In my atheist phase, the opposite dynamic occurred. The future was a source of frustration and depression, because it meant the end of my existence. I clung to the present with futile urgency, unable to stop it racing forward to my inevitable doom.

Since I'm still going to die, does my new perspective on time really change anything? It does, dramatically, when you put it together with a deeper appreciation of consciousness. The Universe experiences selfhood through multiple points of limited awareness. None of those points is an actual *self*, just a lens of limitation for the true self, which is the Universe. You, the Universe, exist in an ever-changing present, peering out of the eyes of every conscious creature. So when a life ceases in the present moment, all other life continues in the present moment, and all life is you.

The whole notion of self as an independent separate entity only appears when we believe in time. You can't invent your identity without including the backstory that forms that identity. Without reference to those memories there is just consciousness happening now. Have you ever had the experience of being totally absorbed in an activity? Is there any self there? No. There's certainly conscious activity, but this activity has no sense of itself as an entity until the moment its attention is diverted from the present moment to where it was before or where it wants to be later.

Life is the story of an eternal present, not the story of a past-present-future narrative. In your story, each moment of time is significant for its own sake, not just to take you to the next event. Why do we obsess over extending our personal identities indefinitely in time? If we think our personal story should have an everlasting duration, what about the stories of every cat and dog? What about the stories of every conscious organism on every life-sustaining planet, from an infinite regression and succession of universes? That's got to be one hell of a storage compartment. And for what purpose, since the Infinite (that's you!) has an infinitude of experiences still in waiting? It makes much more sense to accept that we're supposed to hold life lightly. We're supposed to be able to enjoy it and let it go. Nothing is meant to be permanently recorded on the pillars of eternity. The recording of "you" would eventually become too big to be meaningful.

The events that make up the story of my life are meaningful for as long as my brain is able to sustain them as recallable memories. Our individual filmstrips are continually in flux as we make new memories and forget old ones. It's a huge error to think that life is only meaningful when it is remembered forever. The phenomenon of memory is far more playful than that.

What is actually lost at death? One of the lenses of awareness through which you, the Universe, are peering ceases to function. The ego that formed around that lens and the reel of memory attached to it disappear. Meanwhile, it's still the present moment and you're still here peering out through every other lens.

In closing, I should admit that I do think it's possible time exists as a real dimension. If that turns out to be the case, nothing I've said about the primacy of the present moment changes. The only difference is that every moment is equally the *definitive* present moment. For instance, there is a Darryl Sloan in 1980 who can remember things about the Darryl of 1979 that I cannot. There is a Darryl experiencing the present in 2030 (hopefully!) who has memories of a Darryl experiencing the present in 2020. And from my perspective, here in 2017, I'm experiencing the present, too, but those other Darryls view my present experience as the past or the future. When you take into account these multiple vantage points in the time dimension, it becomes possible to notice that there is no need to give your own particular present any more primacy than any other manifestation of the present, nor do you need to view all those other perspectives as different presents. *You*, dear reader, certainly don't believe that 31 January 2017 is the present, because you are reading this at a later date, but I assure you that *I* do. You think that I am writing these words to you from the past, but it looks to me as if all the people reading this book are in the future. Why is your present any more definitive than my present? It all depends on your vantage point in time, and they all appear to be as good as each other. Essentially, the little marker we were moving along the filmstrip doesn't exist in one spot, because it's *everywhere*. All of time exists in *this moment*. Think of time like a movie on a DVD that you've been watching for the past half hour. The whole story exists right now on the disc, even though some of it is in your memory and some of it is yet to happen.

What are we to make of a person who feels an inexplicable feeling of dread while stopped at crossroads as the traffic lights turn from red to green? The driver is frozen with fear and can't bring himself to press his foot on the accelerator. A few seconds later a high-speed collision involving two cars happens right in front of him. The driver who remained stationary says to himself, "That would have been me." I'm not describing a documented case, but there's no shortage of testimonies like this involving precognition or presentiment. If there is truth to any of these claims, the implication is that one's future can affect one's present, which means the future is real even before it happens. Time must exist as a dimension. The field of parapsychology holds the potential for giving us solid data on this dilemma, but for now the jury seems to be out.

So time might exist as a real dimension of the Universe, or as a purely mental abstraction. Using my earlier analogy, the dilemma is basically: the DVD may exist, or it may not. It's very hard to say for sure, because reality functions just fine, either way. This chapter went through a couple of rewrites over the years, because I couldn't make my mind up. I have a personal preference for the view that the DVD doesn't exist. Believing in the DVD gives the ego a place to preserve its identity indefinitely, while making here and now feel like an arbitrary point in the story. Direct experience feels like playback, because whatever is happening has (from another point of view) already happened. On the flipside, not believing in the DVD helps loosen my attachment to my personal story, because the so-called past has no actual existence and the future is truly unwritten. This also makes me feel deeply grounded in direct experience as the only reality.

Of course, reality doesn't bow to our personal preferences. Using Occam's Razor, the non-existence of time is the more elegant of the two viewpoints and there is currently no convincing data that contradicts it. But even if time does turn out to be real, that doesn't negate the key insight I wanted to get across: the only moment that is real is the present moment. Past, present and future are really present, present and present.

Most people live with a conditioned sense of awareness that (1) everyone is separate from everyone, (2) everything is separate from everything, and (3) every moment is separate from the rest. You might say we have a wrong view of mind, space and time. When these three areas are understood at a deep level, they become puzzle pieces that fit snugly together and allow us to see a profound truth that will have a deep influence on our lives: I am you, you are me, we are everything, and everything is one, forever.

THE FLUX OF LIFE AND DEATH

IT comes naturally to identify your entire sense of self with your individual mind – your own unique ego with its personality and character traits. Often we indulge in the notion of our personality freeing itself from the body at death and moving on to other experiences. But the personality is purely brain-based, as we have covered in a previous chapter. A mother who loses her teenage son in an accident will not find that same quirky, mischievous personality waiting for her on the other side, because the attributes that made her son the person he was are physical, not spiritual, in nature. This also means she won't be on the other side waiting for him, either, which makes the whole notion of an other side rather pointless.

Science shows there's a lot about you that is provably material in nature, and everything that is material perishes. When you die, say goodbye to your brain and everything you used it for. After death, we're done with thought and personality. Do you think you'll continue to be a man or a woman, mentally and emotionally, after you shuffle off this mortal coil? Why would you be, when everything that dictated those qualities has turned to dust? So who exactly is the *you* doing the shuffling?

This casts clear, rational light on our typical assumptions about the essence of what we are and about what lies beyond death. When I die, there's so much that I tend to think of as *me* that I'll be leaving behind. When I die, just what will I be? Because there doesn't seem to be much left of me to *be* anything. Ghost stories and near-death experiences abound, but there is overwhelming evidence in favour of the view that the mind is entirely dependent on the physical brain. Where there is no brain, there is no mind.

This is initially puzzling, since we have already established that consciousness has metaphysical roots. "But if my personality must go, then what's left?" you cry. "If all I amount to when I shrug off this body is some bland, unthinking self, then death might as well be oblivion, for all I care."

The dismay you might feel about this arrangement is simply a result of identifying who you are with the wrong thing: your personality, your ego, your sense of being a unique individual, different from everyone else around you. The solution lies in understanding what it means to say, "I am the Infinite." This requires making a profound shift in your sense of who you really are. Death *is* oblivion – for the false egocentric self that you invented then clung to as if it were a thing-in-itself. There is no "bland, unthinking self" that continues after death. When you reason in that fashion, you are slipping into the cultural trap of modelling consciousness in the manner of mind-body dualism. Death is not the freeing of a soul from a fleshly prison; it's merely the closing of an aperture.

Imagine a mother showing her adult son an old photograph that was taken at a Halloween party when he was just four years old. "Don't you look cute in that outfit?" the mother says. The photo shows three boys standing side by side. One is dressed as a witch, the other a vampire, and the third a goblin. All three faces are concealed behind masks. The boy, now a man, has no memory of the party, or of which costume he wore. His mother clearly knows who she is looking at, but her son can only think, "I could be any one of those three." Here is an image of a boy who was once very much alive, with a four-year-old personality to match, but everything that made him who he was, physically and psychologically, has changed to such a degree that he essentially no longer exists. The development of the boy into the man was a transformation of such a magnitude that not even the memory of the boy now remains in the man.

"But it's still the same *person*," you may object. Well, what do you mean by person? You are using the word as if there is a *constant* within each of us, an identifiable soul that exists apart from the experiences that give rise to individual personhood. No such constant exists in a meaningful way.

Imagine a thirty-year-old man who crashes his car and suffers a severe head injury that causes him to lose his entire memory. Nevertheless, he gets on with his life and starts to make new memories. At age seventy he dies, having never recovered the missing decades. One body containing two distinct lives – and two deaths. For all practical purposes, the first man died at thirty, because everything that gave his identity substance vanished. Shall we say he died without a soul, since the soul would undoubtedly have to continue its journey with the second man?

We see that it is impossible to think of the idea of *person* without reference to the experiences that define a person. The soul, distinct from the contents of the mind, becomes a meaningless concept, because what we are really attached to, as the self, is the personality (including its memories) that gives substance to our identity.

The really interesting observation is that our personalities are continually changing and our memories are continually leaking away. When I was ten years old, I could recall a lot more about when I was nine years old than I can today. Presently, in 2017, I feel very attached to who I am and the recent experiences of my life, but in 2030 I might only be able to recall a small fraction of what happened in 2017, and the intervening life experiences may turn me into quite a different person.

This all begs the question: what are we really trying to hold on to? We conceive of the soul and the afterlife, so that we can give our individual personalities permanence and thus inject meaning into our lives. But right here, in our mortality, we can see that our personalities and life experiences have no importance beyond their immediate and short-term usefulness. We throw away memories that lose importance to us and we remould our personalities according to our changing needs. When we compare self to self across a large span of time, the transformation can be so profound that the one is not recognisable as the other.

The factor that separates one person from another is the individual experience of body/mind. The factor that unites us – what we all have in common – is consciousness. Not *a* consciousness, in the sense of an entity; we all simply share in the phenomenon of conscious awareness. Regardless of where you are and who you are, you are *conscious*.

A roadblock in our understanding arises when we add *ness* to *conscious*, turning it into a noun. I've spoken about the trick played on us by nouns in a previous chapter, but the point bears reinforcing. Since consciousness is a noun, we say "my consciousness" and "your consciousness," as if consciousness is an object that each of us owns and we all have a different one. Consciousness really should be a verb, and we ought to think of our identity in the manner of a verb, because we are changing from moment to moment. I am not a consciousness; I am consciousness-ing. It looks inelegant on paper, but it's the truth, just like you would say, "I am mov*ing*," "I am walk*ing*," "I am think*ing*." Nothing about your identity is stationary. You're not a permanent or even semi-permanent *being*; you're a fluid *doing*.

There are innumerable manifestations of consciousness going on in the world right now. The problem is, we think of these individuated processes as actual entities in themselves called *I* and *you*. We even reinforce this error by using the words I and you to refer to individual persons. We have to, or we can't communicate effectively. But it's a false sense of self we're referring to when we do this.

There's a useful analogy that can help us see past this shortcoming of language. Imagine a bucket full of water. The water represents the hidden unified state of the Universe, the fundamental Ground of Being behind everything that we see. Stab a hole in the bottom of the bucket with a knife. This represents the birth of a human life; the water that flows from the hole is the consciousness of that life. Now stab a second hole. This is a second person; see how he has his own unique consciousness stream. They appear separate if you look at the underside of the bucket. But when you take notice of the water in the bucket, you see that the streams are the same water. I like this analogy because it involves a flow, and that's what consciousness is; it's a *doing*, not a *being*. There is no need to invent an entity where there is only an aperture.

The great lie is that you are nothing more than your tiny little isolated mind. When the body is about to die and the personality panics because its existence is about to be terminated, that terror only happens because you've wrongly identified yourself as your limited physical mind. You are bigger than your individuality. Death is not the termination of *you*. It's the termination of a mere shell that you are using; it's the falling of a leaf from a tree whose life continues to flourish.

All afterlife myths are the result of a failure to understand that there is more to you than your individual personality. The personality, like the body, is part of the shell. When you understand that you are the Infinite, that all consciousness is one, that every moment is now, what use is heaven? In fact, you come to realise that the very idea of heaven is a tragic misdirection from what is truly real: life in the here and now. The true afterlife is the next generation, right here in the material world, not your present ego shunted onto some higher plane of existence. Each self-aware child is your*self* in another guise. From another point of view, your life already *is* the afterlife – of all the humans that have gone before.

Reincarnation is another unnecessary concept born out of the fear of the cessation of consciousness. The "soul" is said to be engaged in a journey of evolution by experience, moving from life to life. But why is this necessary? Reincarnation teaches that my soul chose to incarnate as Darryl Sloan specifically to have the experiences that it knew this lifetime would provide. Yet when I look at the world as a whole, every body/mind is simply *conscious*. Life does not resemble a supermarket where individual souls purchase experiences. What store ever sells all its stock every moment of every day? A life is conceived; consciousness begins to flow with a blank slate. It's as simple as that. Reincarnation is only a crafty relabelling of the human ego as *soul*. It is a failure to realise that the ego is a fleeting expression of identity and the future an imaginary construct. There is only *one* existing in an ever present *now*.

To belabour the point, don't fall into the trap of viewing consciousness as an entity. You may say, "I get the idea that I am not my personality; I am consciousness, distinct from the identity of the mind. But *my* consciousness is not *your* consciousness. We are still separated from each other. You are not conscious of what I am conscious of." Well, when you say "*my* consciousness," whose consciousness do you mean? The typical answer would be: "The consciousness belonging to this body." The *self* is viewed as the body, in this context. But notice that we can equally say "*my* body." Whose body? "The body belonging to this consciousness." The self is viewed as consciousness, in this context. Did you notice the subtle switcheroo? We're not actually pinning down our identity in a meaningful way.

So we might propose: "There is a deeper *I* that has a body and also has a consciousness, both as distinct possessions." Shall we call that the soul? But if it's distinct from consciousness, then it has no structure, so is it even real? Body, mind, consciousness, soul – how many additional layers of personal identity should we invent to find out who we truly are? The philosopher Alan Watts illustrated this difficulty with a limerick:

There was a young man who said, "Though
It seems that I know that I know,
What I would like to see is the I that sees me
When I know that I know that I know."

When you attempt to pin down the self as an entity, the only place you end up is in an unending recursive loop. Whenever you think you see the self conceptually, you are forced to notice that you appear to be a self who sees that self. The reason why we can't find a solution to this is because we're looking at consciousness all wrong. We thought we could understand it because we wrongly assumed it was a tangible entity. Consciousness is the mysterious *doing* at the basis of everyone's existence. There it is in Will's head, there it is in Henry's, and there it is in yours – not three conscious entities, but the *process* of consciousness manifesting in three locations. And the transcendent mystery from which this limited space-time-bound process springs is the real you. We don't know what it is, except to say that you're it. So simple and yet so hard to grasp.

Imagine yourself old and frail, lying on a bed, your final breath imminent. A friend is holding your hand to comfort you. Are you worried about what will happen when you cross over to the other side? Are you scared that maybe there's nothing there? Personally, I'm highly confident that individual consciousness terminates at death, but this perspective causes me no fear or sadness. You see, the person holding your hand, the friend who will still be sitting there when you are gone, is also *you*.

When you've loosened your grip on your individual ego enough to truly understand this, then you won't need to believe in heaven or reincarnation, because you will see that every life that ever was, is, and will be, is *you*. Your death, as an individual creature, is nothing more than a small break in the continuity of your endless life, where a temporary personality and a set of disposable memories are snatched away before you're quite ready to part with them. Since you've already reshaped your personality many times, from infancy to old age, and forgotten a huge percentage of your life, you really have nothing to lose. Death is only stealing from you what you would naturally dispose of in time, if you were somehow able to live for several more centuries.

Similarly, bereavement occurs when the process of consciousness that remains intact (that is, the surviving friend or relative) is forced to cope with this break in continuity with the process of consciousness that dissolves (the deceased). And so, consciousness experiences sorrow. The suddenness of the moment of death is what makes it seem so horrible. When a mother watches her son change from infant to adult, she doesn't experience grief at the loss of the infant, because the transition is slow and smooth. But imagine the baby was magically transformed into his thirty-year-old self from the future. How do you think the mother would react then? Would she be content that her son is still the same *person*? I think not. An event like this would be a break in continuity comparable to bereavement, which would result in the mother screaming the house down: "Where is my baby? Give me back my baby!"

Nothing is permanent. *Nothing.* Everything and everyone changes. The changes are easy to swallow when they come slowly. Death is merely a sudden point of change, nothing more. Western culture, with its lack of understanding about this, turns death into an unnatural horror. We know it's going to happen to us one day, so all we can do is choose not to think about it. To make life tolerable, we pretend we're never going to die. But death is not an unnatural horror; it's an essential part of the cycle of life, and the thought of it should not fill us with dread. This dread causes us to cling fiercely to life, instead of holding life lightly. I'm not suggesting that we should start casually stepping out in front of moving traffic. There is middle ground to be discovered here. What a weight off our shoulders, to enjoy living while knowing there is nothing to fear in dying. When you finally see past the illusion of your personal identity, you've found the key to laughing in the face of your mortality.

THE DUALITY DILEMMA

E ACH human being is not an individual soul; he is the Infinite focused to an area of limited awareness within space-time. That's a fairly accurate summary of the preceding chapters, in scientific language suited to modern Western ears. This notion of an underlying non-duality is certainly not new. It was first expressed in the West by the ancient Greek philosopher Parmenides. In the East, it appears within a branch of Hinduism known as Advaita Vedanta. The *dvaita* in Advaita means *two*, and *a* is placed in front to denote *not*; in other words, non-duality. Hinduism has a long-established vocabulary for the very concepts I've been discussing using unwieldy Western terms: *Brahman* is the Hindu word for God, but not in the monotheistic sense of a divine personality. It means *that which cannot be imagined*. The word *atman* refers to the core of one's individual being – the idea of a real you beyond mind. There is even a term for the material world viewed as illusion: *maya*. In Advaita, a liberated human being is one who has realised Brahman as his own true self: atman is synonymous with Brahman.

When one perceives the fundamental non-duality of all things – between oneself, the Universe, and "God" – one is still faced with the predicament of continuing to exist in a state of apparent separateness from the world. What precisely is to be done about this? If you're in the habit of reading literature on non-duality, or listening to various teachers, you'll see that not everyone addresses this dilemma in the same manner. Loosely speaking, there are two overall approaches, one of which I aim to show is wrong.

First, let's deal with the incorrect version, the one that misses the real meat and potatoes. Here, the goal of atman is to return to Brahman. The ego is viewed as a misbehaving, illusory thing that prevents man from awakening to the realisation of his true divine nature. The claim is that Brahman is separate from atman at the outset, but this duality can be transcended so that all which thereafter peers out from behind a pair of eyes is Brahman himself. Individual self-consciousness is transcended and cosmic consciousness takes its place. There is no longer any feeling of oneself as an individual. This is liberation, awakening, enlightenment, and you are forever free from the suffering of the mind. The usual method of achieving this "awakening" is by a meditative practice.

You will find this sort of "spirituality" promoted by teachers whose public personalities are of a particular type: they project an image of serene, saintly otherness. And the underlying message is: "You, too, can be like me." Zen Buddhist Brad Warner, in his book *There Is No God and He Is Always with You* (2013), colourfully refers to this as *enlightenment porn*. Pornography teases you with lots of phoney superheated sex that you're never going to experience in real life; in just the same way, enlightenment porn shows you a glorious state of mind that you're never going to attain – because it's an act.

Non-duality teachers who claim that they've attained a permanent state of egoless awareness make hypocrites of themselves every time they comb their hair or put on makeup, because those are the actions of consciousness regarding itself as a bodily entity distinct from the world. Such teachers say lines like, "There's no one here. There's just what's happening." In a sense, this is true, but I find myself wanting to ask, "If there's no one there, why did you go to a professional hair stylist?" The honest answer is: "I was viewing myself as an individual and I wanted others to perceive me as beautiful." And so we see that very little has changed. I once listened to a non-duality teacher talk about the experience of rejection in relationships. She said there was no need to feel rejected, because there was no one there doing the rejecting. It sounds like a nice get-out clause from the harsher aspects of relationships, but if the teacher were consistent, she should apply the same reasoning to all of our interpersonal experiences. For instance, if you see someone crying, you shouldn't do anything to comfort him, because there's no one there who needs comforting. Any comfort you provide would only serve to reinforce the ego, so you'd be doing him a disservice. Is it truly desirable to become the sort of person who attends a funeral and feels no heartache for the loss of a loved one? And so we see that a truly consistent egoless awareness wouldn't just take away our suffering, but would also flatten the entire spectrum of our emotional life and turn us into disconnected observers of every experience. The more progress you make in this direction, the less human you would become.

Here in the West, we are especially prone to pursuing non-duality in this fashion because we carry with us the baggage of our Christian heritage. In Christianity, God is separate from man, so we think that union with God is a quest each person must undertake, a prize he must win. But this premise is entirely wrong. There never was any separation between a creator and his creation; there is just the fundamental Ground of Being, which is you, without condition.

So the second, alternative approach to non-duality recognises no existing separation between Brahman and atman, and therefore sees no need to seek Brahman. Atman is Brahman already. In Western terms: you do not need to become one with God by achieving something, because you are God already. You can't *not* be God, even when you fail to realise that you're God.

There is no separation, whether you recognise that or you don't. God is not "up there" gazing down, he's "in here" looking out. Any sense of him being up there is merely due to the lingering influence of monotheism. There is nothing outside of you that you need to seek union with by denying your individual sense of self. The individual sense of self *is* Brahman. So, instead of trying to transcend the ego, one's natural actions are to balance it and enjoy it.

There is no metaphysical change to your being that you need to pursue. However, there is still *something* to do. An ego that realises the true nature of itself as the Infinite is of a different character from an ego that views itself as an isolated entity imprisoned between the eyes of a meat machine. While you can't ever become "cosmic consciousness" in the flesh, neither are you merely an individual. You are playing the role of an individual while knowing you are more. So you will naturally take care of yourself as an individual, and you will care about other individuals, just as you would be doing if you knew nothing about non-duality. But knowing about non-duality gives you an edge. You can't use it to avoid the slings and arrows of life, to eradicate emotions like sorrow and anger. You will, however, be able to deal with all of this in a more constructive manner.

When I was about twelve years old, I recall walking home from a friend's house on a dark evening during the Halloween period. On the way, I ended up surrounded by four or five slightly older youths who were up to some traditional October mischief. The guy in front of me was wearing a jacket that bulged out at the level of his stomach. He put his hand inside the zipper and extracted an egg. Presumably he was carrying quite a few in there, unboxed, and the only thing preventing them from falling out was the elastic around the bottom of his jacket. Calmly, he extended his arm and cracked the egg on top of my head. I felt the cool slime soaking through my hair. The group sniggered. I endured this treatment in silence, too scared to retaliate, verbally or physically. A moment later, they let me go, having had their fun.

But that was not the end of the matter, psychologically speaking. They humiliated me! They humiliated *me*! I've no idea how many times I replayed the scene in my imagination, changing the details. When they surround me, I see myself shoving the guy in front, causing all the eggs inside his jacket to smash, spoiling his clothes. Then I run like hell, thinking, "Explain that one to your parents." In my fantasy, I don't think about much beyond the immediate gratification of getting the better of my opponents. It doesn't occur to me that the rest of their egg supply would probably have ended up decorating the front of my house, *if* I managed to make it home without getting beaten up. Nor do I think about what would happen in school the following day when the bullies make it their business to track me down and have their revenge. Although they had made me feel like a coward, the strategy I employed was exactly right for getting out of the situation with the least damage. But try telling that to the wounded ego. My futile compulsive fantasies occurred because of the belief in a separate self. But who is this *I* that feels it must defend its wounded pride? It's not a real entity at all. The only true *I* is everything. Grasping that makes a big difference to the quality of consciousness. In your own life, and in a multitude of contexts, you can probably find numerous examples of the runaway ego taking control of your emotions. Putting this voice in its proper place is one of the big benefits of understanding non-duality.

However, I want to be careful to avoid exaggerating this advantage. There are spiritual teachers who will try to convince you that it's possible to avoid all negative emotional states in life. This is not true, nor is it even desirable. For example, when someone tries to take advantage of me, I feel a rush of anger, regardless of the fictional status of the ego. This is a normal, healthy physiological call to action, urging me to confront the person in the interests of protecting myself. Subduing my anger in this context would only serve to make me a bigger target. The emotion is functioning perfectly.

Let's use a more dramatic example. If someone were running towards me brandishing a knife, face twisted in a malevolent snarl, and if I happened to be carrying a loaded gun, is it my responsibility to say, "Please go ahead. I will not resist you, for we are all one"? No, I will aim the gun at the centre of his chest and pull the trigger. We have to understand that there is a sense in which life is both sacred and disposable. The Universe makes it that way. At a fundamental level of being, everything is one, but when that oneness manifests itself as separateness, this introduces a playfulness into reality. It may seem perverse to refer to death as playful, but this truly is the correct way to see it. Life, across the entire animal and plant kingdom, is continually destroying and creating. There could never have been any evolution without a prodigious amount of death to facilitate the trial-and-error nature of that process. You can't sustain your body without stealing life from life. So the basic rule of life is to love when it's advantageous to love and to destroy when you have to destroy. There is no cosmic consciousness that negates any of that. Think of all life as a single organism attempting to continually re-shape itself using strategies that are both cooperative and hostile.

The notion of universal love is a false ideal peddled by enlightenment pornographers. It's easy for them to sell this, because we only ever see them lecturing to an audience or giving interviews, where the worst that could happen is a little unfriendly heckling. I imagine it's not easy to put this ideal into practice if you happen to be a soldier on the run behind enemy lines. But there is really no contradiction between understanding that the Universe is non-dual and having to take a life. We think there is, because we used to believe in a God who made a clear distinction between good and evil, and he parked himself exclusively on the side of good. So we think that we, as the Ground of Being, must be like this imaginary God. Not so. Non-duality includes *everything*. If it includes compassion, it also includes aggression. Life and death, beauty and horror – nothing is excluded.

I used to think that I had to achieve a certain level of moral fortitude before I would be worthy enough to experience authentic spirituality in my life. "Oh look, I've been good today. I'm making progress. Maybe now I'll start to feel really spiritual." The foolishness of this became clear when I realised that the goal I was striving for was already in place – without effort, without attainment, without time. I'm the Infinite; I've never been anything else and neither have you.

Life demands that we interact with each other as separate entities, but I can view myself as an ego with a crafty twinkle in my eye, understanding that there's more to the game of life than merely self versus other. What I know from day-to-day experience is this: the more forgetful I am of my oneness with the Universe, the more prone I am to feeling restless, bored, resentful, or angry. The ego always wants to be right, to defend its pride, to have its own way. When we remind ourselves that it's not fundamentally real, then it stops needing to be validated in these ways. The more I focus my mind on the interconnectedness of life, the more contented I am; the more I focus on the importance of my ego, the more agitated I am. Importantly, *I* make the decision about where to put the focus. And it was never a choice between being cosmic consciousness or being an ego. Those are false alternatives. Ego is the aperture through which cosmic consciousness peers, and the narrowness of that aperture is what seduces consciousness into forgetting its cosmic nature. Regularly contemplating the oneness that underlies the duality of experience has a very positive effect on daily living. Granted, there may be circumstances where it is entirely appropriate to feel angry or fearful, but more often than not I find myself blowing things out of proportion and getting stupidly obsessed over trivialities. This is the ego running amok. And when I remind myself that the separate self is an illusion, my mind is drawn back towards a state of serenity, realising that there is nothing to be upset about.

Meditation may be useful in maintaining this kind of awareness. Books upon books have been written on this subject, so an anecdote here will hardly suffice, especially from someone like me who has undertaken very little formal practice. But what I do know from life experience is this: there is a psychological toxicity that accumulates when the mind is continually being bombarded, whether that is from stress at the workplace, or spending too long in front of videogames, or any number of factors. Whether one is sitting crossed-legged facing a wall, or walking through peaceful surroundings, the absence of stimulation gives the mind an opportunity to recover its natural equilibrium. Conversely, when the ego is being swept along in an endless stream of stimulation, it has no opportunity to reflect and see its true nature clearly.

I haven't prioritised meditation in my life because I've always been an obsessively introspective person. It already comes naturally to me to be watchful of my state of mind. My Christian background, with its focus on self-examination, served to increase this skill. But not everyone is like me. I would hazard a guess that extroverts find this insight particularly hard to grasp, because they habitually focus their attention on the exterior world of experience. They spend their lives being carried along by the mind's activity and completely self-identifying with every thought that arises. Meditation is a way of breaking through this illusion, because it forces you to sit with nothing else but the contents of your mind for company. You try to observe your thoughts, and you experience first-hand how easy it is for thoughts to carry you away. So you try again. And within mere minutes, thoughts once again seduce you away from your position as observer. But eventually you become more skilled at staying put. And you may ask yourself, "Who is this that is observing the mind?" Habitually, we think of the contents of the mind as *internal* to the self and the world as *external* to the self. But when we practise observing the mind without judgment, we are opened to the realisation that the contents of the mind are just as external as the contents of the world. External to what? To the real you beyond personal identity. Becoming aware of yourself in this fashion is what makes all the difference.

Notice that this is a far cry from the "enlightenment" described in my description of the erroneous form of non-duality. I acknowledge that emotions such as fear, sorrow and anger have their legitimate roles to play in our lives. Enlightenment is not going to save me when I am being pursued down a dark alley by an assailant. However, in the more general dramas of life, non-dual awareness helps us maintain a calmer and happier psychological state. Unfortunately, the enlightenment pornographers take this benefit and exaggerate it, promising far more than they can deliver, trafficking in bliss while refusing to acknowledge its fragility.

The Universe exhibits the appearance of separateness, a multitude of diverse forms given substance through temporal duration. Historically, the human race has put the suffering of material existence down to a fall from grace, but our present scientific understanding of the nature of energy allows us to see that this was certainly not the case. All things are composed of energy. Physical activity requires the expenditure of energy. Therefore, in order to continue to exist, creatures must acquire more energy from elsewhere, taking it by force. While all things are essentially the self in other guises, existence in space-time is not possible unless one views the Universe in terms of I and not-I. Life is unavoidably a game of the self against the self, but is felt as the self against the other. This adversarial arrangement is integral to the nature of energy right across the Cosmos; it did not happen as a result of a metaphysical mishap on one little planet. And so, it no longer makes any sense to view this life of separation and suffering as an aberration. There is no undoing a fall that never happened, no reclaiming a union with God that was never lost.

Does it make any sense that we would be granted individual consciousness just so that we might flee from it? Brahman individuates itself into atman, then atman cries, "What the hell did you do that for? I don't want to be here! Take me back!" The quest to dissolve the ego will ultimately lead you to an existence of obsessive meditation at the expense of living, where you permanently sit crossed-legged on a mountain, or live in a cave, devoid of any vital existence. On the opposite extreme is the sociopath, viewing his own ego as the centre of the Universe and placing no value on others. The only sane, productive stance is a balance of the two polarities. It is completely unnatural to seek an experience of non-duality, even when one recognises the underlying non-duality of all things, because the entire Universe has been striving outward (into form), not inward (into formlessness).

The phrase "an experience of non-duality" is actually absurd, when you examine it closely. Experience, by definition, is the relationship between he-who-experiences and that-which-is-experienced. It's dual in nature. Non-duality is not an *experience* that the ego encounters. There is only a realisation of what underpins the duality, and that realisation is not something that makes the duality disappear, nor is it something that requires a transcendental experience to grasp.

That said, it *is* possible to have experiences of a numinous nature. In my mid-twenties, when I was a Christian, I went through a period of great emotional suffering. I was deeply in love with a woman, thought I had found the person I would spend the rest of my life with, when out of the blue she ended our relationship, leaving me feeling confused, betrayed and heartbroken. The year that followed was the most difficult of my life, as I struggled to recover emotionally. What I did was turn to God for help. I don't mean that I read my Bible and received comfort from this or that verse of scripture. I got into the habit of going for walks late in the evening, heading for somewhere quiet and private and close to nature. Here I would sit down and simply allow myself to become aware of God. Every evening for about two months during that rock-bottom period, I experienced the reality of God in a potent and profound way that I never once did at church. It wasn't a feeling or a sensation, and it certainly wasn't audible contact with a divine personality, like Saul on the road to Damascus (Acts 9). It was an intuition, as if a veil had been lifted from my mind, allowing me to "see" something that was normally hidden from view because of our ever busy lives. I knew that God was everywhere, all around me, in everything, and I felt completely and utterly loved without judgement. This wasn't like tuning in to an astral plane, or something of that nature. All I saw was the physical world around me, and it appeared to my senses exactly as it had always appeared. Except that what once seemed mundane now seemed fantastic. I would look up at the stars with a profound sense of awe at the divine and think, "How can people not see this?" But of course they don't. In day-to-day life, most of our attention is devoted to our chattering thoughts, our sensory experiences, our restless strivings, not to our ability to intuit outside of these parameters. For a time, I was living my life in a subtly altered state of consciousness brought on by emotional trauma. As a Christian, I interpreted this experience as communion with God, but what I was really doing was getting away from my suffering ego and connecting with a bigger sense of reality that made the pain tolerable. This doesn't mean that the Christian God is the one true God, although you can see how an experience like this would make most Christians unable to think anything else (including me, at the time). The important point to notice is that regardless of the subjective interpretation one places on such an experience, *something* profound was happening.

When Eckhart Tolle recounted his own rock-bottom experience at the start of *The Power of Now*, I instantly identified with it and drew parallels with my own experience, right down to the bliss he uncovered through abandoning his ego and expanding his sense of self. But I am not attached to the memory of this experience as a phenomenon I need to keep chasing. For me, the bliss was only a temporary measure, a band-aid to help me through a difficult time of life. It was not something that I was supposed to spend all my days wallowing in, like some drug-induced high. In fact, it dissipated naturally as my emotional state recovered and my attachment to worldly affairs re-formed.

Despite Tolle's emphasis on achieving a blissful stillness in the now, there remains an inexorable forward motion to existence that pulls us away from our attempts at stasis, forcing us to live as consciousness propelled in time and space, individuated from the whole, at the mercy of a hostile world. We should not see this arrangement as unnatural, but as a means to a vital existence, filled with all manner of adventure.

Numinous experiences are beautiful, but they are not as special, or as necessary, as some teachers make them out to be. They are certainly not enlightenment itself, for the simple reason that you can't realistically hold on to them. As experiences, they're not even truly non-dual, in the strictest sense of the word. Finding an altered state of consciousness that removes separateness is fundamentally impossible. As soon as your individual consciousness experiences a deeper level of reality, you've already distinguished yourself from the whole and created duality, because there is still *you* and *the experience* – that makes two. The quest to defeat the ego is really the quest to defeat consciousness itself: death, in other words. Anyone who pursues non-duality via meditative trance, or psychoactive drug use, is attempting the impossible. Any accomplishment in this endeavour will merely be a halfway house. The true exit was always obvious, and equally undesirable.

Atman doesn't get to transcend itself and encounter Brahman, because atman is Brahman already. The self doesn't have to go through an experience of transcendence because the only self that is real is already peering out from behind your eyes. "I want to become one with the Universe," you might say. You already are! There is no becoming. The Universe *is* non-dual in nature.

Imagine there is a higher plane of existence that we can reach with our minds. It doesn't matter what images you invent, as this is merely a thought experiment. Just visualise yourself in a realm vastly different from everyday experience. Notice how there is you (the subject) and where you are (the object). This is how consciousness works. The term *pure consciousness* is a meaningless abstraction. Now, come back to the real world, put this book down for a moment, and look around you. Once again, there is you (the subject) and where you are (the object). If there were an astral plane inhabited by other forms of consciousness, wouldn't that realm be just as solid to them as our realm is to us? And isn't the world around you absolutely marvellous, filled with wonders? It's easy to forget that, because familiarity breeds contempt. So, what's the fascination with "higher" consciousness? Isn't this life, right here, right now, a spiritual experience in just the same way that any other experience of consciousness would be? If you're looking for the spirit world, just open your eyes; you're already in it.

Furthermore, let's remember that the Universe's desire to experience itself began as a non-local field of primordial awareness that sought to focus itself locally. This focusing process began with cellular life, and it took billions of years for the primitive awareness to develop into the richness of human consciousness. When we desire to escape from "ordinary" consciousness and return to oneness, we are facing the wrong direction entirely. The Universe spent aeons refining base organic material into the marvel of the human form, both body and mind. The Universe is interested in evolution, not devolution. That means continued refinement of the physical form and of *individual* consciousness. Eckhart Tolle, at the close of his book *A New Earth* (2005), tells us we are on the verge of evolving into a new state of consciousness, where the ego is finally defeated. This is nonsense. As long as you are a body/mind creature, you will have a sense of ego. You will have to deal with an "outside" world that doesn't always have your best interests at heart, and you will have to steal energy from other forms of life to survive. There isn't a new Earth coming; there isn't a new consciousness on the horizon. There is only the continuing forward motion of evolution, including the evolution of consciousness (which is synonymous with the physical evolution of the brain). We don't choose our own evolutionary path. Evolution is caused by the pressures of a changing world and the ability of organic matter to randomly mutate. When a mutation provides a better chance of survival, it thrives and eventually becomes dominant. Tolle doesn't understand evolution, because he doesn't seem to be interested in real science; he prefers to wallow in a web of philosophical abstraction that is divorced from the observable world. The ego is a demonstrably successful product of evolution. That makes it the hero of the story, not the villain to be vanquished. The ego should be tamed, not killed, and taming it is just a matter of correctly understanding the nature of oneself.

The ego gets a bad rep in spiritual circles, as if one can pin the blame on an entity of some kind. But the ego is not real; it's merely a concept we use to denote our sense of individual consciousness. When an ego is conditioned to view itself as an entity located within a body, that misinformation provides the impetus for it to grow in a self-absorbed direction. But a healthy ego understands that it isn't real in the form of an entity; it knows that it is just a lens for the Universe to experience itself. As such, it knows that it *is* the Universe.

I've come to realise that the reason there are two opposing approaches to non-duality is because there are two types of person. There are those who wish to opt into life and those who wish to opt out of it. The opt-ins enjoy the experience of ego, accepting the highs and lows, pleasures and pains of life. The opt-outs strive to defeat ego, because they've had enough of suffering. I find it interesting that I had my own numinous experience at a time when I would have given anything to get out of my own head. Recently, during a discussion with an opt-out person, my opponent said, "I don't like not being in control," which I thought was very telling. Lack of control over one's circumstances causes anxiety, and anxiety is suffering. One solution is to opt-out; seek to transcend the mind by pursuing a subdued life of inward contemplation with a minimum of worldly attachment and outside interference. I'm clearly in the opt-in category. I embrace my lack of control, with all its potential for joy and disaster.

I think we can learn a lot from young children here. When a child gets up in the morning during his summer break from school, he doesn't say to himself, "I need to sit quietly and meditate for thirty minutes so that I can make myself feel okay during the day." No, he jumps out of bed and embraces life with reckless enthusiasm. While meditation has benefits, don't become obsessed with it to the point where it replaces living. We all end up with a degree of psychological damage as we accumulate life experience; it's unavoidable, because not all of our experiences are pleasant and not all of our choices are wise. It could be that you've failed to heal some personal wounds that are causing ongoing suffering. So day by day you choose to opt out of fully living.

The goal of our individual lives is not to escape from the everyday experience of consciousness; it's to live as an individual while deriving psychological benefit from understanding that the self-other duality of it is really non-dual. That sounds like a contradiction, but it's actually no more irrational than the statement: "The world appears flat, but I know it's round." There is the immediate experience and there is also the understanding of what's truly going on behind the experience. Notice that the understanding doesn't change the nature of the experience; your eyes still perceive the Earth as flat (assuming you're not reading this book aboard a space station). Don't seek numinous experience as if that's going to be the Big Answer, because you won't get to keep it. What's much more important than any fleeting experience of the divine is to understand that life is divinity, even when it doesn't feel like it. The true nature of reality doesn't change just because it's veiled from us.

OUT OF NO-THING EVERYTHING COMES

I MAGINE there was no Universe. What sort of mental picture comes to mind? Total blackness extending in all directions to infinity – that's the typical answer. We take all the planets, stars and galaxies and we make them vanish, leaving behind an endless expanse of empty space. We think in this fashion because most of us are referencing what we were taught in school science, where the nature of reality was never explained as anything deeper than atoms and molecules stacked in a three-dimensional arena – the Universe according to Newton, which every modern physicist knows is outdated.

In our present mental exercise, although we've successfully done away with all the matter of the Universe, we've left behind a ready-made *container* for it (space), as well as a mind contemplating this container (that's you). Despite there being no Universe, notice how you've accidentally invented the concept of colour – specifically black, as something definite and distinct from white. But the absence of the Universe is more than just the absence of *things*. If we think of an expanse that is black in colour, where all the laws of physics still apply (for want of a few objects to float about), then we are not thinking deeply enough about this situation.

No Universe means no forms, no laws of physics, no arena of empty space, no distinction of anything from anything. Absolute nothingness – which is not the same as an endless expanse of physical space that is waiting for something to pop into existence. For the purposes of this chapter, we shall call this profound absence the Void. It is, of course, the very same concept that I've been calling the Infinite throughout this book and Brahman in the previous chapter. The most interesting aspect of the Void is that it is incomprehensible to the mind. The mind wants to differentiate and categorise, but the Void resists our attempts to imagine it. We may think of it as endless black, or we may think of it as blinding white. It is neither, for without a Universe, there is no distinction between light and darkness. If we could imagine the Void, it would not be the Void; it would be the form of a thing distinct from some other thing.

There's an old philosophical expression: "Out of nothing nothing comes" (*ex nihilo nihil fit*, for those who like their Latin). It is commonly used as a defence for monotheism. It has a certain logic to it, but it is equally true to say, "Out of nothing *everything* comes." It all depends on what you mean by nothing. Do you mean a container of empty space (which is a thing), or do you mean the absence of form itself (which is truly *no-thing*)?

The Void may be described as the formless essence from which the Universe springs. In Eastern thinking, this is acceptable, whereas in the West, people tend to scratch their heads at the notion of something coming from the Void; they feel that there must be an eternally pre-existent God who creates the Universe. This objection only occurs because they've been conditioned to think of the Void as mundane empty space. They ask, "How can a Universe come from nothing?" It didn't come from nothing; it came from no-thing. The Void is the incomprehensible mystery behind the Universe. The Westerner then suspects, "Isn't this just a fanciful way of saying that the Void is God?" Well, yes, but it's more accurate to say that God is a fanciful way of describing the Void.

The monotheistic concept of God is full of detail and complexity. He is a conscious being who is good, just, holy, loving, all-powerful, all-knowing, all-seeing. "The attributes of God" is a common term in Christian teaching. God is anything but Void; he's an actual person. A Christian commonly argues, "How can something as complex as the Universe exist unless it was created by God?" The atheist counters, "So who created God?" The Christian answers, "God was not created. He is eternal, having no beginning or end." But the atheist recognises that this answer is a cheat, because the Christian originally argued that the existence of complexity requires explanation, then he presented a *complex* being as the answer and changed the rules to suit himself. It's clear that if we are to use the word God in an intelligent manner, we cannot refer to a complex entity with mental faculties, emotions, desires, ethics. We must view God as an incomprehensible higher order of reality, an impenetrable mystery, an unknowable otherness, *void* of all categories that apply to space-time. God isn't nothing, but he/she/it is certainly no-thing. The Void, the Absolute, the Whole, the Infinite, the All, the Ground of Being – these are all much purer terms than God because they strip away the excess baggage.

So the Void is no-thing, but it is equally everything, because everything that exists came out of it in the Big Bang. A tricky question arises here. How did sequential time (as we experience it) begin? How does the Void start time, when starting is an act that takes place *in* sequential time? Time already had to exist for time to exist. Confusing, I know! But the question is only problematic if we believe in the existence of time as an actual dimension. A dimension is something real that requires explanation. On the other hand, if time isn't real, then it doesn't require explanation. *Change* is real, and that's all we mean by time: the measurement of change. Without change, nothing could exist, except perhaps a Universe or a God in freeze-frame, incapable of motion or thought, no more alive than a photograph.

This reminds me of a recurring nightmare I had as a child. In one version of the dream I'm on my bicycle, pedalling frantically down an empty street, attempting to outrun a strange phenomenon that's sweeping along the landscape behind me, getting closer by the second. It looks like a gigantic shimmering curtain that I can partially see through. Somehow, I know that its function is to devour time. If it overtakes me, I will be frozen in time forever. And then it happens. Everything abruptly stops moving, including my body – just like hitting the pause button on a DVD. I can't move my arms and legs, can't even shift my gaze as much as a millimetre. There is no pain, but I'm stuck in a manner more profound than any bodily paralysis. My first thought is, "Okay, maybe I can just ..." And then there is a terrifying realisation: my consciousness is stuck inside a single slice of time and it can never become unstuck, because there is no time here to unstick me with. The curtain isn't just freezing matter and letting time tick on; it's literally freezing time itself. This fills me with the horror of knowing that rescue is impossible. I will never die and I will never move from this spot, for all eternity. That was the most terrifying dream I've ever had, because it was like being in hell; I can still vividly recall the relief of waking up from it. Although the idea of remaining conscious while stuck in time is pure fantasy, it illustrates a powerful point. Where there is no time, there can never be time.

So the way out of the philosophical problem of the origin of time is to accept the premise that there never was a moment of creation when time began. Time/change existed before the Big Bang. The Void has always done what it is doing and it always will. All we can say is that it is the nature of the Void to unfold temporally and spatially, simply because we observe that this is what is happening. After all, here we are.

Ultimately, the manifest Universe will come to an end. It is predicted there will either be a Big Crunch to match its Big Bang, or a Big Freeze. An expanding Universe filled with physical bodies of finite energy must finally succumb to its own gravity and collapse in on itself, or burn out. The latter scenario appears to contradict what I've been saying in previous chapters about the eternal nature of energy. But the energy itself doesn't vanish; it only becomes unusable. This is what's called *entropy*, the observable principle that order tends towards disorder. Entropy is why the pyramids of Egypt don't look as pretty today as they did when they were originally built, and they can't magically spring back to their former glory.

The inevitable end of the Universe sounds depressing, but it isn't, really. Whatever shape that ending takes, the Universe will simply return to the state it was in prior to its emergence: Void. And since the Void brought forth the Universe once, it seems natural that it can, and will, do it again – and again and again, forever. It may be that the Universe is cyclical, oscillating from Big Bang to Big Crunch to Big Bang, like breathing. Or it may be that multiple universes come and go like bubbles on the surface of boiling water; they form, they expand, they burn out – many at the same time and many more in an eternal succession.

This is all speculation, of course, but the view that the Universe is a once-only phenomenon is likewise unproven. If the latter seems like the most natural, logical position, that is likely because you've inherited the Judeo-Christian view of time, as a structure that had a definite beginning and is moving towards a once-for-all-time goal. You were subjected to this conditioning by virtue of your place in Western culture, whether you were raised as a Christian or not. Once this becomes clear, a comparison between the linear and cyclical views of time reveals the latter to be much more logical.

Our experience of time is filled with cycles. You inhale, you exhale, then you inhale again; you eat, you excrete, and you eat again; night follows day and day follows night, as you sleep and rise; the tides of the ocean move in and out from the beach; the moon goes through its phases; each year the same four seasons occur, during which time a great deal of life will grow, thrive and die, only to be reborn annually. The duration of a human life appears to be linear, moving from the energy of youth to the frailty of old age and eventual death. But from a wider perspective, even this is part of a cycle, as we give birth to our replacements, who later give birth to their replacements. The evolution of life appears to be linear, but even this may be part of a larger cycle. Consider the dinosaurs. When they were wiped out, the evolutionary process merely suffered a reboot, and this time large mammals emerged. And if we are stupid enough to wipe ourselves out, something else will evolve in our place. The Western mentality, with its linear view of time, is always restless, because it feels there is a destination to strive for, but it has no idea what this destination is. In reality, there is no linear goal to life. We would be a lot less agitated if we saw our purpose as relaxing into the natural rhythms of life, right here in the present. To do that, we have to understand time as cyclical. And when we do, it's not a big stretch of the imagination to conceive of the entire history of the Universe we inhabit as one cycle in an endless succession.

To the Christian, I imagine the cyclical perspective is unsatisfying. Christianity views fleshly existence as a training ground. Mortal life is lived in order to die and finally get satisfaction in the next life. The idea of mortality being continually recycled for all eternity is abhorrent to the Christian, because he has been conditioned to hate his earthly life of sin and suffering. Those of us who love life, and who understand that all life is *I* in manifold guises, can take delight in the Universe's ever changing shape. On such a grand scale as the birth and death of endless universes, it is actually a comfort to know that each of my tiny little lives must forget the others it has lived and know nothing of its future lives. True eternal life is to know that I am all that ever was, is, and will be – without consciousness being crushed by such a colossal weight of experience. When this is truly grasped, it is deeply liberating.

When I first understood the Infinite as my true identity, I thought of it as a vast collector of experiences. I took comfort in the idea that nothing I experienced would ever be lost; the Ground of Being, the real me, has instant access to it all. But I've come to see that I was missing the point. Consciousness happens right here, not "up there," and with good reason.

There is an elusive insight to be gained in watching a young child experience the world. Everything is new and exciting. The adult realises that life cannot be like this for him, at least not nearly as often, because he has lived so much already. Life has become duller because he has already experienced much of what it has to offer. He has memories that he treasures, many that have leaked away through inattention, and others he wishes he could forget. And although he has a lot of living yet to do, he sees something marvellous and desirable about a child starting from scratch. He might even experience a degree of envy. And then it hits him: this is just as it should be. Our lives are supposed to be recycled like this, the burdens of our memories lifted off so that we can experience it all again, only differently.

The cyclical nature of the Universe implies that it is not heading for an ultimate destination where all of its striving comes to a finish for all time. If the Universe is cyclical, then it is not purpose-driven towards a final goal, such as the Christian's Judgement Day and the subsequent creation of a permanent and lasting paradise.

The religionist's stance is nothing more than a desire to freeze time at a point where conditions are ideally suited for him. But time is merely a synonym for change, and change is the cornerstone of existence itself. Without time, without change, there is nothing at all.

This is perhaps why we cannot visualise heaven without secretly thinking of it as boring beyond belief. Can you imagine a life that consists of praising God for all eternity – a life devoid of conflict and adventure, where joy is never as joyful as it was on Earth, because you can no longer experience the transition out of sorrow? Can you imagine what it would be like to go on accumulating memories for a trillion years without any of the drama that makes life interesting? Heaven starts to sound suspiciously like its opposite, hell. And in heaven, what would become of the memory of your earthly life when it is buried beneath the weight of a trillion years of memory collecting? And what tedious, dreary memories they must be, in a world without drama.

When we desire to live forever, we don't realise the full extent of what we're wishing for. We're hoping to preserve our individual existence like a photograph, to stop time, to stop change – when existence itself *is* change, and forgetting is as much a part of change as remembering. And what is death other than a form of forgetting, with birth bringing renewal?

It is absurd to ask "What is the purpose of the Universe?" This is merely another way of framing the question "What is the finish line for the process of change?" But the end of change means the end of time, for time and change mean the same thing. When there is no time, there can be no material form. And so we are left with emptiness. There can be no eternal freezing of the Universe at some mythical ultimate objective, otherwise there is no Universe.

In searching for the meaning of life, we should not be looking to the future, for if there is no ultimate objective, then the future holds no key to the meaning of our individual lives. There is no future and no past outside the recording device of your brain. If we are to attach meaning to our lives, that meaning must be accessible in the only moment that's real: *right now.*

Every experience of your life, and every life, is the eternal flux of the Universe. The Void manifests itself as seemingly individual parts and gazes at itself as though the things it is looking at are separate. In doing so, the Void becomes something tangible. If it did not play this game with itself, the Void would truly be nothing. It would not even be conscious, for when there is nothing to be conscious of, there is no consciousness. In a manner of speaking, the existence of "God" is as dependent upon the Universe as the Universe is upon God. If God were not engaged in this adventure of duality, he would be comatose – we might as well say non-existent.

But we must be careful not to rely too much on anthropomorphisms, which are merely crude approximations of the ungraspable. It is too easy to slip back into patterns of Western conditioning and to think of the Void as a divine personality presiding over creatures in a fatherly fashion. The Void, as its name implies, has no form. Out of this mysterious non-dual essence, patterns arise and descend eternally; whole universes come and go in a dance that had no beginning and will have no end. You are that dance. There is no divine consciousness with which to seek union. There is nothing else to find except YOU, right here, right now, for always. You are formlessness made real through an infinitude of forms across an eternity of change.

When I first grasped the idea of non-duality, I thought of it as a higher order of reality that I had to reach – a transcendent realm where Big Me "up there" orchestrated the lives of all the little mes "down here." I didn't realise it, but I was still suffering from a lingering monotheistic outlook. Now I realise that there is no Big Me presiding over the Universe. Consciousness is entirely dependent on the subject-object duality of the Universe.

Non-duality is a slightly unfortunate term, because we instinctively think that duality is its opposite. This is how we treat all other words that can be preceded by *non*. Sense and nonsense; existence and non-existence; conformist and nonconformist – all of these are opposites. But non-duality, when correctly understood, is the unique idea of oneness that has no opposite. If it *had* an opposite, it wouldn't be oneness. The duality that we experience is not separate from the non-duality "underneath." There aren't two realities, above and below. Duality is merely the manner in which a non-dual reality manifests. As such, duality and non-duality are one and the same. One of the drawbacks of our reliance on words is that we unconsciously fall into the habit of thinking exclusively in a manner dictated by existing language structure. This is why it's so difficult to wrap our minds around non-duality. Practically speaking, we see duality all around us, so we mistakenly think that the non-duality is something else that we have to discover under the surface, when the duality *is* the non-duality. Nothing is separate.

One of my first insights into non-duality was that the physical Universe had an illusory quality. And while that is true, I now see that the illusion of the material world is the very basis of consciousness. Heaven, paradise, nirvana – whatever you want to call it – is right here in the adventures of our earthbound lives. Heaven is a walk on the beach with the wind blowing through my hair; it is the scent of cocoa rising from the cup on my desk. No pretentious poetry is intended here. I have literally arrived at the place I was seeking. In fact, I've been at the destination all along, only I couldn't see it for what it was. I thought duality was something I had to escape from, but escape to what – to the formless essence of the Infinite? What is that? It is me, it is everything, but it is also nothing at all – unless there is the appearance of duality to give it form. I was trying to get to somewhere, only to realise it's right here under my nose. It always was and always will be.

Each day of your life is like the Universe in miniature. It begins, it is filled with experiences, it ends, and it begins anew. There is no more profound meaning to life than to wake up in the morning and ask yourself: "Now, what interesting things shall I do today?" I find it heart-warming that all this deep philosophising takes us right back to what comes naturally to any child on his summer break from school. And I find it hilarious that this oh-so-serious pursuit of truth has no more ultimate significance than a kid playing with toys. If there is any value in what I'm doing here, it consists in helping adults to become less serious and more playful in life.

Perhaps it is too much for the scientist to muse upon the depressing realisation that the great body of knowledge to which he dedicates most of his life must ultimately come to naught. What about the revolutionary, whose life is dedicated to making a positive impact on the world? What's it all for, if everything perishes?

This is certainly a depressing situation, if you view the Universe as a once-only phenomenon. When we face the inevitability of the end of everything, all our serious strivings become no more important than a child at play. But when the Universe is understood as cyclical, the darkness is banished, because the one factor that remains, when all else is lost, is the singular *I* at the heart of existence itself, and that I is *you*. You are basically a child at play who never truly dies. All your noble endeavours should be undertaken with a lightness of spirit, valued for their temporary significance alone. In other words, what we do matters for the time in which it matters, and then it doesn't; at another time and place, in a future Universe, something else will matter, until it doesn't. Life should be understood as a big game we're all playing, one that never had a beginning and will never have an end.

GENESIS REBOOTED

I'M against imposing any ideology on young children, because they're not capable of critical thinking. Nevertheless, children will ask those amazing questions, like "Where did the world come from?" and "Where was I before I was born?" and "Where do people go when they die?" Here in the West, unless you raise your child by turning your home into his prison, he's likely going to be conditioned by the Christian myths that permeate our culture. The child will be exposed to them through television programmes, youth clubs, schools, and other outlets.

These myths retain some value when they are viewed as man's attempt to reach out to God, rather than the revelation of God to man. However, Bible mythology is noticeably outdated in light of modern science. I want to outline an alternative myth that takes our discoveries into account – one that starts with the familiar word God, but goes in a new direction; a meaningful story that doesn't insult the intelligence or get bogged down in all the technicalities that have plagued this book.

I don't recommend reading the following myth verbatim to young children, because some of the words will be unfamiliar and confusing. I struggled to find a child-friendly vocabulary when writing this. Nevertheless, you may be able to extract something valuable from the narrative to help you give meaningful answers to your children. Adults who resonate with monism, but struggle to wrap their minds around it, might find this more helpful than some of the more intellectual chapters already digested.

Note that what follows is merely myth, and it relies heavily on anthropomorphism – describing the Infinite as if it's humanlike. I've resisted using the word God throughout much of this book, and now I'm going to wholeheartedly break that rule. But a little metaphor never hurts (except when you don't recognise it as metaphor). This approach may help you bridge the gap between the familiarity of monotheism and the strangeness of monism. Unlike Genesis 1, the following myth is compatible with modern science, providing a better basis for understanding the Universe than ancient Hebrew scripture.

* * *

There was no beginning; there was always God. He was all-powerful, but that didn't mean anything because there was nothing for him to have power over. He was all knowing, but there wasn't anything for him to know about except himself. He was all seeing, but he felt completely blind, because there was nothing to see. His presence was everywhere, but everywhere was nowhere, because nothing else existed except him. Although God was the Supreme Being, residing in the blinding glory of his own eternal existence, this was meaningless, because there was no one and nothing below or above him. He felt as small as an unborn baby asleep in its mother's womb. His life was utterly lifeless.

So he thought, "I will create." But there was a snag: he didn't have any material to work with. He didn't even have any space to put anything. All that existed was God, so anything he made would *be* himself. He tried creating something, but it was impossible, because it could not be separated from the light of his own presence. Then he thought of a neat trick. He did something that was not quite an act of creation, but a pulling back of his own being, forming a bubble of absence.

As a test, he pushed his presence into one side of the bubble, to see what absence felt like. It didn't feel like anything. There was nothing to see, just like before. While continuing to gaze into the bubble, he decided to peer into the opposite side at the same time. Suddenly, a face appeared, as if out of nowhere. "Who are you?" God cried out. The shape responded, "Me? And just who are *you*?"

God pulled back in alarm. Looking across the bubble, he hadn't been able to recognise himself. The experience was terrifying and exhilarating and immensely interesting. In an existence that consisted of nothing but himself, he couldn't imagine anything more interesting – except perhaps doing the same thing on a much larger scale. So that's just what he did.

God threw his presence into the bubble with reckless abandon. And the more of himself he inserted, the larger the bubble grew. The effect was like a massive explosion. He saw himself in all of the individual pieces, but none of the bits realised that they were him. Some fragments fought each other and destroyed themselves, yet this destruction was also a transformation into something new. Those fragments that got along were especially interesting, because they started forming strange and fascinating relationships.

Eventually this settled down into planets that orbited around stars, which arranged themselves into galaxies. This stability was always under threat by the sheer diversity of all the things that now existed. Sometimes a huge chunk of rock would collide with a planet and cause massive damage. Occasionally a star would become so heavy that it would collapse in on itself and start pulling in anything else that got too close. The Universe was a fencing match between order and chaos, with neither side ever able to win outright.

Even more interesting events started happening on the surfaces of some of the planets. Tiny cells worked together, established a rapport with their environment, and eventually built themselves into creatures. Their lives were just as chaotic as the rest of the Universe. They discovered they had to eat other living things just to stay alive. All sorts of variety emerged, some creatures learning to collaborate with other species, while others opted for a more isolated and aggressive approach. Those whose bodies were structured in a manner that gave them an advantage in fighting or defence got to survive, while the weaker forms died and were never seen again. Even this only made the situation more interesting, because over time the creatures took on more complex and amazing shapes. One of these was humankind.

As God watched the lives of the humans, he saw them loving and hating and creating all sorts of drama. He knew that every one of them was himself, but he didn't tell them the big secret; the whole game had depended on this pretence from the beginning. But these creatures were persistent. Some of them figured out the truth just a little bit, and they would try to talk to God as if he were a separate person from them. Others attempted to reach him using meditation techniques or mind-altering substances.

"But who or what do you expect to find?" God felt like asking them. "I *am* you. And if I wasn't down there having these wonderful experiences as you, I would be all alone forever in a great big nowhere. Don't you get it? There's nothing 'up here' with me. *You're* what makes me truly alive. So stop trying to find me; you *are* me. I put you down there so that *I* could live."

Some, in their quest to find God, got hung up on mystical experiences and spent their lives pursuing those, not realising that the whole point of living was to have a life. Some spent so much time contemplating another plane of existence that they spoiled life by neglecting to live it fully.

Human lives were not built to last, and people were sometimes glum about that. They felt that they should go on living forever. This was an understandable feeling, since they were God-in-disguise. Some humans overcame this sadness by making up stories about going to a better place when they died. Others saw themselves as jumping into a new body when their present life was over. But the really smart ones understood that they were inside every body at the same time, only the experience of unity was walled off – except in those occasional weird moments when one of them could tell what another was thinking, or when they made something happen that wasn't ordinarily supposed to be possible. They were God-in-disguise, playing a game of separateness. They realised that they didn't have to worry about their little life winking out. It was just like forgetting one experience to make room for new ones. After all, they were everybody all at once.

Just like bodies, God didn't make the Universe to last. Eventually he will pull all the separate parts of himself together again, and there will only be him alone, as it was before. And that situation will be as uninteresting as it always was. So he will play the game again. He always has and he always will.

LIFE IS PLAY

WHAT is the meaning of life? Many people would say, "I haven't got a clue," which, on the surface, seems like a fair and unpretentious answer. You may not be aware of it, but you have, consciously or otherwise, placed a meaning of some kind on your life. And that meaning is expressed in what you spend your life pursuing.

A person who knowingly destroys his health with dangerous illegal drugs has decided that life isn't worth preserving. A person who stands on a street corner shouting to the world about the wrath of God has decided to give himself completely in the service of a deity. A person with a big house full of expensive treasures has decided that wealth is what matters. A person with an extensive library of books believes in the pursuit of knowledge. The list goes on.

Unless you spend your whole life standing completely still, then you have injected some kind of purpose into it. It could be one particular aim, or a mixture of pursuits. Since no one ever came along and said, "Here is the meaning of life," you took it upon yourself to get on with the business of living – and living for *something*.

But maybe it's not true that no one told you the meaning of life. Maybe something was being said, but you just never consciously took notice. For instance, you're born into life in the Western world. It's all playtime for a few years, then at age five your parents hand you over to the education system. This system instructs you with information that will help you survive in later life. The aim, according to the education system, is to be as smart as possible, get as qualified as possible, so you can get the best job possible, and make as much money as possible. As you progress through school, six or more hours of your life, five days per week, are devoted to this goal. The pursuit is done in competition with those around you; somebody's got to be first in class, and somebody's got to be last. Life becomes a game of survival (or success) of the fittest.

I'm a realist, and in the real world not everyone is born equal. Some are imbued with a greater capacity for intelligence than others; some are physically stronger than others; some are more coordinated than others; some are more creative than others; some are more beautiful than others. The harsh truth, visible across the whole animal kingdom, is that nature stratifies itself. There are winners and losers. But competition is only half the story. In prehistoric times, the life of the tribe depended upon working together and sharing resources. Each new life was valued for what it would contribute to the whole. Contrast this with today, where each individual competes against others for gainful employment. All the way through school, he has a sense of how unnecessary he is, because he knows there are more people than jobs. Instead of collaborating for the benefit of the tribe as the hunter-gatherers did, we are individually alienated and set against each other. And in a world where material values reign supreme, the winners are those with the most expensive cars and the biggest houses. So many of us unthinkingly subscribe to these values, not realising that whatever you devote your life to becomes your life's meaning. Whatever path you choose, you should walk it *consciously*.

I played the competitive game because I had to, because the modern world is the way it is and you either sink or swim. I don't regret for a second investing three years of my life to obtain a university qualification that allowed me to pursue a career in computing. Once qualified, I recall that I applied for two particular jobs simultaneously. One of them was a much higher-paying job than the other, but a lot less fun. If I had been offered both jobs, I would have chosen money over fun, because that's what material values dictate. That was the decision that never asks the question, "What am I living for?" I'm relieved that I was only offered the fun job, because back then I didn't have the sense to say, "I don't like the way modern Western life works. I'm going to live it with other priorities."

Look how many of us spend forty hours or more a week exhausting ourselves doing something we hate. We assume we need all that money, but if we allowed ourselves to think outside of the box of the hive-mind of society, we might see ways to change our lives. It might be as simple as reconsidering our addiction to lottery tickets, or how many electronic gadgets we buy.

I personally went as far as questioning my need for the ownership of a car. Almost all of my life's activities take place within my local area, and since I didn't have a family to support, I realised that I could do almost everything by bicycle. I could save a lot of money, maintain my health, and reduce some of the admin of life; there was nothing to lose and everything to gain. So I made the move from four wheels to two.

I realise it's not practical for everyone to give up cars. But our lives are soaked in unnecessary materialism of one kind or another. Hypnotised by our television screens, we buy, buy, buy, then work, work, work, so we can buy, buy, buy. And it rarely seems to hit home that our way of life is like a prison without bars. I have a five-days-a-week job, like most people, but if I didn't enjoy it, I would be asking to have it reduced to four days, or maybe even three. And yet there are people who grasp at every opportunity to work overtime, despite doing a job they hate. In the great pursuit of wealth, your life can easily become something that is barely fit to be lived. You may not think you know the meaning of life, but the zeitgeist has been dictating a meaning to you your whole life – and not a very healthy one: "He who dies with the most toys wins."

The reason why it's so easy to become materialistic is because of the value we place on *material*. But what is the material Universe? It's like a frequency your consciousness is tuned to. It has no more solidity than a videogame. The pursuit of wealth in the real world is the same in principle as scoring points in a game. In life, you can use your wealth to buy a new car; in a game, when you accrue enough points, you might have the choice of equipping your character with a variety of power-ups. The game ends, and the points vanish. Likewise, life ends, and all contact with your wealth is gone forever.

Oh sure, your wealth still exists in the world, and you may feel a sense of satisfaction in leaving it to your sons and daughters when you die. But let's take a look at the way of life you're perpetuating. You're born; you have a few years in which to enjoy a childhood; then the business of making money begins. At some point, you may get married and start a family. Instead of enjoying your money sensibly whilst looking after your family, the system dictates that you must make more and more money, to invest in your children's futures. So you work harder and harder, thinking about your kids needing cars and college later on. Now there is no room left for you to have a life of your own – to pursue what *you* want to do. This kind of altruism may sound commendable on the surface. But in living like this, what are you really offering your kids? A chance to live in exactly the same manner you're living – to have a brief childhood followed by a long life of slavery to the system, as they seek to do for their own children what you did for them.

In principle it's good to labour for your family's future, but it's important that this doesn't get out of control. There is a fine line between planning for the future and simply being *enslaved* by the future. It's important to understand that the future, being the future, never arrives. Tomorrow never comes, as the saying goes. Wealth, instead of being used for what it is – a means to an end – becomes the food for an insatiable imaginary monster called the future, who must be fed by you, then by your sons, then by their sons, into infinity. All the while, everybody's thinking, "We're getting there. We're going to make it." But nobody has any clue what *there* means. People blindly invest their time increasing their wealth, with no sense of a practical limit on what they need. Later, they die with lots of unspent money, unable to get back the time they wasted amassing it.

If we want to live a life that has any meaning, we need to first have a life. And that means living in the now instead of being a slave to the future. It may sound selfish to claim the right to enjoy life in the now, but if you deny that right to yourself, you perpetuate the system that denies it to your children, too.

Imagine going to the cinema, and right before the lights go out, an usher walks in front of the screen and says, "Excuse me, ladies and gentlemen, I would like to take a moment to tell you what this film is about." He goes on to provide a rough plot summary, leaving out only the ending. "Now that I've saved you the trouble of watching the movie, we'll just roll the last five minutes." You would feel cheated, wouldn't you? Why? Because you know that the purpose of watching a movie is not merely to get to the end. The purpose is to experience each moment of the whole for its own sake. When you watch a movie, you are getting something out of every part of it. The same is true when you read a novel or listen to a song. And the same is true of life, for your life is a collection of experiences laid out in exactly the same manner. It's not about where you're going, but about what you're doing each step along the way.

One of the most fundamental reflections about life that I can make is: "I am the experience of consciousness." The purpose of life, then, is to have experience. But what experience in particular? Well, does it have to be only one? Life offers a great deal of variety, and maybe that's the point. Ask yourself, what it is you want to do with your life? Okay, then. Create *that* experience.

But what do we do instead? We buy into the con that the Universe is three-dimensionally solid, that matter is what matters, then we work long and hard to claim ownership of a little piece of the physical world for ourselves. Believing it to be fundamentally real, we fail to realise that we can own *nothing*. All we can do is experience.

Imagine a man who lives in an overcrowded city full of buildings so tall that he can barely see the sky; he has a high-paying job that he hates, drives a flashy car, and owns a luxurious apartment filled with expensive treasures. Then imagine a man who owns almost nothing, lives in a small house made of palm branches, works for a pittance as a fisherman; he wakes up every morning to the view of a spectacular beach and ocean, and as he goes about his working day, he enjoys the sensation of the boat bobbing upon the waves, the feel of the warm sun on his skin, and the smell of salt water in his nostrils. One of these men is considered rich and the other poor. But from a deeper point of view, possessions are nothing more than experiences in waiting. If I buy an expensive car, I am paying for the repeatable experience of driving that car and enjoying the feeling of status that it gives me. If I purchase an expensive ornament for my home, I am paying for the repeatable experience of the pleasure of gazing upon it. That's what *ownership* boils down to. All of life is, in a sense, holographic. Notice how the poor man "owns" the experience of gazing upon the ocean – a repeatable pleasure utterly denied to the rich man, who wakes up each morning in his expensive apartment without a view. When you really understand what ownership is, at its core, it's not so clear who is rich and who is poor. This illustrates the folly of the mindless pursuit of wealth.

But take care that you don't make the opposite mistake of demonising wealth. If you happen to be lucky financially, there is nothing noble about forcing yourself to live an ascetic life. Asceticism can easily turn into just another ego-driven activity, where you get to feel superior to all those greedy, rich folks. Pleasure is pleasure, whether it comes from spending money or not. So if you've got money, enjoy the experience of using it; if you haven't got it, enjoy whatever other experiences come your way. The key is to understand that *everything* in life boils down to experience.

When I make decisions that affect my life, all I'm doing is reshaping the hologram, creating new experiences. And there will come a time when the collection of memory fragments known as the life of Darryl Sloan terminates. But what does that matter to me? I am the Infinite and Darryl Sloan is merely one of my manifestations.

From the perspective of the time-bound ego, look at how slippery the reality of the present is. No sooner have you grasped it than it becomes the past. The apparent solidity of the present moment becomes nothing more solid than a stored memory in the blink of an eye. Think of a cherished memory from the distant past that you wish you could relive. That memory is no further from you today than it was the very second after you lived it.

When we ask ourselves "What is the meaning of life?" that's usually the ego asking if there is a special reason for its individual existence, or wondering if it's supposed to be doing something in particular with this life. But when you ask that question, see yourself as the Infinite, having an infinitude of experiences past, present and future. The question "Does God have a plan for my life?" (or "Is there a particular life-plan for this incarnation?") takes on quite a different spin, doesn't it? As the Infinite, I am every person who ever gave his life heroically, every person who ever killed another in cold blood, every loving husband, every rapist, every person who ever lived long or died tragically in childhood. There is only one.

In full awareness that you are the Infinite, what sort of an experience should you choose for yourself in this life? I think the truth is we knew the answer to that question when we were children, before the system got hold of us and moulded us into its image of what a person should be. There is something simple and profound in watching a child at play. We're told to grow up, get serious, and start making lots of money, but that's all misdirection. A kid knows what it's all about without having to be told. He's just creating with his toys, drinking in the wonderful cocktail of the holographic experience. A child who builds a sandcastle on the beach knows he cannot take it home with him and cares nothing for the fact that the sea will wash it away later. Yet he continues to build, not bothered about the futility of it. The act of building needs no more justification than the creation and enjoyment of experience in the now.

How many children have been exploited because of the pursuit of wealth? How much of the planet has been devastated by human greed? How many wars have been started because someone in a position of power decided he wanted to own a bigger slice of the hologram? We are living in a materialist paradigm that is not only wrong on a purely intellectual level, but its aberrant nature is revealed in its self-destructive consequences.

The Infinite has no ultimate purpose. I state this confidently because I recognise that the idea of purpose is connected to the erroneous view that "time" has an ending. Time is just the present. The Universe, as a temporal manifestation of the Infinite, has a visible purpose: the motion of all life towards survival and wellbeing. Our purpose as creatures, then, lies in flowing with that arrangement. Parents know this intuitively, in the joy they experience through their children; doctors feel it when they help the sick; scientists sense it when they improve the world with new discoveries. But don't make the mistake of taking that sense of purpose too seriously. Ultimately the manifest Universe will come to an end, only to begin anew.

Adults, raised to serve self-centred material values, perpetuate madness. Children are the truly sane ones, because they haven't yet been manipulated to forget the truth: *life is play*. The beauty in this tragedy is that you can reclaim that truth for yourself any time you want. The trick is to notice it.

PART THREE
UNCHARTED TERRITORY

In science, as in politics and religion, it is a lot easier to believe what you have been taught, than to set out for yourself and ascertain what happens.

Upton Sinclair, *Mental Radio*

Science of today – the superstition of tomorrow. Science of tomorrow – the superstition of today.

Charles Fort, *The Book of the Damned*

THE UNCONSCIOUS, AT YOUR SERVICE

W E have five senses – sight, hearing, smell, taste, touch – which we rely on to give us information. Yet we know that there is much more going on around us than we can perceive. For instance, all around me are the various frequencies of the radio and television stations broadcasting to my area. These frequencies pass through the walls, and even through my body. The "machinery" of my body is not designed to pick up these signals, and so it's as if they don't exist. However, a different sort of machine with different sensory apparatus – a television or radio with an aerial – will receive those frequencies and interpret them into usable information.

The experience of being conscious is an experience of limitation. Our consciousness is tuned to the physical Universe and our sense of sight is able to receive only a miniscule part of the electromagnetic spectrum known as visible light.

This understanding should give pause to those who think exclusively in terms of material minimalism: "If I can't detect it, it isn't real." It's all well and good that we know about radio waves today, but imagine trying to explain them to someone in the 15th century: "In the future, people will have little boxes that they hold up to their mouth to talk to each other. I could stand at the far side of the lake over there and talk to you as if I were standing right beside you. The box changes your speech into an invisible wave that flies out in all directions, travelling much farther than your voice can extend. And the other box receives the wave, changes it back into sound, and speaks it into the air so that the other person can hear it with his own ears."

A reasonable person of the time period might reply, "Little boxes that can listen to you as if they have ears, then throw your voice over great distances, and even speak back to you as if they have mouths – how ridiculous! What proof can you offer me of this nonsense? I don't believe it." In this case, allowing yourself to be led by evidence alone would have brought you to the wrong conclusion. Absence of proof is not proof of absence, and yet many people continually treat evidence as the singular factor in determining what is both true and untrue, possible and impossible, ridiculous and sensible.

We should not be so quick to label something as impossible when it may simply be undetected. As conscious entities, locked into a specific range of perception, we simply have no way of knowing what exists outside of us that we are not perceiving. We may make certain discoveries with scientific instruments, and we have (gamma rays, X-rays, ultraviolet, infra-red, microwaves, radio waves), but we never know how much or how little there really is going on. Reality may well be far more multi-dimensional than we realise.

Another aspect of our limited range of perception is our limited focus of attention. We are always focused on one thing or another, never on many things at once. I cannot watch a movie on television while writing this book. It's impossible for my mind to attend to the two activities simultaneously. I might attempt to switch between two things periodically, but attention is always on one or the other. I can play the piano a little, with *both* hands, which appears to defy this logic, but always my focus is on one of the hands, while the other plays a repeating pattern that I have trained my mind to handle without the need for attention. As we experience life and accumulate memories, those memories are not ever-present with us, but go into storage. They are only useful to us when accessed and focused upon afresh.

You've probably heard the term *subconscious* or *unconscious* mind. What exactly is it, and do we possess one? Well, what *precisely* it is remains something of a mystery, but you'll get a sense of it by example. It's undeniable that we do possess an unconscious mind, since it can be shown that we use it every day, mostly without realising it.

Your conscious mind is aware of only a fraction of the information that is presented to it in your moment-to-moment experience. You might go out for a walk and not notice the sound of birdsong. You might be so engrossed in a television programme that you don't notice someone in the room asking you a question. You may have listened to a song fifty times but never noticed a subtle bassline until one particular moment when your attention is drawn to it. When you drive a car, countless aspects of your environment slip by while you concentrate on the road ahead; they are within sight of your eyes, but there is no opportunity to pay them any attention as you navigate the twists and turns of the road. The conscious mind is stuck in five-sense awareness and able to pay attention to only a narrow band of those five senses at any moment.

The unconscious mind, however, sees it all, making a permanent recording of everything that the conscious mind misses. It is not restricted by a focus of attention. Think of the unconscious like a dark attic with all sorts of stuff lying around in it, and the conscious mind like the beam of a flashlight illuminating only one spot.

Critical thinking is a process of the conscious mind. The unconscious, on the other hand, has no sense of judgement whatsoever. It is like a robot. If someone says something to us, or we read a piece of information, the conscious mind is able to actively judge the worth of that message and decide whether it is true or false. But if the message goes straight to the unconscious by bypassing conscious awareness, the unconscious will automatically and passively accept it without our awareness.

Why does the mind work in this unfortunate way? Actually, if it didn't function in this manner, we would be in real trouble. When I was a child, learning to type for the first time was a frustratingly slow process. I would rove my finger over the keyboard for maybe five seconds, just looking for the V key. With continual practice, I learned to memorise the layout and find the keys at a much faster pace. But something more than memorisation was also taking place. In the early days, I still had to consciously direct each finger to each key, but in time it started to happen automatically. What I was doing, without realising it, was training my unconscious mind. You can think of the unconscious as a faithful servant who constantly pays attention to what you're doing, always on the look-out for repetitive patterns, so that it can take some of the workload off your conscious mind. Nowadays, in my typing experience, there is a direct connection between a simple intent of the will for a word to appear on the screen and its appearance. My fingers do my bidding with little or no conscious thought. If you're reasonably good at typing, try it. Think of a sentence, type it on your keyboard, then afterwards reflect on how aware you were of what your fingers were doing. I'm betting not a lot. Amusingly, I sometimes have the experience of a wrong word slipping out through my fingers. I don't mean a typing error like "trudt" instead of "trust"; I mean something like "trash" instead of "trust," where a totally different, yet perfectly formed, word from the one intended pops out. It's as if the unconscious mishears me and grabs the wrong word from my mental dictionary.

Driving is another good example. If you're an experienced driver, you will remember the hardship of learning to drive. It's especially difficult here in the United Kingdom, where automatic gears are not the norm. You have to learn the correct order of three foot-pedals (clutch, brake and accelerator) and the positions of five gears – oh, and not forgetting reverse. While remembering those, you have to know how to properly lower and raise the clutch while changing the gear, simultaneously steering and paying attention to the road. When you become an experienced driver, the whole car just feels like an extension of your body. You barely have to think about what your limbs are doing as you navigate. You can even give most of your conscious attention to a conversation with a passenger. All of this is possible because you have successfully trained your unconscious to handle what your conscious mind originally had to perform on its own. If we didn't have an unconscious mind to aid us, every trip in the car would feel like your first ever driving lesson.

I once had an amusing experience not long after I moved house. It was my habit to drive home from work at lunch-time, so one day I got in the car and started driving, not giving conscious thought to where I was heading. I ended up pulling into the driveway of my previous house before I realised my mistake. I had literally said to my unconscious, "Take me home," and my unconscious followed the old program it had been trained to perform while my conscious mind occupied itself elsewhere (probably doing some dangerous daydreaming). This shows just how elaborate our unconscious programming can become.

The unconscious is what regulates our bodies; we do not need to think in order to breathe. Certainly, we can consciously take control of our lungs at any time, by choosing to take a shallow breath or a deep breath. But we don't have to. We won't die if we forget to breathe. Actually, strike that – we *will* die if we forget to breathe. But it's the unconscious that remembers for us and does it on our behalf. Some claim to be able to regulate their own heart rate and blood pressure by the same principle of wresting control from the unconscious.

We all make use of our unconscious every day, without thinking about it. It is a faithful servant that makes life so much easier. Without it, life would be an intolerable drudgery, if not an impossibility, as our every motion would require our full conscious attention.

There is a downside to having an unconscious mind. It tends to make the world a duller place. New experiences can be stimulating, but once they are repeated several times, they lose their excitement. This is because the unconscious notices a pattern, learns it, and all but has the experience on your behalf.

I once lived in a neighbourhood that I detested for three years. When I finally had opportunity to move back to the area where I grew up, one of the first activities I did was to get on my bicycle and go riding through the nearby countryside – something I had done often in my youth. The experience was utter bliss; I had missed this simple pleasure so much. However, now that I have repeated this experience hundreds of times since, it has lost much of its excitement. This is because my unconscious has spotted the pattern and taken over. Contrast this with the excitement of a dog, whose much simpler mind never fails to be enthralled by its surroundings each time it goes for a walk to the same place.

You can, however, prevent the unconscious from stealing the vitality out of your experiences. Some years ago, I took the notion to record a little video of my local countryside. As I cycled around looking for interesting scenes to shoot, I found myself suddenly getting excited by the simplest things, such as a particular view of dead leaves on a lawn, with the sun shining through the branches of a tree. Items that I ordinarily took no notice of became extraordinarily interesting. What I had done, without realising it, was prevent my unconscious mind from living on my behalf.

Aldous Huxley, in *The Doors of Perception* (1954), describes the experience of taking the drug mescaline as a kind of hyperawareness of everything being utterly fascinating beyond belief. It's as if the robotic side of consciousness was temporarily disabled, allowing every perception to be fresh.

I recall having a similar experience in my teens, obtained without the aid of drugs. One of my ears had become completely blocked with wax to the point where I could hear nothing through that orifice. I lived with it like this for a couple of months and adjusted completely – to the point where monaural hearing felt completely natural. I could get by with one working ear, and didn't really miss stereo sound; even listening to music with headphones felt natural with only one ear functioning. When I finally went to the doctor to get the ear canal cleaned out, the experience of regaining the use of a second ear was exhilarating. Directly afterwards, I found myself walking around the town centre, drinking in the sheer pleasure of all the crisp, clear stereo sound. I was listening to nothing more than car engines and chattering shoppers, but the sounds became utterly new and fascinating. Of course, once I got used to hearing with two ears again, the experience turned stale. The robot had taken over.

The unconscious lives vast portions of our lives for us. One way to prevent this – to turn mundane experiences into exciting experiences – is to start taking notice of your surroundings again. Force yourself to become conscious of what is going on in your sensory experience; be in the moment.

Unconscious and its older synonym *subconscious* are merely mythic labels that Western science invents to account for the behaviours of the mind that happen unconsciously or *sub*-consciously – *below* awareness. In composing a meaningful model of the mind, there appears to be *me* existing in a state of limited cognition and limited perception, and a more mysterious me working behind the scenes.

Talking to ourselves is something we do often without realising it. I might say to myself, "What's the name of the actor who played Obi-Wan Kenobi in the original *Star Wars*? I can't remember." Anything from a moment to several minutes later, the answer will pop into my conscious mind, as if from nowhere. "Alec Guinness." Now, the next time you have a conversation with yourself like that, ask yourself what process you went through to recall the information you wanted, because I have no idea what I did beyond simply creating a request for information. The unconscious just seems to get on with the task, and then it gives you the answer when it's done, sometimes at a completely unexpected moment. Spooky. Notice also how this talking to oneself is an admission of there being two aspects to you: an up-front part doing the experiencing of the world and a behind-the-scenes part doing the work. See how we naturally think of both parts as *me*.

We should be careful about viewing this inner duality as two distinct entities. The behind-the-scenes aspect of the mind is nothing more than a subservient robot, while the up-front aspect acts as a scanner on the world. Consciousness itself is a singular phenomenon that arises within this mental arrangement; it's not as if there are two persons inhabiting one body. We only think of the unconscious as separate because we have a tendency to identify the self as the scanner. This does not mean that the unconscious is literally a separate self. While the unconscious acts as a faithful servant to the conscious mind, we must remember that we are merely modelling the mind in a way that helps us understand its workings. It's all *you* – singular.

∗ ∗ ∗

There is a scene in the 2009 remake of the movie *The Day the Earth Stood Still* where Jennifer Connelly and Keanu Reeves pull into a car park at night. The camera is positioned in front of their car, looking in through the windscreen. As the vehicle grinds to a halt, the reflection of a huge letter M crawls up the glass, a yellow M with very familiar curved peaks. If you've seen the movie, do you recall having this huge McDonald's advertisement thrust in your face? If you spotted it, good for you, because you weren't supposed to. It's what's known as a subliminal, which means *below threshold* – something that's designed to get into your head by bypassing the critical faculty of normal conscious awareness. Most people have heard of subliminal messages, and the example that probably comes to mind is a lightning-quick message flashed across a screen – gone before you've time to read it. That certainly is a subliminal, but subliminals are also much more crafty than this.

In the above movie, the attention of most viewers is on the conversation Jennifer and Keanu are having, not on the McDonald's logo. Typically, we look through the glass, not directly at it. Someone may ask, "What's the value of an advertisement if no one pays attention to it?" But when you understand something of the nature of the mind, then it becomes clear that it's precisely your lack of attention the advertisers are counting on. The unconscious mind, your faithful servant, makes a perfect recording of everything you experience, regardless of your focus of attention.

So the darkened room of your unconscious now has a big letter M lying around among the other junk. What difference does that make? How can that influence you to rush out and buy a Big Mac? What value has a logo without a sales pitch? Ah, but there *was* a sales pitch.

Picture this: you're sitting at home, warm and snug in your living room, tucking into a snack, while *The Day the Earth Stood Still* is pouring out of the TV across the room and into your eyes. While you're in this feel-good state, a big McDonald's logo is staring you in the face, but you don't see it. Your unconscious, however, sees all. Always trying to take the workload off your conscious mind, your unconscious forges a link between the pleasurable emotional state and the McDonald's logo, because it thinks that's what you wish to happen. Later, when you drive your car past the local McDonald's takeaway and you spot that big letter M on the building, you may start to feel good and have no idea why. It's really your unconscious dictating the feeling, because that's what your experience taught it to do. The effect is so subtle that you don't even ask yourself why you feel good.

Of course, one subliminal message in one movie isn't going to have much of an effect. A cumulative effect is created by the constant repetition of the same theme, again and again, in other movies and during commercial breaks. Just look at how often we are subjected to advertisements. Every ten to fifteen minutes of air-time is interrupted by three to five minutes of advertisements. The commercial breaks are usually broadcast at a higher volume than the programme and are often timed to coincide with breaks on other channels, in case you switch. None of this, I'll wager, is by accident.

Ask yourself, how many television advertisements are designed to *inform* you, whereas how many are designed to make you *feel* something? With this in mind, you can start to appreciate the importance of a company having a distinct, simple, identifiable symbol on their products and services. In time, your unconscious learns a clear message from the experiences you feed it, and it starts to tell you: "McDonald's makes me feel good." And unless you've educated yourself with the likes of Morgan Spurlock's documentary *Super Size Me* (2004), which exposed the horrors of the fast food industry, then you have no reason not to follow what makes you feel good. "Big Mac and fries, please."

Around 2008, in the UK, there was a television advertisement for the new cervical cancer vaccine that was being introduced for teenage girls. Did this advert inform the public of the medical facts about cervical cancer and the vaccine? No. Instead, it staged a little feel-good play, where a schoolgirl sang a song with words like "Had the jab we need; girls feeling safe," combined with images of her playing netball with her friends on the school court. This was aimed at teenage girls and was designed to stimulate the positive emotions associated with fun school activities, then transfer those emotions to the cervical cancer vaccine, regardless of what the viewer does or doesn't know about the vaccine. The only useful information in the advertisement was an Internet address at the tail end, where you could go and get the facts. I mean, really, who keeps a notepad by their armchair to take down web sites while they watch TV? Based on the content of the advert itself, it was essentially saying, "You don't need to think. Information is irrelevant. Just feel how we want you to feel." How about instead using those thirty seconds to properly inform the public about the risks of developing cervical cancer and about the side-effects of the vaccine? Then mothers and fathers can make an informed choice about whether to have their daughters vaccinated. But no, the National Health Service prefers to subject schoolgirls to mind control, to lull them into feeling positive emotions instead of presenting impartial freedom of choice.

Another alarming TV advertisement was a recruiting drive by the British armed forces called Start Thinking Soldier. The advert dramatised a combat scenario in the style of a first-person shooter videogame, using the television screen as the eyes of the soldier. It was clearly designed to appeal to the young male gaming generation. The viewer is reminded of the good feelings associated with playing games – the adrenaline rush of full-on virtual combat, the pleasure of outwitting an enemy with superior tactics. The unconscious is then encouraged to link the real-life combat shown on the advertisement with the good feelings of videogames. The message is clear: "You like videogames? Well, if you want the ultimate adrenaline rush, sign up for the armed forces." No useful information; no critical thinking encouraged. It's all feel, feel, feel. "Feel what we want you to feel. You're the donkey; just follow the carrot we're holding in front of your nose. No need to think." Remember, this isn't an advert that's trying to make you change your brand of fabric softener. It's using the feeling you get from killing videogame characters and attempting to associate it with the killing of real people in real war.

These are not sinister exceptions in an otherwise clean and safe world of advertising. This is how the whole advertising game is played. It's the straightforward and informative adverts that are the exception. Emotional manipulation is the norm. Ever watch a television advert and you thought it was completely daft? Doesn't matter. Did it make you laugh? That's what mattered. Can you even remember what the product was? Doesn't matter. Your unconscious took note of that brand logo, and rest assured you'll feel good when you see it again. Why would a company pay thousands of pounds to parade a celebrity in front of your nose for thirty seconds when a second-rate actor would do just as well? You won't feel the same way about Joe Bloggs as you do about Bruce Willis (advertising Aviva insurance), Ewen McGregor (Davidoff Adventure fragrance), Samuel L. Jackson (Virgin Media broadband). We've all had experiences with celebrities before, because we've enjoyed their movies, appreciated their recipes, tapped our feet to their music. Their presence in an advertisement is not to inform you; the advertisers know that if you like the celebrity, it's easy to transfer that feeling to the product he's peddling. There's often no *rational* reason to like the product, and there doesn't need to be, because human beings tend to blindly follow their feelings and not examine how those feelings arose in the first place.

Advertisers manipulate your unconscious mind into feeling good about a product or service, regardless of what you know or don't know about it.

This is how the wool is pulled over our eyes. This is how we are treated like sheep every day. This is how we make decisions without any awareness that a great part of the decision-making process is being done for us – below threshold. I encourage everyone to start watching their televisions in a radically different manner. In movies and dramas, keep an eye out for those product placement logos. In advertisements, always ask, "What am I being encouraged to feel right now and why?" When a subliminal is spotted, all its power over you is instantly gone, because the critical thinking of the conscious mind now has its say. And if you want to go as far as tossing your television in the trash, the world may laugh, but I won't be joining in.

The film *Dawn of the Dead* (1978) is, on one level, just a horror movie, but it also happens to contain a profound subtext. Four humans take refuge in a shopping mall from the undead hordes ravaging the world. From the safety of the roof, they gaze at the zombies who wander aimlessly about the car park. Fran asks Stephen, "What are they doing? Why do they come here?" Stephen replies, "Some kind of instinct. Memory, of what they used to do. This was an important place in their lives." In another scene, another survivor, Peter, says, "They're after the place. They don't know why; they just remember – remember that they want to be in here." Fran asks, "What the hell are they?" Peter says, "They're us, that's all." In other words, when Peter looked at the brain-dead behaviour of the zombies, there was no significant difference from the behaviour of an average human being.

We're zombies! To one extent or another, we've been lulled into becoming mind-controlled non-thinking zombies by a rectangle that sits in the corner of the living room. We think we have free will, unaware of how often we're actually reacting to emotional stimuli that have been craftily implanted in us. The mind control of advertising can only be described as genius, since it can manipulate you to do something whilst you feel it was entirely your own free choice.

A little knowledge is a dangerous thing. In the realm of big business, in the hands of people with questionable ethics, this deep understanding of the human mind becomes a tool for the exploitation of the human race. Be vigilant for their invisible schemes.

*　*　*

I once knew a young woman who found it extremely uncomfortable to be photographed. At first, I thought her reaction to cameras was based on insecurity about her appearance, but I later learned from her that the origin of her fear lay much deeper. As a young child, her parents had hired a professional photographer for her birthday party each year. It was always the same man, a bearded individual whose physical appearance frightened the child. Naturally the photographer was never seen without his camera. And so the girl's unconscious mind associated the negative emotion she was feeling with the camera as well as the man. When this experience was reinforced over a few years, the same emotions subsequently occurred when any camera was pointed at the girl, regardless of who was holding it. The unconscious, in an attempt to be helpful, was now dictating the experience it thought the conscious mind had asked for. It's exactly the same underlying principle as what happens when we learn to drive or when we are subjected to subliminal advertising: the unconscious looks for repeating patterns of behaviour and starts to perform them on behalf of the conscious mind.

As an adult, the woman was completely aware that her fear of cameras was irrational, but the feelings persisted regardless of what her conscious mind knew. A camera appeared, and the unconscious said, "Oh! There's a camera pointed at me. I know what I'm supposed to feel: fear!" The conscious mind says, "Stop it. This is irrational. There's no reason I should feel like this." And the unconscious replies, "Sorry, but I already know what I'm supposed to be doing." The mind works this way because it's meant to. Ordinarily, it's helpful to be able to bypass conscious awareness; it's why typing this chapter into a computer took a couple of days instead of a month. If it were easy to retrain my unconscious, I would be able to regress my typing skills just by telling my unconscious to forget them. Let me test that … Foiled; I'm still typing as rapidly as ever. That's why the unconscious isn't listening to the conscious mind, even when the conscious mind attempts to correct it. One way to remove the old unwanted program is by the use of the same method that put it there in the first place: repetition.

To cure a phobia, teach your unconscious a new experience. The most direct and difficult way to do this is to confront the fear head-on by performing the action that makes you afraid. At first, the irrational fear will hit you in the face, but as you repeat the experience again and again, each time pushing the fear away and denying it, eventually the unconscious will accept the new behaviour pattern and remove the old.

There is also an easier way. Not only does the unconscious pay attention to what you experience through your five senses; it also pays attention to what you imagine with your mind. For instance, a man can experience sexual arousal either by looking at an attractive woman or by imagining an attractive woman. In both cases, the unconscious takes the image and triggers the body's sexual response. It's important to realise that the unconscious is never actually responding to something outside of you. We see, not with our eyes, but with the visual cortex at the back of the brain. The unconscious makes absolutely no distinction about whether your attention is focused on information that flows into your brain from the outside world or information that you manufacture in your imagination.

Fantasies are powerful, not just in terms of sexuality. The woman with the camera phobia could try imagining herself being photographed and getting great enjoyment out of the experience. She could make up any imaginary scenario, be it walking on a beach or modelling on a catwalk. It's important to be vivid and to inject positive emotion into a fantasy. Relax as deeply as you can when doing this; lying in bed at night, just before falling asleep, is a great time, because there is less mental chatter getting in the way. When you do this again and again, your unconscious will take note and eventually overwrite the old program with the new one.

Emotion is the key. When using your imagination, it is important that you *feel* rather than think. Thinking does not get you through to the unconscious mind, because the unconscious mind does not rationalise. Unhelpful emotional responses, such as phobias, occur because of your own suggestibility. That same suggestibility is the very tool you must use to undo them. But there is one subtle difference: this time it is a deliberately induced and consciously directed suggestibility. Do not accept what your mind dictates you should feel, if those feelings are demonstrably irrational. When you are weary of continually striving against unhelpful emotional responses, recognise that these feelings are being dictated by your unconscious, and you can reprogram it using your imagination.

In this endeavour, take care that you do not attempt to suppress entirely proper emotional responses. Spiritually inclined persons are particularly prone to holding idealised notions about human nature that are divorced from the reality of what we are as a species. Anger is a favourite "defect" that we target in ourselves. To get rid of our anger, we stick a plug in it and congratulate ourselves on our spiritual progress. But the energy behind the emotion continually strives to discharge itself, on any available target. Persons with anger issues are living with a store of unresolved anger that keeps leaking out. I understand why anger is regarded as a negative emotion, because it can so easily lead to a loss of self-control. But it's really just a call to action, coming from a region of the brain that's older and more basic than the area where we do our complex reasoning. Anger should be respected as a legitimate human emotion and allowed to discharge through responsible confrontation. Even more desirable is when anger can be resolved using thoughtful reanalysis of a situation, because sometimes our anger stems from our own stupidity and we just need to think smarter. Either way, suppression is not the solution. Sometimes it is our unrealistic view of human nature that needs fixing, not our emotions.

* * *

Sexuality is an area of human experience where the unconscious plays a significant role. Psychologist Jesse Bering, in an interview recorded at the Festival of Dangerous Ideas in 2012, related the particularly tragic story of a boy whose first experiences of masturbation revolved around the discovery of photos of naked women in a medical textbook that belonged to his father. These happened to be pictures of amputees. The boy experienced a natural attraction to the female form, but while stimulating himself, his unconscious mind, incapable of judgment, associated all aspects of the image with erotic arousal, including the absence of a limb. As a result, he developed a paraphilia (an attraction to something outside of what is normally considered sexually stimulating) and knew of no means to undo it. Later, he married a woman who had a missing limb. When she eventually found out about his condition by discovering amputee pornography on his computer, she divorced him because she felt deceived. From his perspective, his sexual inclination was a source of great shame, not something he felt he could share with her. This is an example of the unconscious mind leading us in an unhelpful direction, crystallising our erotic impulses into a distorted shape.

Many of us have developed sexual kinks of one kind or another. This is nothing to be ashamed of; it's merely the natural outcome of our self-directed sexual curiosity. But the example above should make us cautious about what material we allow into our minds. Pornography, for instance, ranges from typical nude poses to truly bizarre sexual practices. However, before we make a universal condemnation of all pornography, pause for a moment and consider: what do you think would have happened if the boy above had found a copy of *Playboy* in his dad's belongings instead of the medical textbook? He likely wouldn't have ended up eroticising the stumps from missing limbs, because his unconscious mind wouldn't have forged that link.

Ironically, it was a climate of sexual repression that created the conditions leading to the boy's distorted sexuality, albeit accidentally. Before we swing the other way and give pornography an unequivocal thumbs-up, imagine what might have transpired if the boy had instead discovered a fetish mag featuring a paraphilia? As long as he found the women in the photos to be stimulating, there's a fair chance the paraphilia would also embed itself in his sexual makeup, because that is precisely what happened with the medical textbook.

Additionally, it's not just outside influences that distort our sexuality. Sometimes the wellspring of the problem lies within ourselves. Imagination is just as powerful as physical imagery. Whether you indulge in strange fantasies about sex or watch unusual sex acts with your eyes makes little difference to the brain; it will respond to either stimulus.

We have already discussed television advertising as a form of mind control, where the unconscious is lulled into associating pleasurable emotions with visual stimuli. The same principle is at work in pornography. Sexual arousal, particularly during orgasm, is a deeply suggestible state; in the throes of passion, the thinking mind is not getting in the way. This makes it relatively easy for our sexual inclinations to be reshaped, to our detriment, by the whims of pornographers or the fancies of our own imagination.

Why do pornographers produce unusual material? They do it because there is a demand for it. A better question, then, is: why do people seek out unusual pornography? It may surprise you to learn that this is not a new trend in human sexuality. The most shocking excesses of modern pornography are fully present in the Marquis de Sade's erotic play *Philosophy in the Bedroom*, first published in 1795. The root of the problem lies with the human race's odd obsession with sex. Every animal species integrates the sexual instinct as an ordinary part of its life, except man. Man takes sexuality, invents all kinds of rules and regulations for sexual conduct, manufactures all sorts of taboos, and engages in all manner of shaming. In short, we have a deeply unnatural relationship with our own sexuality.

I've thought a lot about when, how and why human sexuality took this unusual turn, and I've come to the conclusion that it was likely due to the noblest of intentions. One of the chief concerns of religion in general is to aid mankind in reaching its highest ethical potential. Self-control is vital in this pursuit, because we experience impulses that are unruly. And nowhere do we feel less in control of ourselves than in the arena of sexuality. I could cite myriad examples, but one will suffice. Imagine a single man who experiences lust for his best friend's beautiful wife. The evolutionarily older and more basic reptilian and limbic regions of the brain are screaming, "She's gorgeous! Take her now!" Simultaneously, the more recent and complex neo-cortical region looks on in horror and guiltily responds, "I mustn't betray my friend!" Our sex drive is powerful. It doesn't care about our ethics; it doesn't even care about whether the object of its attention would be a compatible personality to live with; it just wants to make more humans and it will happily derail our lives to accomplish that, if we let it. So you can understand how human sexuality historically came to be viewed as an enemy of our wellbeing and progress. This is not a development unique to Western culture. If we look to the East, the monks of early Buddhism were required to be celibate, just like the Christian monks. This did not apply to the common people of either culture, of course. But the point is this: the type of person who was most concerned with "spiritual" development was the most anti-sex. And while the common people would have largely continued to satisfy their carnal cravings, this could no longer be done without the feeling that the monks were morally superior for their abstinence. That's my best speculation on how the link between sex and shame was forged.

Parents, today as in the past, sorrow over the impending loss of their child's "innocence." But the opposite of innocence is, of course, guilt. During puberty, a person becomes *guilty* of turning into a sexual being. This is not something we usually admit outright to ourselves; if we did, we would see how absurd it is. Instead, we blindly inherit a vague and incomprehensible feeling that we've been corrupted in some way by puberty. When you take something naturally exciting, like sex, and associate it with sin, that doesn't prevent people from exploring their sexuality. Instead, the excitement of sex is combined with the thrill of breaking the rules, giving you a doubly potent emotional cocktail. The existence of so many rules also promotes addiction, because any natural desire that is frustrated tends to become an obsession. Christian teenagers get the rawest deal of all, as they listen to pastors preach on the evils of lust. The greater the taboo, the greater the desire. The "sickness" that the pastor wants to cure is only exacerbated by his particular medicine.

Why is it that a man finds an accidental glimpse up a woman's skirt far more exciting than viewing a woman in a bathing costume? This is rather odd, since in both cases the same amount of flesh is visible around her nether region. But one scenario is socially acceptable and the other is not. A peek at something inappropriate provides a greater emotional charge than, say, a biology textbook with a full-frontal nude of a woman.

We've become a species of sex addicts because we've associated sexuality with taboo, enabling us to increase the excitement by breaking the taboo. However, when you break the same taboo often enough, you begin to feel that you're not really doing anything naughty, so you look for another taboo to break. And so begins the process of our sexual appetite becoming stranger and stranger. The excesses of pornography aren't the problem; they're just the most visible symptom of the problem.

We are all sexually dysfunctional to one extent or another. Our culture taught us early in life that the most exciting sex is *wrong* sex – a lesson that only the human animal learns. This attitude of mind will not be undone until we've learned to sever the link between sex and shame – to make sex ordinary again. This is not an easy task for an individual today, if it's even possible. The real winners will be future generations, living in a more sexually intelligent civilisation, uninfected by shame. But we have quite a way to go.

Look at the topsy-turvy nature of our present culture's sexual attitudes. A fifteen-year-old boy looks at a fifteen-year-old girl then remarks to a male friend, "She's sexy." We say that's acceptable. But if a thirty-year-old man looks at a fifteen-year-old girl and thinks, "She's sexy," he'd better not say that to anyone for fear of being branded a pervert. But in reality, the primal appeal of the female form does not change as we get older. In high school,

I liked girls who were my age; I also thought my English teacher had great legs. This didn't make me a pervert. Neither is it perversion when an adult finds a teenager attractive. Even without makeup and sexy clothes, a girl in her mid-teens possesses womanly curves that are designed to appeal to the male of our species. But a grown man is expected to pretend that he doesn't find her appealing, because that's what polite society dictates; he should be thoroughly ashamed of himself for feeling attracted to this "child." What am I advocating here – that men should seduce underage girls? No. Having an age-of-consent law is a positive move for civilisation that I fully respect. I'm simply saying that a man doesn't have to feel ashamed of his natural desires. It's perfectly possible to acknowledge that a girl is desirable, while also acknowledging that she's immature and respecting the fact that she's under the care of her parents. Being honest about the primal side of one's nature doesn't make anyone a pervert. Shame shouldn't be part of the equation. In fact, it's shame that turns a girl's ordinary desirability into an obsessional complex. She is desired all the more because she is taboo.

The Marquis de Sade probably regarded himself as someone who was sexually liberated, but the opposite is true. He talks about how man should follow his natural appetites without restraint, but he is unable to distinguish nature from his own personal sexual neuroses – the latter being symptoms of his obsession with sex, and his obsession being a symptom of his cultural conditioning. A truly liberated person is not one who revels in how shameful sex is, but one who has broken the link between sex and shame.

I once got into a debate about hardcore pornography. At the time, I argued that it was unethical on the grounds that quite a bit of porn portrays women like human ashtrays. My opponent kept coming back to me with the objection, "Why is it wrong? What if I enjoy being humiliated and degraded during sex?" And I had to concede, there are such individuals. How can I tell them they're doing something morally wrong if it's something they want and they're not being harmed against their will? Eventually, I realised that this wasn't a moral issue at root. It was about psychological abnormality. For instance, there's nothing evil about having an attraction to amputees, but you wouldn't wish to develop that paraphilia on purpose. When a person enjoys sexual humiliation (or its counterpart, sadism), it's not morally reprehensible, but it *is* a manifestation of how we've learned make sex more exciting by making it feel wrong. We can accept this, if we wish, but wouldn't it be better for one's overall psychological health to try and fix the root problem from which such symptoms spring?

The popular justification of sexual excess is not a true liberation from sexual repression. It's a consequence of the sense of shame we've thus far failed to outgrow. It used to puzzle me that a massive hardcore pornography industry exists in the United States, when the country has such a large

Christian population (70.6 percent of citizens, according to Pew Research Centre in 2016). But now I get it: those with the most taboos about sex will naturally have the biggest obsession with sex. The real challenge is learning to integrate our sexual nature into our lives in a sane, healthy way. The erotic beauty of the human body should be enjoyed without shame, whether that is in the form of gazing at a beautiful woman on the street or viewing "dirty" pictures on the Internet. Pornography only becomes detrimental when its consumption is fuelled by the excitement of breaking taboos. If you have a problem with porn addiction, the main lesson you need to learn is that you're not actually doing anything wrong. Once you truly accept this, the urge to compulsively consume pornography wanes.

What if living through years of sexual obsessiveness has already caused deep psychological changes? Is it possible to take your mind down an avenue that leaves you scarred for life? Unfortunately, yes. In the case of the man with the amputee paraphilia, he appears to be stuck with it. Unlike phobias, which can be conquered with a bit of effort, it does not appear to be easy to reprogram one's sexuality once the initial programming has taken root. Pandora's Box, when opened, stays open. The mind isn't a spiritual entity that exists independently of the brain; the desires of the mind are a reflection of the physical structure of the brain itself. What we don't often realise is that we had a *conscious* hand in the manner of our own brain's development as we were growing up. The desires we now experience as adults are hardwired into our grey matter.

The brain does have a remarkable ability to modify its own functions, called neuroplasticity. An episode of the television documentary series *Extraordinary People* (2007) entitled "Living with Half a Brain" tells the story of a little girl named Cameron Mott who started displaying the symptoms of a rare brain disease called Rasmussen's Encephalitis when she was just three years old. The only cure was a radical surgical operation called a hemispherectomy: the complete removal or disconnection of one side of the brain. As predicted, after the operation Cameron suffered paralysis along one side of her body. You could be forgiven for thinking that this paralysis would be permanent, given that the side of the brain which had controlled the functioning of that side of the body had been obliterated. But shortly after surgery, the doctors were encouraging her to try and move her limbs again. Slowly but surely, with great persistence, her limbs came back to life. They never reached one hundred percent of their original dexterity, but they were far from paralysed. The undamaged side of Cameron's brain had reorganised itself to perform new functions.

However, neuroplasticity has limits. I am reminded of the case of Oxana Malaya, a Ukrainian girl whose abusive parents put her outdoors, making her live in a kennel from ages three to eight, where her primary company was dogs. She was found in 1991, barking like a dog, unable to speak, and walking around on all fours. Now an adult, Malaya has learned to talk, but she remains cognitively impaired and lives in a mental institution. The perverse living experience she was put through in childhood caused her to forge a distorted sense of identity which became hardwired into her brain and could not be completely repaired.

Most of us, given a choice, would probably prefer not to be lumbered with a paraphilia. But if it happens to be too late, it's important to realise that these "deviant" desires are usually quite harmless, unless they are accompanied by an irresponsible attitude or a lack of empathy. For a thorough treatment of paraphilia, I recommend *Perv: The Sexual Deviant in All of Us* (2013) by Jesse Bering.

Far too often, an unusual sexual desire is met with moral outrage by the masses, when it's really just a matter of aesthetics. The paraphilia affects no one; it just seems a bit disgusting to normal people. Does that make the sufferer an evil person? Of course not. Unless he is doing something that adversely affects the lives of others, there is no reason he should be condemned or condemn himself. He is just an ordinary person whose unconscious mind has taken a wrong turn.

* * *

When our unconscious works against our wellbeing, in any aspect of life, it happens because we've undergone an experience that the unconscious misinterprets. Sometimes the experience is purely accidental and sometimes it's deliberately engineered to exploit us. It's not easy to reclaim control of yourself when the enemy is inside you. The first step is to acquire a deep knowledge of the workings of your mind; we've now got that covered. Then we need the wisdom to recognise and avoid detrimental experiences.

The basic lesson to learn about the dangers associated with the unconscious mind is this: whatever you repeatedly draw into your mind, either through the eyes or the imagination, moulds the behaviour patterns that later emerge from it. If you are careful, the unconscious is your faithful friend, happily working on your behalf, helping you get the most out of life.

THE SURPRISE OF PSI

HAVING arrived at an understanding of the Universe that transcends the materialistic assumptions of classical science and the dogmatic claims of authoritarian religion, it was perhaps inevitable that I turned my attention to a sphere of research that is condemned by one camp as ridiculous and the other as taboo: parapsychology.

If the apparent solidity of the Universe is more akin to a hologram, where everything is one beneath the surface, then perhaps it might be possible to generate an effect in that Universe without the cause being in its immediate vicinity: action at a distance. Similarly, if all consciousness is one essence beneath the surface, it might be possible to communicate information from one mind to another over distance, without the use of the body's five senses.

Psi (Ψ) is the twenty-third letter of the Greek alphabet, from which we get the term psyche. Psionics refers to the study and practice of using the mind to induce paranormal phenomena. Psionic practices are generally divided into two categories: extrasensory perception (ESP) and psychokinesis (PK). The former is concerned with effects that occur within the mind of the participant, where he obtains information that he ordinarily shouldn't be able to know. Examples are intuitive hunches, telepathy, precognition. The latter is concerned with causing an effect in the material world itself, such as moving an object. Psi is the mythic label given to the unknown agent that allows such effects to occur. Nobody knows what psi is, how it operates, whether it is a force, a substance, or something much more mysterious. We merely perceive its existence by virtue of the empirical reality of the effects themselves.

The word psychokinesis comes from two Greek words: psyche (mind) and kinesis (motion). Alternatively, there is telekinesis, where tele is Greek for distance, referring to the movement of an object without direct touch. The two terms are interchangeable, although the latter is generally regarded as a sub-category of the umbrella term, psychokinesis, which also covers pyrokinesis (fire movement), hydrokinesis (water movement), and many more terms. Personally, I prefer to stick with psychokinesis, which has an air of respectability, given the likelihood that many other kineses have no reality outside of role-playing games. Whichever word we choose, let's be clear from the outset that what I am talking about in this book is specifically the movement of an object generated by the will, without a helping hand from any currently known forces.

Such effects are not possible in a purely materialistic paradigm, so it struck me that if I could obtain empirical evidence of psychic phenomena, this would provide the strongest possible basis for the alternative worldview I'm suggesting. In a sphere of activity populated by charlatans and snake oil salesmen, I knew this was a tall order. In fact, I may not have given it such a high degree of attention, were it not for a personal experience I had when I was thirteen years old.

My school friend Andrew claimed that he could move objects with his mind. He never made a big show about it, so one evening I nagged him until he demonstrated it for me. If he had been intending to create a hoax, his ability to do so was hampered by the fact that I gave him no opportunity to plan. This wasn't even taking place in the familiarity of his home, but in another friend's house. Those factors only occurred to me later. There and then, being a naïve teenager, I already half believed him, and I was excited that I might just see something amazing.

We were alone in the living room. It was late in the evening, dark outdoors. Andrew turned off the lights, then turned on the TV and muted the sound. He found a box of matches, lifted a coffee table over to the armchair next to the telly, and sat down. I was on the sofa at the far side of the room.

Andrew placed four matches in a square on the table. "Don't watch me," he said. "Look at the TV, or you'll put me off." He leaned forward, with his elbows on his knees and his hands resting on his temples. He remained perfectly still, bathed in the flickering light from the movie that was showing.

As requested, I diverted my attention to the television.

A couple of minutes later, Andrew took his hands away from his face and looked over at me. "There you have it."

One of the matches was sitting askew.

"No way," I complained. "You moved that when I wasn't looking."

Andrew sighed. "All right, then." And he placed his hands back on his temples.

This time I was going to watch, regardless of his instructions.

After about a minute, the match moved slightly. Some seconds later, the same match moved again. And again. Sometimes it would roll a few centimetres; sometimes it would turn slightly. I appeared to be witnessing some sort of force that acted in short bursts.

Andrew kept going until the match rolled so far that it reached the edge of the small table and rolled off. Then he gave his attention to the next match and repeated the routine. The same with the third and fourth matches.

I was ecstatic. For the first time in my life, I had witnessed the paranormal and I now knew for sure it was real.

Andrew's friend arrived back shortly afterwards and I told him all about it. Andrew then gave the demonstration a second time. After that, his friend's sister arrived home, and we asked Andrew to show her, too. He did so. If it was a hoax, it was faultless, three times in a row.

Not long after that, I started trying to do PK for myself, in a half-hearted sort of way. I had no idea how to go about it. I remember sitting in an exam hall in school, having finished my paper, spending the remaining time staring at my eraser and willing it to move – which it didn't.

Any time I tried it, nothing happened, bar one particular occasion. Nothing moved, but something else happened that scared me. After going to bed one night, I decided to leave the light on and stare across the room at the switch, to see if I could turn the light off with my mind. As I lay there, becoming more and more relaxed and focused, I noticed a change in my perception of the room. My vision seemed blurry at the edges, while the centre remained in focus. I wondered whether this strange effect had anything to do with finding some special state of mind that would allow me to perform PK. Another part of my mind was worried that if I succeeded, I would plunge the room into darkness and scare myself silly. I hadn't really thought this through. But this strange altered perception of the world was too interesting to ignore. I felt that I could go deeper into this state and, simply by continuing to concentrate, I did.

I only have my memories of what happened next, and memories can be easily distorted with time, but I'll do my best to accurately recall the experience. There was a sort of shift inside my head. I felt like I was all mind and no body, although whether I lost the ability to move my body I don't know; my guess is probably not. The sensation was something like dizziness, but not quite. Looking at the light switch was like looking down a tunnel at it. I can't properly describe it, because it's not a sensation that happens in normal, waking consciousness.

After five to ten seconds in this state, I had the horrifying thought, "What if I can't get back to my body?" I wouldn't necessarily call what happened an out-of-body experience, but that was the thought I had at the time. And that was enough to make me call it quits.

I blinked and shook myself back to normality. I was excited and scared, thinking that maybe I had come close to actually performing PK. I recall it was difficult to get to sleep that night, not because of the excitement, but because every time I put my head on the pillow, I felt that strange state of mind creeping back over me. I thought, "If psychokinesis is this scary to learn, I'll stick with the familiar."

After that experience, once in a blue moon, I would sit still and focus all my attention on something. Shortly, I would start to feel that familiar shift in perception, then I would quickly stop. I knew the frightening experience was lying in wait if I ever wanted to experience it again, and I sure didn't. Essentially, fear won the battle over curiosity, and I never made another serious attempt at PK after that – not for twenty-three years.

There's more than a fear of altered states of consciousness that lay behind my abandonment of PK for over two decades. In part, I simply got on with my life and didn't give it a great deal of thought. But another large factor was that, aged seventeen, I had become a Christian. It wasn't until I finally shed myself of this, as well as materialistic atheism, in my mid-thirties, that I finally became interested.

Since I don't have a Christian worldview, I'm not predisposed to viewing paranormal abilities as originating from God or Satan. The word paranormal is also widely misunderstood as synonymous with supernatural. But the prefixes *para* and *super* do not carry identical meanings. The Greek *para* means beyond, and so, paranormal refers to whatever phenomena lie outside of science's *current* ability to explain. This does not mean that such phenomena will never be explained, or that they are not real. By contrast, the Latin *supra* (from which we get *super*) means above. Supernatural refers to that which is above nature, not subject to its laws. The supernatural may break nature's laws without apology, whereas the paranormal exists in harmony with them. For instance, if something like levitation were conceived of as supernatural, no energy would be required to perform such a feat. However, if it were viewed as paranormal, it would require a great deal of energy, because the force of gravity must be overcome with an opposing force. If there ever turns out to be any truth to such a phenomenon, I would side firmly with the latter perspective. As a non-religious person, I do not believe in the supernatural, nor do I see any evidence of the genuinely miraculous. The paranormal is quite another matter. There is only one coherent multi-dimensional reality, including the small fraction of it that we comprehend and label science. When something that has been classified as paranormal becomes better understood, it then ceases to be paranormal and joins the ranks of the normal. Demonstrating a walkie-talkie in the seventeenth century would have been paranormal back then, wouldn't it? Furthermore, the religious authorities might have drowned you in the lake for practising witchcraft. When a phenomenon is classified as paranormal, it usually joins the ranks of the forbidden (if you're religious), or the ridiculous (if you're scientific). This gives you a bias about what it is before you've even investigated it.

If PK is a reality, it must be admitted that dabbling in such a phenomenon is a leap into the great playground of the unknown. The big question is, how much of a leap is it safe to take? To my astonishment, I learned that Andrew paid a price for his own journey into the occult. I have no idea how great a leap he took, or what practices he was into specifically, but there was a cost involved that he never saw coming. I don't share Andrew's present Christian convictions, but I will share with you what he went through, in his own words:

"The stuff I was into came back to haunt me, so I have no issue believing that there is a whole spiritual 'science' that we in the West have little knowledge of ... Is there another world out there? Sure. The Bible's pretty clear that it exists, and you only have to look at any of the thousands of new age mysticisms (or, indeed, old age ones) to see that. The problem is that man is too fallen to play with them beyond a certain level ... I came to understand some of the power I was actually playing with. Went through a messy period of demonic intervention – terrifying until I learned to cling to the promises of God ... Is it possible that there are things you can do beyond the physical experience that will have no effect on your salvation? Possibly. Probably, even. Do I know where the line is? Hell no."

When I quizzed Andrew for more details, he provided the following startling clarification (emphasis mine): "Suffice it to say that I had a few hitchhikers for the sins of my youth, and they were a bit upset about the [Christian] path I was taking. Life turned distinctly unpleasant for a few weeks. Eventually, I had an intervention, where I got the elders to pray for me, and a couple of folks who had experience invited me over and prayed it through. *The garden at the front of their house burst into flames.* You see, when you play with those sorts of forces, you invite them into your life. It's not possession, but they have their claws in you anyway, and you often have no idea what you are inviting to stay when you mess with it. It doesn't require you to believe in God or any religion, but the invite is there nonetheless."

Obviously, I can't report a startling claim like this as if it constitutes evidence. But speaking for myself, I simply have to take my friend seriously. That said, the sheer convenience of the fire erupting *outside* the house (where it would destroy the shrubs but not the sofa) isn't lost on me, and makes me wonder if Andrew was being sold a little snake oil. I simply don't know. All things considered, it makes me cautious, but not so cautious that it kills my curiosity. It may seem like I'm disregarding Andrew's experience by ploughing ahead with my own psychic experiments, but his warning is well taken. In our tendency to dabble, I think it's important that we take note of the advice and warnings of others who have gone before. My experiments into PK are based on the complete absence of any accounts of harm resulting from this specific practice. If your own efforts lead you to the same discovery, please do not let your excitement cause you to dive fearlessly and recklessly into the complete unknown without any knowledge of what you are doing.

The story I've just told you about Andrew, in addition to the one I'm about to tell you about my own dabbling, could be a complete fiction. You are naïve if you simply believe me, because I have offered you no evidence. The bottom line is, you'll never know unless you do this for yourself. That's where we're going with this.

WEIRD SCIENCE

Y view that everything in the Universe is one was a massive step away from the thinking of the masses. Was I stupid, or crazy, or both, to feel so convinced that I was right, against the massive followings of contemporary science and ancient religion?

My one glimpse into the weird – into the perspective that the world was perhaps stranger than what conventional thinking allowed – was Andrew's demonstration of psychokinesis. So I decided: "I'm going to do it. I don't know how, but if one person can do it, so can another. I want that evidence in my hands and I'm not going to stop until I get it."

But where was I supposed to begin? Having no one to teach me, not knowing of any respected literature on the subject, I turned to that familiar research tool: the Internet. I understood immediately that there was no way to tell good information from bad; the Internet is the great free publishing playground of every seer and jester on the planet. I didn't have much enthusiasm for wading through lots of suspect PK training guides, but one avenue that did pique my curiosity was video. The Internet video giant YouTube was awash with demonstrations, many of them easily debunked. I did, however, notice that there was an interesting device cropping up again and again. It was called a psi wheel.

Here's how to make one. Cut a square out of a piece of paper or aluminium foil. You can actually use any thin, flat material. Foil is particularly good because it's very light. There's no importance to it being metal and, helpfully, it's non-magnetic. The size is also relatively unimportant; try 10 cm by 10 cm, if you like. Fold the square across the diagonal to make a triangle. Unfold it. Fold it across the other diagonal. Unfold it again. Squeeze gently along each fold so that the centre of the square rises up like the tip of a pyramid.

Take a sewing needle, or anything with a sharp point – a cocktail stick, perhaps. I don't recommend using the tip of a pen; I have successfully used a pen, but some pens have a lot of friction, which will make success more difficult. You need to come up with a way to keep the needle pointing skyward. So, find something you can use as a base to prevent the needle from falling over. A piece of BluTack will do. Or attach the needle to something with sticky-tape. My usual method is to thread the needle through a pencil eraser. Finally, balance the square of paper or foil on top of the point, and your psi wheel is complete. You can find the psi wheel (sometimes called the chi wheel) for sale online as a commercial product, but it's so simple to make one yourself out of household materials, and the homemade version will be every bit as effective.

The online videos showed people causing the psi wheel to spin without touching it. Some cupped both hands around the wheel; others used only one hand. Some made gestures with their fingers; others kept their hands perfectly rigid. Still others kept their hands well away. And even more impressively, some appeared to be able to generate movement with a transparent cover, such as a glass bowl, placed over the apparatus.

Obviously a piece of paper suspended on a single point of friction is very easy to move by conventional forces. Small drafts of air blowing through the room cause dramatic movements, as do convection currents from nearby heat sources. Unfortunately, the air around us is constantly shifting, and if it's moving enough to push the psi wheel, that's a huge problem. There's even something a little unintentionally deceptive in the design of the psi wheel. We tend to judge matters on what we see rather than what lies beneath. So when you see dramatic movement on an object of significant size, it's easy to forget that there's nothing more than a pinhead holding the object in a fixed position.

Sceptics have suggested numerous elaborate controls for such an experiment, but there's a fairly simple one that covers most bases. Record your experiment on video. Immediately afterwards, walk away, but let the recording continue for, say, thirty minutes. Then you're in a position to compare the movement that occurs naturally with the movement that occurred when the mind was introduced. Other factors, such as the heat of the human body in close proximity to the psi wheel, must also be taken into account.

That said, I knew enough about physics to recognise that a pyramid and a propeller are not the same object – at all. The aim is to make the psi wheel spin continuously in a single direction for an ongoing period of time, and that requires a greater force consistently striking one side of the wheel than the other. A force striking the whole wheel should cause haphazard movements. This simple observation has been almost universally ignored by sceptics with whom I have debated. Yet another example of people with a rigid worldview paying attention only to what defends their stance instead of examining all the data on display.

I understood what the purpose of the psi wheel was from the start. Back in my teens, on those few occasions when I had attempted to move an object, I gave no consideration to matters like mass and friction. When I was attempting to move an eraser across a desk by the power of thought, what if I really was exerting a genuine force, but it was too weak to have an effect? Maybe moving the eraser by thought was like trying to lift a double-decker bus with your bare hands. Now consider the psi wheel. If there is any way to determine whether the slightest force, no matter how insignificant, is being projected from my mind, what better way to find out than by using a light object on a single point of friction?

So I placed the psi wheel on the desk in front of me and willed it to move. I decided not to use my hands at all, since Andrew hadn't used his hands to move the matchsticks. Lots of questions occurred to me. Do I focus my attention on a tiny piece of the psi wheel and imagine a force hitting it? Or do I think of the psi wheel as a whole object and simply imagine it turning? Does it happen naturally or do I need to enter some sort of trance? Do I need to strain myself mentally or gently think about what I want? What exactly do I do with my mind to make this happen? I didn't know. So the only course of action was to play with different approaches and see if anything gave me results.

I tried for about an hour, to no avail. Then I successfully focused all my attention on the psi wheel for a period of a few minutes and I felt the beginnings of that frightening state of mind I experienced in my teens. But as an adult, I didn't feel afraid. This time the altered state of consciousness wasn't as profound as what I experienced all that time ago, and was actually quite slippery to hold on to. In any case, the psi wheel remained completely still.

It was a few minutes after emerging from that altered state that I made the wheel move. It gave a bit of a twitch, and another. I didn't know what I was doing to cause this. I wondered if my leg against the table had caused the movement. So I moved it away. Again, I was able to move the wheel a fraction. I wondered if my breath was affecting it. I covered my mouth and nose with my sweater, blew out a couple of big breaths to make sure nothing would get through the fabric, and nothing did. Sure enough, I was able to make the wheel move once again. It was a difficult experience to quantify, because sometimes it would work, then a few seconds later it would fail. Then I could get it to work again. I managed to get the wheel to move about a centimetre one way, then a centimetre the other way, back and forth several times in quick succession. I was determined to do a full counter-clockwise revolution. But I found it hard to keep the motion going, and also hard to get the direction the same every time. Although I didn't manage a full revolution, I did manage a one-quarter turn in the direction I intended, in several "pushes." After that, I couldn't do anything more.

While this was happening, I was thinking about the possibility of a draught from the door that I had left open behind me. I didn't want to get up and close the door during the experiment, so I decided that I would leave the wheel set up afterwards to see if any drafts affected it later. The wheel never moved in the slightest, despite me walking about the house, opening and closing other doors and causing air currents. When I got up the next morning, the wheel was in exactly same position as I left it the previous night.

During the experiment, the movements had been small and didn't always happen when I willed them. It was hard for me to figure out exactly what I was doing to create the movement. It didn't seem to be about willing something really hard. If anything, when I applied extra mental pressure, that seemed to stop the wheel working. I didn't know exactly what mental muscle I was flexing, so to speak, but I was confident that I was genuinely flexing it.

I was over the moon about this discovery and could barely contain my excitement. And yet, after a short time, I doubted. After all, I wasn't doing this in anything remotely resembling laboratory conditions, and I hadn't even taken all the steps I could have taken to ensure that my environment wasn't compromised by known forces.

For the next three weeks, I kept trying, and I could get little or nothing to happen. Maybe the first session was a fluke and I was only fooling myself? Possibly, but I refused to give up easily. Every day, I sat down in front of the psi wheel for the best part of an hour, determined to get somewhere with this, wishing I could put my finger on exactly what I had done with my mind to make it happen the first time.

Finally, after twenty-one days, it happened again, and much more profoundly. I was holding the psi wheel in my hand, gripping the eraser between my fingers, and it was simply, inexplicably, rotating for no good reason – not the sort of revolutions that occur when an object is gradually winding down to a standstill. There was something perpetual in the movement. Of course, it should be noted that my hand was under the psi wheel; the body generates heat, and heat naturally rises. However, on this occasion I was also able to make the psi wheel spin by placing it on the table and putting my hand to the side of it, rather than underneath. Interestingly, I got very dramatic spin by holding the psi wheel close to my forehead.

It was important to test all of these results against conventional science. On another occasion, I placed two glasses of boiling hot water right beside the psi wheel and recorded it on a camcorder for twenty minutes while I left the room. The wheel didn't budge. I once saw a debunker enclose a psi wheel in a complete circle of glasses filled with boiling water, and the psi wheel *did* spin. He accepted this as proof that psi was nothing more than an effect of heat. He didn't seem to notice that when a genuine experimenter attempts PK, he isn't using a ring of hot glasses! Of *course* heat can move things; that was never in doubt. But just how much heat does a human hand produce? My name isn't Johnny Storm, the Human Torch. If my two glasses of boiling water failed to move the wheel in the slightest, and yet my much cooler hand succeeded in moving the wheel dramatically, clearly whatever I was witnessing was more than a mere thermal effect.

I decided to be similarly rigorous with the matter of air currents. I started wearing a mask at times when practising. I would record what I was doing, then allow the tape to continue recording for twenty minutes after I had finished and left the room, to verify that natural air currents caused no significant movement on the psi wheel.

Static electricity was another possibility for a conventional explanation. If you run a comb through your hair and hold it close to the psi wheel, you can make the psi wheel move. This works for paper wheels as much as foil. It even works when the wheel is covered by a glass bowl. However, the effect caused by static is quite recognisable: the static pulls the nearest prong of the wheel towards the comb and holds it there. It's a force of attraction only and it doesn't generate spin. The only way you can use static to produce spin is to move the source of the static about. Even then it's very difficult. This is one reason why I advise people not to move their hands about when doing PK. I've successfully jerked a psi wheel under a plastic cover by simply changing the position of my fingers, but once I wiped the inside of the cover with a damp cloth, removing all trace of static, the wheel wouldn't budge. Be rigorous with your environment.

Magnetism is another force to consider. When watching an unrelated documentary on television, I caught a snippet of information that pricked my ears: the human heart generates a magnetic force that can be measured by instruments up to six feet away from the body. I wondered if I had found the natural explanation for PK. But just like static, magnetism attracts (or repels). Compass needles do not spin. They find north and stick with it. How could the magnetism of the body cause an object on the table in front of me to spin? It didn't make sense.

I took into account every conventional explanation I could think of – chiefly drafts, convection, static electricity and magnetism – and all of them failed to explain the results I was getting from my experiments. And the longer the experiments went on, the more dramatic the results became. In the beginning there was little or nothing. Then I could make the psi wheel spin occasionally. Then I could make it spin regularly. Then I could make it spin almost any time I wanted it to. In the beginning, it was difficult to make the wheel spin in the intended direction, but over time I seemed to develop better control. In the beginning my hand needed to be quite close to the psi wheel, but at other times I could achieve spin with my hand held farther away, and eventually I could sit a couple of feet away, with my hands in my lap, and cause the wheel to spin.

Even with all this evidence, there was still a nagging doubt. I wondered if there might be something conventional that I had missed – perhaps some minor aspect of thermodynamics that would eventually come to my attention and explain all of this in terms of known physics.

I finally extinguished the last flames of my personal scepticism when I got the psi wheel to move under a big glass bowl. I had been doing PK for nine months before finally reaching this stage. I started using a big bowl because I had tried often enough with a little bowl and got nowhere. Whether size had anything to do with it, I don't know. All I know is that finally, for no apparent reason, the psi wheel started rotating inside the glass. As always, I held my hand completely still on the outside. On a later occasion, in keeping with my tradition of being rigorous, I laid a scarf on the desk first, so that the edges of the bowl would compress the material and prevent any air whatsoever from entering or escaping. After testing it with a few good, hard breaths, I repeated the experiment, and again I was able to make the psi wheel spin. At my current level, performing PK under a glass cover does appear to require a certain something extra, as it only works on a semi-regular basis and usually only gives me a quarter turn. I am at a loss to comprehensively explain what that something extra is.

With increased distance from the object, as well as physical barriers around the object, comes hindrances to success. But on one occasion I got some peculiar results that confounded my expectations. The psi wheel beneath the glass bowl began to rotate right, then left, back and forth repeatedly, regardless of what I was thinking and regardless of whether I was in the vicinity. This effect kept up for over five minutes, gradually winding down. This threw all my data about distance into disarray. Was I witnessing genuine PK of a level I had never before achieved, or had I missed something mundane? In time, I realised my mistake. Prior to the experiment I had been using my laptop computer on the desk. I had switched it off and pushed it out of the way before beginning the PK experiment. What I failed to notice was the presence of residual heat from the laptop lingering in the desk. This heat then rose and generated movement on the psi wheel. It just goes to show how easy it is to unintentionally fool yourself. At least I was suspicious enough of my results to discover my blunder. But happily, this mistake was not something that affected all of my glass bowl experiments, because I found I was still able to do it while taking this factor into consideration.

The observation "What I couldn't do earlier I now can" has been characteristic of this journey into psionics from the beginning and is completely at odds with any conventional explanation.

SCEPTICISM ON STEROIDS

SINCE I began experimenting with psychokinesis, I've uploaded to the Internet several video demonstrations. These have attracted many responses from both believers and sceptics. I've risen to the challenge of the sceptics' objections so often that I've seen a definite pattern emerge. It goes like this:

First the sceptic claims that what I'm demonstrating is a purely conventional force – accidental drafts of air and convection are the favourites. He confidently asserts that I am deluding myself and that what he is seeing is perfectly mundane. If, at this point, I say nothing, the sceptic will walk away supremely confident that he is right, having done *no testing whatsoever* to verify his claim. The sceptic often claims that it is my responsibility, not his, to present evidence, because he's not the one making a truth claim. But when he suggests an alternative explanation, he is indeed making a truth claim, and it must be verified. My claim is only that we are witnessing something that is anomalous to conventional explanation, by virtue of the fact that we are not able to find one.

When I point out the factors that rule out the sceptic's claim, based on how rigorous I've been with my environment, the sceptic then plays a little mental game of hopscotch and immediately jumps to the next conventional explanation, again believing it without testing. And once more, I point out the flaws in that theory, and he tries to hop again.

When he eventually realises there's nowhere left to hop, he says something like, "Okay, if this is real, why don't you make it levitate? Then I will believe." Well, of course I can't. He moves the goalpost so that he can feel justified in dismissing the *actual* anomaly that's presented to him.

When I press for an explanation for the anomaly at hand, the sceptic often resorts to saying something like: "Well, I'm sure there's something perfectly ordinary behind this," or "If you're so sure this is real, how come you haven't claimed James Randi's million dollars, hmm?"

James Randi is a stage illusionist who became a professional sceptic. He does a wonderful job of exposing the tricks of fraudulent psychics who attempt to pull the wool over the eyes of the public. For a time, his organisation, the James Randi Educational Foundation (JREF) hosted an ongoing contest: the One-Million-Dollar Paranormal Challenge. The website said, "We offer a one-million-dollar prize to anyone who can show, under proper observing conditions, evidence of any paranormal, supernatural, or occult power or event." The contest was active for many years and no one was able to claim the prize.

The first issue I had with sceptics who liked to taunt me about the JREF Challenge was that, nine times out of ten, they hadn't even looked at the entrance criteria. If they had, they would have seen that JREF does not accept just anyone. You have to be publicly known for your paranormal ability. This means JREF's modus operandi was not the examination of small, interesting anomalies that offer clues about the nature of reality, but knocking big-time psychic fraudsters off their thrones of deception – Uri Geller being a prime example and favourite target. To JREF we owe a debt of thanks, because we can now be reasonably sure that anyone claiming to be able to, say, levitate himself off the ground at will is lying. Otherwise that million bucks would have been long gone. If there is any substance at all to the more dramatic psi manifestations, such as poltergeist activity, it is extremely doubtful that such phenomena can be harnessed and reproduced at will in a lab.

My own experimentation tells me that psi is quite real, but is very limited in scope and difficult to reproduce on demand. In this sense, it is not akin to a purely predictable natural law. Its reality can only be attested through statistical analysis. And this is something that JREF was not set up to handle. If a "contestant" couldn't checkmate the organisation with something grand, JREF wasn't listening.

A proper scientific investigation into a psychic phenomenon should involve ongoing tests over a lengthy period, a keen interest in any findings that are anomalous to conventional explanation, and a compilation of statistics that compare the results to chance expectation. In fact, the twentieth century is littered with many such investigations, yielding a wealth of statistical evidence in favour of psi. Dean Radin, in his book *Entangled Minds* (2006), compiles a fascinating catalogue of them.

Furthermore, when you introduce money, you compromise objectivity. The nature of any contest is to make the prize exceptionally hard to get, so the criteria for winning is naturally set much higher than it would be in a genuine laboratory experiment, where there would be interest in dispassionately looking at all data, large and small. If a series of lab tests on telepathy resulted in a hit-rate of 55 percent, where chance expectation should have yielded 50 percent, it's an indicator that something weird may be going on. Of course, it's easy to get a figure like 55 percent if you've only done a handful of tests. Someone tossing a coin ten times might make seven correct guesses of the outcome (a 70 percent hit-rate), but toss it five thousand times and you'll end up very close to 50 percent. In a telepathy experiment, if the figure stays close to 55 percent after a huge number of tests, this is a powerful indicator that something unusual is happening –

something slippery, hard to replicate, and prone to failure, but quite real, as evidenced by the unbalanced statistic. 55 percent, however, is not going to win you a million bucks.

What's interesting to note is that sceptics will quote JREF like it's the final word on truth, when it's merely one organisation with a long-standing reputation for debunking career psychics and other attention-seekers. People who make false paranormal claims for personal glamour are contemptible, and I'm happy that James Randi exists to put them in their place. But it must be noted that this is Randi's *only* aim. The results of his challenge do not constitute a thorough examination into psychic phenomena.

In all fairness, the question must be asked: if there is an empirical reality to at least some psychic phenomena, why haven't they become a recognised part of science by now? I believe a large part of the answer lies in the fact that the world is caught in two widely held paradigms, one that has been around for thousands of years and is now diminishing (authoritarian religion), and one that has been emerging for the past few hundred years (material minimalism). Religion often renders psychic abilities as taboo:

When you enter the land the LORD your God is giving you, do not learn to imitate the detestable ways of the nations there. Let no-one be found among you who sacrifices his son or daughter in the fire, who practises divination or sorcery, interprets omens, engages in witchcraft, or casts spells, or who is a medium or spiritist or who consults with the dead. Anyone who does these things is detestable to the LORD ...

Deuteronomy 18:9-12

All kinds of occult practices are mentioned, and they are listed alongside child sacrifice. It doesn't get clearer than that. According to Christianity, all such activities are evil. I'm guessing most people who practise PK aren't claiming it's an ability bestowed by the Lord. In the minds of Christians, then, that leaves only the devil. When I was a Christian, I didn't crystallise it in my mind in such concrete terms, but there was enough of a negative association there for me to at least categorise PK as best left untouched for reasons of safety.

Later, when I was an atheist, what did I think about PK? With religion out of the picture, all that was left was materialistic science. And what do you do with that big word paranormal when you believe only in science? Unfortunately, paranormal and supernatural tend to be viewed as synonyms, and both are equally classed as an offence to science. Science teaches and demonstrates that we live in a Universe based on strict, unbreakable laws. Detectable material reality is the only reality. From faith healings to demon possessions, and everything in between, including PK – they could be only one thing: fraudulent.

If you are a materialist, paranormal abilities don't sit well with your view of reality, and so they are often declared fake by default. When evidence of their reality is staring you in the face, you make every effort to squeeze that evidence into a conventional mould, regardless of how poorly it fits. If you are a Christian, paranormal abilities are declared forbidden. They are kept out of reach, and so they are never investigated.

Belief systems create bias. So often, when we think we're engaged in learning, what we're really doing is seeking to add to what we so overconfidently think we already know. This is why I neither investigated, nor took seriously, PK, in all my years as a Christian or atheist, despite being blown away by a demonstration of it when I was thirteen.

Never underestimate the power of a faulty paradigm to crush the truth. The greatest example of this is the heliocentric model of the solar system devised by Copernicus in 1514. He was not the first person to suggest that the Earth revolves around the sun. This honour truly belongs to the Greek philosopher Aristarchus in the third century BC, but the idea failed to gain support in his day, even with his contemporary philosophers. Isn't it amazing that a man can be right about something this important, and yet he ends up standing completely alone with the truth for the best part of two millennia?

Another possible reason why psychic phenomena are not accepted in mainstream science is because the effects are not easily controlled or reproduced on demand. Consider a husband who experiences an inexplicable feeling of dread that something unfortunate has happened to his wife. Soon after, he learns that she was in a car accident. Given that an intuition of this kind cannot be explained by mainstream science, it must be conceded that the husband experienced extrasensory perception. But he has no ability to reproduce such an effect in a laboratory, for the benefit of curious scientists. Poltergeist activity has traditionally been reported around children. The common explanation is mischievous spirits, but a better explanation may be unconscious psychokinetic activity triggered by the children themselves. They appear to have no control over the timing of these PK manifestations. So you can appreciate the futility of moving children to a lab and expecting results on demand. This drawback does not necessarily mean that the phenomenon isn't real; without direct experience, we simply don't know. This is also the case with my personal PK experiments. In a rigorous test environment, such as a psi wheel beneath a glass bowl, I can achieve only occasional success. I suspect that ESP and PK have never entered science because they are not easily replicated. They don't conform to predictable scientific principles; they originate in the mysterious darkness of the unconscious mind, of which we are only scratching the surface in our attempt to understand ourselves.

And yet I am also confronted with the remarkable example of my old friend Andrew, who demonstrated PK three times in a row. That certainly fits the definition of replicable. So I am left scratching my head, to an extent. All I know for sure is that my personal successes with PK have been intermittent. If I sat down in front of a panel of observers at JREF and attempted to move a psi wheel under a glass bowl, in all likelihood I would fail.

Scepticism is, admittedly, a good practice. Sceptics are highly critical of what they call True Believers, and with good reason. For what is scepticism? It's your mind's way of ensuring that you are not deluding yourself, by demanding that you search for evidence. Even though I value creative, out-of-the-box thinking, I am keen to avoid being deceived by others, as well as avoiding self-delusion. That's what your critical thinking mind is for and it's something to treasure. Scepticism brings you closer to the truth by helping you expose what is untrue using a process of elimination. This is something that is missing from so many people who are open to abstract thinking and have an interest in the paranormal. They go with the creative, intuitive right hemisphere of the brain and suppress the rational, deductive left. And so, they become prey for every "psychic" charlatan out there, unable to discern the truth-tellers from the liars.

Many of the sceptics I have encountered fail to realise that they actually demonstrate perfectly the traits of a True Believer. Their reactions to my PK experiments are loaded with dogmatism. They make definitive statements like "You're blowing on it," or "That's just heat, mate," and then they're happy to simply walk away. No further testing needed, apparently. As long as it fits the materialist paradigm, they're happy to believe anything. The kind of scepticism I've been up against is nothing short of scientism – the new fundamentalism, where the dogmas of religion have been replaced by the dogmas of contemporary science. This is not true scepticism; it is pseudo-scepticism. It's time to restore the word sceptic to its original nobler meaning of one who doubts.

DON'T TAKE MY WORD FOR IT

TALK is cheap. Regarding my paranormal claims, if I simply asked you to take my word for it, how is that anything but an insult to your intelligence? Even video demonstrations of psychokinesis could be easily faked, if I were so inclined. The real evidence, for anyone who wants it, is found in a familiar little three-letter acronym: DIY.

When I began experimenting with PK, I thought the biggest hurdle was going to be achieving the first movement. I assumed that it would be plain sailing after that. What I didn't anticipate was that I would be able to achieve a psi effect, even develop the ability somewhat over time, but still be fairly confused about what the hell it is I'm doing that makes it work. Interested parties who write to me online often expect me to be able to give them a brief instruction set that will allow them to become an instant adept at this, as if it's merely a matter of finding a hidden switch inside your head and flipping it. The execution is not quite so easy. And there is no substitute for stubborn persistence. My approach, right from the start was: "However long it takes, I'm getting this thing to move."

My usual method (which is probably not the only method) is to visualise as clearly as I can, in my mind's eye, the psi wheel spinning. I tend to picture it as a top-down view, as if I'm floating above it. While I'm doing this, I say inwardly to my unconscious, "Do this. Do this. Do this," for several seconds. Words are not important; I am vocalising a strong intention. This can all be done with your eyes open or closed – whatever helps you to concentrate. PK, in essence, is the projection of your will upon the material Universe, by simply visualising what you wish to occur with single-minded unwavering desire. If you approach the experiment full of doubt, thinking, "This is probably a load of nonsense, but I'll give it a whirl," I imagine you will get nowhere fast. If you think, "I wish I could believe in this, but I just don't," that's not a genuine intention. Scepticism itself is fine, as long as it's a forward-looking scepticism that is genuinely willing to be surprised. Don't assume that any doubts you have will contribute to failure. No one's asking for blind faith, just an openness to possibility.

At this stage, do not expect any movement. After a few minutes of visualisation and intention, think no more about the psi wheel. What is required now is a mind that is relaxed and empty of all thought. It can be useful to focus your eyes on a spot, perhaps a blemish on the table, and keep your mind attentive to it, or you can simply indulge in some idle daydreaming (which is a natural light trance state). You don't have to look at the psi wheel itself; just keep it visible out of the corner of your eye, so that you will notice if something happens. And *if* something happens, the worst action you can take is to change your state of mind in any way. It is tempting to mentally push. Don't do it. Continue to maintain an empty mind. At this point in the experiment, you are merely an observer of something that you have already unleashed. Think of the visualisation stage as an archer drawing back a bow-string, while the emptying of the mind is him releasing the arrow. Whatever happens from here on is a matter for the unconscious mind to execute; the conscious mind does not do the moving. This is simply how I have discovered it to work, after a great deal of trial and error. Perhaps the normal mental chatter of our minds bombards the unconscious with too much work and it can't devote itself effectively to moving the psi wheel. For whatever reason, a relaxed and empty mind works wonders. If you find it difficult to achieve this *focused inattention*, again there is no better way to overcome the problem than persistent practice. You will find that it becomes easier to focus with time, just like any exercise.

I say that it's the unconscious that performs PK. At the moment I'm using the word unconscious as a catch-all term for whatever lies outside of normal conscious awareness. I don't really know what makes PK happen. I only know that it's not my conscious mind that does it. In that sense, it's unconscious. It's possible that the body possesses some kind of natural energy field that the unconscious knows how to manipulate. It's also possible that it's the Infinite manipulating the physical world on my ego's behalf. I wish I knew. I only know that the effects are there, visible in the material world for all to see.

Consider this: If I attempt to raise my own hand with some kind of psychic energy, it will remain still. If, however, I simply *intend* my hand to rise, the muscles in my arm respond and the hand rises. PK works in the same way. There is no psychic energy that you need any awareness of. There is only the will, followed by the obedience of the body. When you will your fist to clench, do you need to know anything about how consciousness interfaces with your brain, how your brain interfaces with your nerves, how your nerves interface with your muscles, to generate movement? No. Everything is taken care of for you at an unconscious level. With the same understanding, when you will the psi wheel to spin, do you need to know anything about how consciousness interfaces with the brain, with the body in general, and with the immediate physical world beyond the body? No. Again, it's taken care of for you at an unconscious level. So don't make it any more complicated than it needs to be. In terms of your conscious awareness, there is only intention and result. It's understandable for a newcomer to assume they need to be instructed in some secret esoteric knowledge. The reality is you don't need to know very much at all to get this to work. And I still don't know very much about it. I am simply confronted with the remarkable reality of the results of it.

One of the most notable aspects of this pursuit is the physiological sensations that occur. With a little practice, you will start to notice the synchronicity of a smoothly spinning psi wheel with a calm, clear-headed state of *no-mind*, where all thoughts are silent and all emotions still. And conversely, you will notice a lack of success when your mind is preoccupied, frustrated, or anxious. It's rare that I'm able to move the psi wheel under a glass bowl without going deeper into no-mind – into a subtly altered state of consciousness where it feels like I'm more than just my mind, as if I've become an observer of the creature that is me. You may find yourself sliding into this "trance" as a natural consequence of your concentration. I know of no other way to trigger it.

The most uncomfortable symptom is headaches, particularly when new to this, or when resuming it after a break in training. These are noteworthy because no part of the process involves mentally straining oneself; quite the opposite. And yet headaches happen. Clearly, something physiological is being stimulated by your will. Perhaps this is analogous to the bodybuilder who resumes his weight-lifting after a break from the gym, and experiences pain in re-training his muscles.

I've noticed that spending an hour doing PK can exhaust me physically. This dramatic loss of energy, in comparison to the body's relaxed posture and the mind's stillness, is unusual. Clearly, a great deal of stored energy is going somewhere. This is true even in unsuccessful PK sessions.

You may sometimes notice a tingling sensation on the palms. I had one very profound experience of this on an occasion when I was attempting to move a psi wheel under a glass bowl. My hand was positioned next to the bowl, through which I was attempting to project energy. I was trying out a method of visualising a blue beam emanating from my palm and penetrating the glass. After several minutes of thinking about this, I became distracted, looked away, and started to daydream. In this light natural trance, without volition, I felt a distinct tingling in the palm of my hand. I immediately looked back at the psi wheel and witnessed it begin to rotate. It turned perhaps one revolution before slowing to a stop again. This was one of my most significant experiences of PK, showing an undeniable link between my mental activity and the effect produced outside the body.

Sceptics should not assume that a psi wheel under a bowl has a purely natural tendency to rotate on occasion. As a test, I carefully photographed the apparatus over seven successive days (that's over one hundred and fifty hours of continuous time) and showed conclusively that it does not whimsically change position, but remains absolutely fixed, regardless of changes in room temperature, sunlight, artificial light, draughts of air caused by the door swinging open and closed, the proximity of my body as I worked on my laptop right beside it, or indeed the electromagnetic field of the laptop itself. None of these factors caused the slightest movement of the psi wheel. (A sceptic on the Internet, in an attempt to debunk me, repeated this test for himself, and curiously did obtain movement by natural causes. However, he had set up his apparatus on a black surface. This converted light into heat, generating convection within the bowl. I had not made this careless error.)

Another unusual sensation is a "vibration" inside the abdomen, around the navel area. I don't feel this during all PK training, but quite often I sense a whisper of it. Only occasionally does it vibrate with any intensity. These are the rare occasions when I am able to successfully obtain movement under a glass bowl. The navel vibration appears to be that little something extra that guarantees success. The most logical assumption I can make is that the navel is the source of energy for psi phenomena. Attempting a harder PK task would presumably require the moving of more energy, hence the intensified sensation. The accurate timing of the vibration with the PK event, again and again, rules out mere auto-suggestion as the explanation for what's happening within the body. It's possibly no accident that this sensation occurs in the very area where food is converted into usable energy for the body.

The key observation about all of these physiological sensations is that you don't *do* something to deliberately stimulate them. These mysterious things happen as a natural, and quite unprovoked, consequence of your intention to move the psi wheel. This would appear to be no different in principle from how brain cells, muscles, bones and skin all marshal together to obey your will when you attempt to pick up an object in your hand, regardless of how much or little you understand about the mental and biological processes that are occurring. And so it is with PK.

When I started out, I had no instruction manual and no expectations about the processes that would, or would not, occur in my body. This gave me an unexpected advantage when I later came to study the writings of others on the subject. When I read of identical experiences, I knew I was learning from someone legitimate. Examples are *The Psion's Handbook* (2004) by Sean Connelly and *Liber Null & Psychonaut* (1987) by Peter J. Carroll.

The most common question I am asked regarding PK is: "What do you think about that makes the object move?" The answer is: "Nothing." The state of no-mind is something that can't be easily explained, because it's not even easily understood by the practitioner, either. It's a bit like a father attempting to explain balance to his young son as he takes him out for his first ever ride on a bicycle. Balance can be experienced, and the knowledge can be passed on by encouraging another to experience it, but it's hard to articulate what it is, even to oneself.

I have received many emails from persons telling me they've tried my technique and discovered PK to be real. Occasionally, however, someone will explain that he has tried and tried and nothing happens. There are a couple of reasons why this might be the case. The big one is the question of intention. Nobody said it was easy to overcome a lifetime of conditioning that's telling you it's impossible. The only way for you to overcome this is to look inside yourself and figure out what might be creating mental blocks. No one can do this but you. Secondly, it's possible there's any number of environmental factors affecting the outcome. The physical exhaustion that accompanies a lengthy PK session probably demonstrates the need for high energy reserves. Are you the sort of person who gets a good night's sleep? Do you survive from day to day on copious amounts of caffeine? How are your health and energy levels in general? These, and other undetected reasons, could be the cause of failure. I can only speculate and so must you.

Ultimately, I reject any notion that I've got some unique superpower – an aberration that I was born with that makes me special. If I were insecure and wanted to feed my ego, I could tell you that. But I have no reason to presume I'm any more or less special than everyone else. After all, we are all manifestations of the Infinite. What I can do, anyone can do. With a little DIY, this amazing discovery is open to anyone who wants it.

I chose to focus on PK, out of a range of alleged psi abilities, because I had seen it done. But I could equally have chosen something else. I've actually made a start with clairvoyance, attempting to mentally "see" drawings that have been placed in envelopes. It's early days for this one, but the results I'm getting suggest more than accidental likenesses. How is clairvoyance or telepathy possible if we are all individuals, completely distinct from one another? Upton Sinclair, in his excellent book *Mental Radio* (1930) offers this hypothesis: "It seems to indicate a common substratum of mind, underlying our individual minds, and which we can learn to tap." A strong pointer, yet again, to the notion that beyond the material realm, all is connected as one.

The moment I successfully achieved a psi effect for the first time, I couldn't help but laugh out loud. Contemporary materialistic science, which so many people pledge unswerving allegiance to as the only measure of truth, had just gone pop. I now had in my hands physical evidence that the Universe was a stranger place to live in than the vast majority of scientists would ever assent to.

The only model of reality where ESP and PK make coherent sense is the view that, under the surface of the visible, everything is one – an interconnected sea of energy that manifests the *appearance* of separateness.

Psi phenomena provide direct empirical evidence for this philosophical worldview. Materialism, by contrast, has no means of accounting for psi other than to render it impossible. If you can obtain experience of psi, either by accident or experiment, you are in a position to understand the nature of reality in a deeper manner than most scientists of the world. And that's no small accomplishment.

I have a hunch that psi is a malfunction of the norm, rather than a skill to be developed – at least beyond a rudimentary level. This certainly accounts for its slipperiness and scarcity. Individuated existence could not function effectively if one mind were continually getting mixed up with another; bodily life would become chaotic if consciousness had license to affect reality at every whim. And so, things are as they are, instead of how they are portrayed in superhero comics. If you lust after *that* kind of power, you'll be grossly disappointed. But more importantly, you'll have missed the point of why this investigation is worth pursuing.

Psi, for me, was the ultimate validation that a person can stand alone from the crowd and be the one who reaches a deeper truth. That's what made me laugh so hard – the absurdity of "little me" being in that position. Yet here I am. Care to join me? Go get a needle and a sheet of paper. Don't believe me; find out for yourself.

LESSONS FROM THE DEVIL

Now that I had experienced the undeniable reality of mind over matter, I couldn't help but wonder whether there was any substance to the practice of magic – not stage magic, but ritual magic, *black magic*, or as the infamous occultist Aleister Crowley preferred, magick. Lighting candles, dressing in black robes, invoking the names of ancient gods – really? Not very scientific, is it? And yet I had to wonder whether the religious trappings were merely the surface dressings over something of genuine rational worth. Perhaps black magic was psychokinesis with dramatics, and maybe I could learn a thing or two about PK by looking at it from this angle. In any case, like a good detective, I would leave no stone unturned.

The first occult text that I came across was *The Satanic Bible*. The Christian might reel back in horror at the very thought of reading such a volume, but there is nothing noble about that level of insecurity. If one wishes to express an opinion about something, it stands to reason he should study it first, so that he will have an *informed* opinion. If the Christian believes his mind is so weak that merely engaging in dispassionate research will compromise him, then I have to wonder how he can feel any sense of security in his existing beliefs, for it is surely unwarranted.

Uneducated assumptions about Satanism go something like this: there are groups of people who meet together in secret cults to worship Satan, the literal being portrayed in the Bible. They engage in orgies, sacrifice animals, and ritually abuse children. This is the sort of worship that Satan likes. In return, he gives them riches, success, and supernatural powers. His followers believe he will take care of them, but the Christian knows that these poor devil worshippers have been deceived and will end up roasting in hell for all eternity. This view of Satanism is based on Christian propaganda, sensationalist journalism, horror movies, and little or no actual research. In reality, such persons, if they exist at all, would not be Satanists; they would simply be immoral and probably more than a little unhinged.

The Satanic Bible was not, as I had assumed, a dusty occult grimoire from the distant past; it was written in the 1960s by a man called Anton Szandor LaVey (born Howard Stanton Levey, 1930-1997) and first published in 1969. Upon reading, one quickly learns that this is not a manual for devil worship, but a philosophy of how to get the most out of one's earthly existence. Spirit is nothing; flesh is everything. Life is about what we do with the here and now. We should indulge our desires, while being careful to avoid the pitfall of compulsion. We should smite our enemies, do unto others as they do to us, because Lex Talionis (the law of the claw) is the law of the natural world. LaVey's Satanism was a philosophy of rational self-interest in a recognisably hostile world.

The Satanist regards the Christian religion as completely false. That includes viewing the biblical character Satan as entirely mythical. Nonetheless, Satan offers a great deal of symbolic relevance, as the outcast (unwelcome in the family of God), the rebel (standing against "divine" tyranny), the individualist (claiming is own autonomy and doing his own thinking), the accuser (exposing hypocrisy), the evil one (defending the animal passions of man). A Satanist is someone who understands that in some defining manner he resembles the fictitious character of the Judeo-Christian devil.

Satanists draw symbolic relevance out of the manifold depictions of Satan, from the Hebrew *ha satan* (the adversary) to the Roman *lucifer* (light-bearer). There is nothing odd about using a mythical character from antiquity purely for its symbolic value. In fact, you will find many examples in the English language. For instance, if I accuse someone of being *mercurial*, I am saying that his character is erratic and volatile. The word is derived from the Roman god of trade, Mercury, and its usage relates to his swift flights from place to place. The planet Mercury is also named after this god, as is the chemical element. When a container is hermetically sealed, does this mean it was made by the Greek god Hermes? When a movie is erotic, does this mean it features the god Eros? When I call someone a vandal, does this mean that he is a member of the ancient Germanic tribe, the Vandals, who in the year 455 sacked the city of Rome? When someone is a narcissist, does this mean that he worships Narcissus, the character from Greek myth who fell in love with his own reflection? When you write down a series of events in chronological order, does that mean you believe in the god Chronos? So you see, we commonly invoke the names of characters and places, both real and unreal, from antiquity purely for their symbolic value.

Simply put, to be a Satanist is to be like the character Satan; as the name implies, it means to be adversarial. The Satanist recognises this trait as something fundamentally important in his own nature. While religions have typically attempted to tame man out of his natural instincts, the Satanist recognises that the adversarial principle is one that permeates all of nature and rightfully belongs in it.

Ancient man attempted to understand his predicament in terms of a fall from grace, a metaphysical event that plunged the world into suffering and death. The Satanist takes a different view. He simply accepts that the way things are is how they are meant to be. He prides himself on seeing the world as it really is, and on accepting that revelation without masking it with self-delusional compensations.

In the myth of the Garden of Eden, the serpent tempted Adam and Eve to eat from the Tree of the Knowledge of Good and Evil in defiance of God. This symbolises the route to knowledge through rebellion against authority, even allegedly divine authority – such as when one resists the demands and threats of false religion. And knowledge is the wellspring of progress. Satanism is not a religion requiring unquestioning, herd-like obedience to a deity; it is an anti-religion, where progress is understood to come through individualism, through following one's own personal path.

When an individual comes to understand authoritarian religion as a tool for controlling the masses, picking their pockets, conquering territory, and hindering the forward motion of human understanding, this causes him to be branded as an enemy of God. And who is the chief enemy of God? Satan, of course. What better title, then, than Satanist?

A Satanist can be a theist, an atheist, a deist, a pantheist, or whatever. This is possible because Satanism is not an ideological endpoint, merely a philosophical foundation, one that empowers the individual to develop his own worldview.

The historical origins of Satanism are obscure, and it is impossible to separate truth from lies, as it was an unfortunate habit of the Christian Church to brand heretics with the label Satanist and to accuse them of strange and perverse practices. Legends of devil worship surround the infamous Knights Templar, but since there were entirely pragmatic reasons for seeking to bring down this religious order, and their confessions were extracted under torture, it's highly likely that the accusations were convenient fictions. Pagans could be thought of as Satanists, since Christianity had changed the old gods into devils. In fact, the term Satanist would seem to have originated with the Church, and there is no evidence of the word being used to denote an actual religion before Anton LaVey codified Satanism in the latter half of the twentieth century. Even Aleister Crowley did not refer to himself as a Satanist; he founded a religious philosophy called Thelema. In medieval times, accusing Satanists of stealing unbaptised babies for ritual sacrifice would certainly have been an effective method of ensuring that mothers had their babies baptised into the Church fast. Satanists were likely nothing more than fictitious bogeymen that helped keep the Christian masses in line. One of LaVey's most famous quotes is: "Satan is the best friend the Church has ever had, for he has kept it in business all these years."

The symbol of Satanism is a pentagram turned upside down. A pentagram is a five-pointed star, usually encased within a circle. In its standard form, with one point facing upward and two down, it represents man as a spiritual being. His head is the upper point of the star, his arms are the two adjacent points, and his legs the two lowermost points. The circle represents infinity or God – that which transcends the natural realm. Alternatively, the five points have also represented the elements from Greek philosophy – the theoretical building blocks of the Universe: earth, air, fire and water (with spirit added as the fifth).

The inverted pentagram has two points facing upward and one down. When any symbol is inverted, it takes on the opposite meaning of the original. In this case, instead of man as a spiritual being, the symbol represents man as a carnal being: an animal. Heaven-focused spirituality is exchanged for the real-world concerns of survival, prosperity, pleasure, and all things animalistic. The priority is this world, not a hypothetical afterlife or a transcendent realm of existence.

Rather than seeing the star as a man standing on his head, the image of a goat's head fits the frame, with the horns occupying the two topmost points, the ears to the sides, and the chin to the bottom. Historically, the goat has symbolised fertility, and the horns communicate defiance. LaVey additionally chose to view the three downward-facing points as a denial of the Trinity (Father, Son and Holy Spirit), making this an anti-Christian symbol.

It should be obvious that it is perfectly possible to appreciate the above philosophy without calling it Satanism. In fact, LaVey's choice of the term, and his creation of the Church of Satan, had a great deal to do with maximising its impact in society by sheer shock value. In this he was successful. But there was a downside. The word Satanism has a tendency to act as a homing beacon for all kinds of undesirable persons. Some call themselves Satanists because it sounds like a glamorous way to justify indecency, vice, perversion, or outright anarchy. While Satanism's ethics accommodate a wide spectrum of behaviour, it emphasises taking responsibility for the consequences of one's actions. The philosophy's identification with evil is more akin to a willingness to be branded as the villain than any actual abandonment of meaningful ethics. Man, conditioned by religion, often characterises his animal side as evil and seeks to cleanse himself of his natural impulses through religious devotion; the Satanist, approving of his natural instincts, approves of "evil" – in terms of how his stance is understood by the Christian masses. Other quasi-Satanists simply enjoy the sinister glamour and have little intellectual grasp of what the satanic viewpoint actually entails. When only a limited percentage of those who claim to be Satanists *are* Satanists in practice, one has to wonder whether the title is worth saving. Then again, this predicament applies to every banner under which people congregate.

A real Satanist is guilty only of the great crime of thinking differently from the masses. To some, that makes him the villain, if for no other reason than "You can't please everybody." So, you understand the mythic relevance of identification with *the* villain. Call it what you will. A genuine Satanist might choose to call himself an individualist. It's accurate, but it's not nearly as stimulating and rich in meaning as Satanist. When you really think about it, is there any other word that would suffice?

LaVey comes under criticism for plagiarising material from Ragnar Redbeard's *Might Is Right* (1896) and for paraphrasing material from Ayn Rand's *Atlas Shrugged* (1957). He also invented some legends about himself, including a previous career as a crime photographer and a fling with Marilyn Monroe before she became famous. See his authorised biography, *The Secret Life of a Satanist* (1990) by Blanche Barton, and *The Church of Satan* (2009) by Michael A. Aquino. Was Anton LaVey serious about his philosophy, or was he interested purely in personal glamour and power? I personally think both. Despite his failings, the merits and demerits of his philosophy should be allowed to stand on rational, not *ad hominem*, grounds. Let the reader make of it what he will.

Satanism was quite influential on me, and I was able to synthesise something valuable from my studies of it. In particular, it provided an effective counterbalance to the unrealistic claims of *white light* spiritual teachers. But Satanism was by no means a perfect philosophy.

The basic essence of Satanism could be used as a purely philosophical foundation, but in the world it also manifests as a movement, having a social and political agenda, with particular views on such hot topics as equality, eugenics, policing. And that's just the Church of Satan. There are other Satanist groups, with different agendas, such as the Satanic Temple, the Temple of Set, the Order of Nine Angles, the Joy of Satan. The more detailed a philosophy becomes, the more freedom of thought it takes from the individual adherent. My own individualism makes me naturally resistant to any form of collectivism. I have no desire to align my loyalties with any political or social movement, to make my intellect subservient to another's. I would become just another follower, defending somebody else's creed instead of defending my own. Paradoxically, the most satanic course of action for a Satanist is to not join a Satanist organisation, since Satanism, at its core, is individualism.

The Church of Satan has always been an above-ground law-abiding organisation, and satanic ethics are generally libertarian. Unfortunately it's all too easy for anarchists (or even worse, psychopaths, such as Richard Ramirez, the Night Stalker) to find symbolic relevance in Satan. For the rest of us, this presents the problem of being branded as guilty-by-association. Then again, that's a bit like saying all Christian priests are child molesters because some Christian priests are child molesters.

Perhaps the greatest problem of all with Satanism is that it has no concept of the *self* beyond an identification with the individual human ego.

A wounded ego naturally seeks to get its own back, so Satanism supports vengeance as the right course of action. There is no understanding that the ego has a false sense of self as an independent entity and this is what causes it to run amok. The Satanist's highest calling is to the preservation of his ego. "What will I get out of it?" is the first question on his mind when any action is contemplated. The goal of life is to accumulate wealth as a means to increase personal happiness. Unfortunately, this does not work as an end in itself, as there are plenty of unhappy rich people in the world. This is because altruism is hard-wired into our brains, just as much as our instinct for self-preservation. We feel more joy when we are kind to others than when we receive a gift.

Being satanic is useful when the world is against you. If you are poor or oppressed and feel that you need to get one up on the world, Satanism will be helpful to you. There is a great sense of satisfaction to be gained in striving to forge a good life for oneself against opposition. But once you've achieved a degree of stable affluence, you will become unsatisfied if you continue indefinitely along a competitive, self-serving path. With nothing to do for the rest of your life but maintain your wealth, watch TV, shop, party, and make love, life starts to feel hollow. This happens because an ego that thinks of itself as real now has to face the fact that it doesn't exist for any purpose outside of itself. Persons who appear to have everything always look attractive to persons who have little, but this is an illusion. We were always meant for selflessness – to understand the ego as a fiction and to live without a sense of separation between oneself and others. Since we derive joy from giving, you might be inclined to think of selflessness as a sophisticated form of selfishness. But this misses the point. Genuine selflessness does not come from a desire to benefit from an act; it is the natural consequence of possessing the understanding that *there is no self.* The psychological benefit to the ego is just a side-effect of that. Satanism, as a philosophy that champions the ego, can only have limited relevance to someone who has seen through the illusion of the self-other duality. I know it is sometimes necessary in life to be adversarial, and this is the value of Satanism. But it is short-sighted to presume that the Adversary is the only character you should ever play in life.

Let me give you an example from personal experience. In 2012, my father's sudden death left me in the enviable position of becoming suddenly wealthy. I was now a forty-year-old with two fully paid-for houses and quite a bit of spending money. I could have quit my job, rented out both properties, and lived on the income from that. Then I would have had all the free time in the world to do whatever I wanted for the rest of my life. But I was smart enough to know that my attachment to my job was more than just for money. I needed my job because I needed to feel useful to the world. I had a role to play and a particular set of skills that others in my workplace didn't have. I mattered to something larger than my own ego. This is particularly obvious to me as a single man with no family. In my home life, I have little in the way of responsibility to others, and when I'm on leave from work, I can easily get depressed from a lack of usefulness. I can try to fill that void with entertainments, but it never works. This illustrates how the self-serving nature of Satanism ultimately fails as a complete way of life.

The final disadvantage of Satanism is that Satan, the Bible character, is still far too alive in the minds of the populace to make his use as a mere symbol practical. When a high percentage of people believe that Satanism is literal devil worship, then for all practical purposes that's what Satanism means. To call oneself a Satanist in public is to invite misunderstanding and condemnation. The Satanist would have to expend a great deal of time and energy fending off unnecessary enemies – energy that could be used for more productive purposes. It's really only pragmatic to use outdated gods, such as the Greek pantheon, as symbols.

Then again, some of the above cons can be pros, depending on how you look at them. I sometimes wear an inverted pentagram pendant, because it reminds me to respect my animal nature, to question all things, to keep my spirituality grounded in the realities of a hostile world, to be fierce in my individualism, to not care what others think of me. Of all the characters of antiquity, Satan is without a doubt the most relevant myth for my life. I cannot help being drawn to him. That undoubtedly sounds sinister to some Christian readers, but I find such a reaction amusing. Sometimes it can be fun to invite condemnation and then privately chuckle to myself, knowing that I have fully seen through a pernicious superstition that ensnares so many people: fear of the bogeyman.

So I do play with the identity of Satanist from time to time, when the fancy takes me. Crucially, it *is* a form of play. All identities are merely masks that we wear; they are not the *self*: Christian, Buddhist, atheist, teacher, guru, fireman, police officer. It's all role-play. A business executive may feel far superior to the cleaner who empties the bins each afternoon, but the reality of the situation is that both individuals are destined to become a pair of grinning skulls, rotting in the ground, their roles equalised in death.

Satanism is role-play in just the same manner. Notice there's no such thing as a Christian skeleton and a Satanist skeleton. So it doesn't make much sense to take our temporary roles in life too seriously. Some Satanists are deeply serious people, feeling that they are part of a special brotherhood, a cut above the rest of humanity. All I see in that stance is yet another pointless pocket of sectarianism boasting yet another enlightenment hoax. For me, one of the main draws of Satanism is that it's a mask you can have a lot of fun with because it's so outrageous. When a Satanist loses sight of that, he's neglecting the one aspect of Satanism that connects it to the meaning of life: playfulness. Let's face it: adult life is often boring, much more so than childhood. So why not make intelligent use of a philosophy that has the added bonus of being stimulating and provocative?

So *that's* Satanism. I haven't even touched on the theme of magic yet, but I felt I needed to explain the philosophy in some detail because, in doing so, I am dispelling the junior bogeyman of Christianity to the world of fiction where he belongs. When you remove Christianity from your life, its superstitions can unfortunately linger; the idea of a literal demonic realm can hang around in the psyche until properly dealt with. Before I knew anything about Satanism, I had read *Practical Psychic Self-Defense* (2002) by Robert Bruce, a prominent researcher into astral projection (out-of-body experiences). Although the author is by no means a Christian, he talks of a hidden realm around us populated by all manner of metaphysical nasties, from astral snakes and spiders to full-blown demons, and he warns against practising the Black Rites. While reading that book, I had a case of the heebie-jeebies worse than what any horror movie ever inflicted upon me. David Icke, a writer who is intensely hostile to Christianity, nevertheless claims in *Children of the Matrix* (2001) that satanic rituals open gateways into another dimension where malevolent reptilian entities find entry into our world, feeding on blood sacrifices and taking possession of human bodies. When I researched Satanism using the source material, rather than relying on the opinions of various occultniks with their pet theories, then Satan and his horde of demons disappeared in a puff of rationality.

WILL THE REAL SATAN PLEASE STAND UP?

I N the Bible, the first historical mention of the character Satan is in the opening chapters of the Book of Job from the Old Testament. "What about the serpent in the Garden of Eden, from Genesis chapter three?" the Christian protests. Ah, but is this really Satan? Try a little experiment with me. Imagine you are a Jew. As such, you don't accept the New Testament as authoritative scripture. Your view of Satan, therefore, may only be influenced by the books of the Old Testament.

The first thing we notice is that Satan is a rather unimportant Bible character, mentioned by name in only three books of the Old Testament. This stands in stark contrast to the countless references to him in the New Testament.

Secondly, a close look at the original Hebrew language reveals that Satan isn't actually a name, at least not originally. The term employed in the Book of Job is *ha satan*, which translates into English as *the accuser* or *the adversary*. The character is given no name and is referred to only by his function in the heavenly court – his job title.

Thirdly, the original depiction of Satan was not as the arch-enemy of God, but as an angel in the service of God. This is very hard for a Christian to accept, but it is undoubtedly what the Book of Job describes, when examined in its original Jewish context. To help you get a feel for this, I will now quote a segment from Job 1, substituting "the accuser" for "Satan" throughout.

One day the angels came to present themselves before the LORD, and the accuser also came with them. The LORD said to the accuser, "Where have you come from?"

The accuser answered the LORD, "From roaming throughout the earth, going back and forth on it."

Then the LORD said to the accuser, "Have you considered my servant Job? There is no one on earth like him; he is blameless and upright, a man who fears God and shuns evil."

"Does Job fear God for nothing?" the accuser replied. "Have you not put a hedge around him and his household and everything he has? You have blessed the work of his hands, so that his flocks and herds are spread throughout the land. But now stretch out your hand and strike everything he has, and he will surely curse you to your face."

The LORD said to the accuser, "Very well, then, everything he has is in your power, but on the man himself do not lay a finger."

Then the accuser went out from the presence of the LORD.

Job 1:6-12

Notice that there is no animosity between God and Satan. Satan stands with other angels and willingly gives account of his activities before the Lord, as one who belongs in the heavenly court, playing the role of prosecutor. Especially telling is his obedience to God's instructions. He sought permission from God before harming Job. To be more specific, it is Satan who instructs God to harm Job: "Stretch out *your* hand and strike." And it is God who gives Satan the responsibility to perform this on his behalf. Furthermore, as you read the rest of the chapter, you see that Satan willingly obeys the prohibition that God spoke: "On the man himself do not lay a finger." A true enemy does not act in obedience to his opponent. A better analogy of the relationship between Satan and God is that of a gangster employed by a Mafia boss.

The depiction of Satan in the Book of Job is in complete conflict with his portrayal in the New Testament as the deceiver and the arch-enemy of man and God.

And I saw an angel coming down out of heaven, having the key to the Abyss and holding in his hand a great chain. He seized the dragon, that ancient serpent, who is the devil, or Satan, and bound him for a thousand years. He threw him into the Abyss, and locked and sealed it over him, to keep him from deceiving the nations anymore until the thousand years were ended. After that, he must be set free for a short time.

Revelation 20:1-3

Christians attempt to harmonise these contradictory characterisations by comparing scripture with scripture across the entire Bible. Typically, it is argued that Satan is indeed the arch-enemy, but his behaviour in the Book of Job is due to God's sovereignty over creation: nothing can happen unless God wills it. But to say that Satan requires permission from God before acting is to make him less powerful than the average human bully, who can punch a victim in the face any time he wishes, without divine consultation. One has to wonder why Armageddon need happen at all, if Satan must kindly ask permission before acting? And what does that say about God, who grants him permission? Of course, this whole interpretation is absurd. The two Satans are fundamentally different in character. This observation holds true whether the above passages are interpreted literally or allegorically.

If the Christian still doubts, he need only ask a Jew. The Jewish view of Satan is vastly different from the Christian perspective, precisely because the Jews interpret the Old Testament in its original historical context, without injecting a new theology into it. To a Jew, the serpent in the Garden of Eden was not Satan, for the simple reason that he is not named as such within the confines of the Old Testament. Comparing scripture with scripture across the two testaments should not be confused with *conflating* scripture with scripture as a method of revising the original meaning of a text, which is precisely what Christians have done.

Some religions, by no means all, have an arch-villain or destructive spirit. Interestingly, the God versus Satan conflict of Christianity is absent from Old Testament theology. In Judaism, evil spirits are depicted as under the control of God, performing a destructive role in his service. They are not a separate kingdom of fallen angels aligned under Satan's rule:

> Now the Spirit of the LORD had departed from Saul, and an evil spirit from the LORD tormented him.
>
> 1 Samuel 16:14

> Micaiah continued, "Therefore hear the word of the LORD: I saw the LORD sitting on his throne with all the multitudes of heaven standing around him on his right and on his left. And the LORD said, 'Who will entice Ahab into attacking Ramoth Gilead and going to his death there?'
>
> "One suggested this, and another that. Finally, a spirit came forward, stood before the LORD and said, 'I will entice him.'
>
> "'By what means?' the LORD asked.
>
> "'I will go out and be a deceiving spirit in the mouths of all his prophets,' he said.
>
> "'You will succeed in enticing him,' said the LORD. 'Go and do it.'
>
> "So now the LORD has put a deceiving spirit in the mouths of all these prophets of yours. The LORD has decreed disaster for you."
>
> 1 Kings 22:19-23

This striking theological difference between Christianity and Judaism usually remains invisible to Christians because, sadly, many have never read the Bible from cover to cover. You can't obtain a clear overall picture until you complete that task. It is also hard for a Christian to reconcile Old Testament demonology with his perception of God as holy and without sin. Clearly, the ancient Israelites did not view their God, the hierarchy of angels, or the nature of sin, in the same manner as the later Christians.

The original Satan was a bit like the character Slugworth from the movie *Willy Wonka and the Chocolate Factory* (1971). Five children win tickets to visit Willy Wonka's highly secretive premises. Prior to the excursion, each child is approached by a man who introduces himself as Arthur Slugworth, president of Slugworth Chocolates Inc. He attempts to bribe the youngsters into stealing a piece of the newly invented Everlasting Gobstopper, so that he can discover the formula and reproduce the product for his own gain. At the end of the movie, this seemingly villainous character is revealed to be secretly in the employ of Willy Wonka, having been given the task of testing the honour of the children. This is very similar to the Satan of the Book of Job. He is essentially an angel with a dirty job. It was only as religion evolved that Satan was rewritten as the arch-enemy of God. Since the contemporary character is divorced from any similarity to his origin, there is simply no doubt that the modern and much feared devil is a complete fabrication.

The repackaging of Satan as the villain of the story most likely came about due to the influence of Zoroastrianism (a religion of ancient Persia) upon Judaism in the centuries leading up to the formation of Christianity. In Zoroastrian mythology, there is a perfect creator god, Ahura Mazda, and a destructive opposing power, Angra Mainyu (or Ahriman). This arrangement puts the Universe into a contaminated, fallen state, where there is a struggle between light and darkness, good and evil. It is the responsibility of each individual to align himself with one of those two sides. The character Satan in the Jews' own religious writings appears to have been used as a best-fit counterpart of Angra Mainyu. But this view did not catch on within mainstream Judaism, only within minor sects, including the followers of Jesus. To this day, the Jewish Satan is nothing like the Christian Satan. In Zoroastrianism we also find the origin of the Christian beliefs in the coming of a saviour, the final destruction of the world, and the resurrection of all the dead.

Consider how Satan and Lucifer are commonly regarded as synonymous. In fact, Lucifer is never once mentioned in the Bible. Well, that depends on which version of the Bible you're reading. You'll find him referred to in Isaiah 14:12 in the King James Version, but not in the majority of the modern translations.

How you have fallen from heaven,
  morning star, son of the dawn!
You have been cast down to the earth,
  you who once laid low the nations!
                          Isaiah 14:12

In the fourth century, St. Jerome produced a Latin translation of the Bible called the Vulgate. In the above passage, he translated "morning star, son of the dawn" as "lucifer qui mane oriebaris," which literally means "morning star that used to rise early." The word *lucifer* was not intentionally transcribed as the name of a being, but as a reference to the *actual* morning star. If you've ever stood outdoors and looked at the sky as dawn breaks, you may have noticed there's one particular star that hangs around for a while after all the others have faded away. Today, we know it as the planet Venus. When chapter 14 of Isaiah is read in full, verse 12 is clearly part of a lengthy taunt against the king of Babylon (see verses 3-4). This is the character to which morning star refers, his defeat being poetically likened to an image of Venus falling from the sky. The Church's misinterpretation of the Isaiah passage, by merging Lucifer with Satan, was entirely unwarranted and erroneous, but it remains a widespread belief today. Many readers will be vaguely familiar with the story of Satan being cast out of heaven because of his ambition to be like God. This "history" of Satan is derived entirely from Isaiah 14, which isn't even referring to Satan. Immediately following verse 12, we read:

You said in your heart,
  "I will ascend to the heavens;
I will raise my throne
  above the stars of God;
I will sit enthroned on the mount of assembly,
  on the utmost heights of Mount Zaphon.
I will ascend above the tops of the clouds;
  I will make myself like the Most High."
But you are brought down to the realm of the dead,
  to the depths of the pit.

Isaiah 14:13-15

The King James Version translates verse 15 as: "Yet thou shalt be brought down to hell, to the sides of the pit." The concept of hell is another Christian modification to the original theology of the Old Testament. The KJV takes great liberties in translating the Hebrew word *sheol* as hell, but the original meaning of the term is unclear and carried no implication of fiery judgement. It is better rendered as the grave, the pit, or the abode of the dead. Its usage throughout the Old Testament clearly shows it to be the destination of both the righteous and the unrighteous after death. To quote just one example of many, Jacob said, "I will continue to mourn until I join my son in the grave [sheol]" (Genesis 37:34-35).

The division of heaven and hell is a later development, which probably came about due to Zoroastrian, and later Greek, cultural influence. The ancient Greeks believed in an underworld that was divided into various sections. Persons of virtue and initiates of the ancient mysteries went to the Elysian Fields; neutral souls were sent to the land of the dead, ruled by the god Hades; the damned ended up in the great pit of Tartarus.

In the New Testament, Hades is the very word used in the text to denote the abode of the dead. The KJV translates this as hell, giving the wrong impression, but the New International Version accurately retains the original Greek word. Where hell is used in the NIV, it is the Greek *Geenna* (or Gehenna in English). "It is better for you to enter life maimed than with two hands to go into hell [Gehenna], where the fire never goes out" (Mark 9:43). If one is accustomed to using the KJV as his primary source for studying the Bible, there are a great many places where an impression of everlasting conscious torment is implied, when no such implication was intended in the original language – including throughout the entire Old Testament. Furthermore, it's not entirely clear that the New Testament teaches everlasting conscious torment. The common assumption about the nature of the soul is that it is eternal, but if you replace that with the premise that a soul can be annihilated, then the true meaning of the references to Gehenna is not so easy to determine. But a full debate on this issue is superfluous to our present discussion. We must deal with the Christian ideas that *have* taken root historically, whether they were originally intended in the scriptures or not.

If God is the bogeyman, what does that make Satan? He would be the junior bogeyman. While God takes care of the big business of deciding whether or not to eternally roast you, Satan is the one who makes sure you keep up your religious devotions, because any slacking off opens the door for him (or one of his demons) to tempt you into all manner of vice and perversion. His aim is to ruin your life and ultimately incite you to damn your soul. In some versions of hell he is being tortured alongside you and in others he is the one doing the torturing. Regular prayer, Bible study, and church attendance are essential to thwart the intentions of the devil. With this mythology of terror firmly in place, your life is well and truly controlled from all sides.

One dilemma I could never solve as a Christian was: "When is the devil tempting me, and when is it merely my own carnal nature?" I couldn't tell. In my attempts to understand my own motivations, the devil usually seemed somewhat surplus to requirements. Sexuality, for instance, is a perfectly ordinary animal drive, but there are some Christians who see Satan at the root of every erotic thought. Demons with names like Lust, Fornication and Adultery are pulled out of thin air and used to terrorise the young into sexual conformity. Or there's the threat of demonic possession to restrain you from seeking knowledge in esoteric avenues of learning. Some Christians even teach that formal meditation is dangerous, as if the only thing keeping the demons out is an incessant stream of mental chatter.

I have never come across a credible case of demon-possession. Forms of mental illness are misdiagnosed by overzealous Christians as cases of possession. And we mustn't forget that epileptic fits were once cruelly treated in the same manner. It's not hard to see why. Christians learned this from the example of their Lord:

When they came to the crowd, a man approached Jesus and knelt before him. "Lord, have mercy on my son," he said. "He has seizures and is suffering greatly. He often falls into the fire or into the water. I brought him to your disciples, but they could not heal him."

"You unbelieving and perverse generation," Jesus replied, "how long shall I stay with you? How long shall I put up with you? Bring the boy here to me." Jesus rebuked the demon, and it came out of the boy, and he was healed at that moment.

Matthew 17:14-18

In modern Evangelical Christianity, demon-possession is part of the showbiz attraction. I recommend looking up videos online of self-styled exorcist Bob Larson for a taste of this. On the Catholic side there is Gabriele Amorth, author of *An Exorcist Tells His Story* (1999). When I read an account of a woman coughing up razor blades, I had a hard time taking this book seriously. Even if I were to accept the existence of a literal devil with the power to break the laws of physics, I can't help but think how weird it is that a person should vomit an object that is man-made in a factory using a great deal of human skill. I ask myself, "Did the blades have Gillette or Wilkinson Sword carved into them?" Even giving credence to the supernatural, would the supernatural really manifest itself like *this*? The scenario just starts to sound more than a little thin, bearing the hallmarks of a conjuror's trick.

If there is any value at all in the term possession, I would say that a person is possessed by *ideas*, not entities. When I am exposed to new information and I am convinced that what I am hearing is true, that information is remembered and thereafter affects my behaviour. Whether I study history, quantum physics, or Zen Buddhism, whatever nuggets of truth emerge become a part of me, take possession of me. Likewise, the Christian, exposed continually to Christian dogma, becomes possessed by it. And judging by the ranting, raving behaviour of some Christians, they mimic so-called *demon*-possession a little more than they realise.

Several months after I abandoned Christianity, one of my Christian friends, angered and exasperated by the changes in me, said, "I don't recognise the guy I used to know." Exactly! As a result of exposing myself to new information, I had started to become a different person. I was, in the truest sense of the word *possessed* – as are we all, by the ideas we have learned in life. The worst kind of possession is manifested in the destructive behaviour of a person who has learned a pack of lies but mistaken it for the truth. The importance of discerning truth from error cannot be overstated.

Satan is not an entity. He is nothing more than the personification of man's carnal nature as a mythical being. I recall a cartoon where a little demon appeared on a man's left shoulder and a little angel on his right. The two tiny characters went to work on the man, each giving different advice, the demon coaxing him in one direction and the angel in another. In the context of the cartoon, it is immediately understood that the demon and the angel are merely colourful depictions of an inner conflict within the man's own mind; they are not actual beings in their own right. In real life, we should know better than to invent spirits that torment us; we ought to realise that whatever inner struggles we face, the demon's thoughts are really our own thoughts, and so are the angel's.

There is no clearer example of this than the popular Christian classic *The Screwtape Letters* (1942) by C.S. Lewis. This is a work of fiction comprised of several letters written by a senior demon, known as Screwtape, to his nephew, a junior demon called Wormwood. The uncle acts as a mentor, advising the younger tempter on how he might secure a human's damnation. Obviously there are no real-life demons with the names Screwtape and Wormwood, nor is Lewis claiming any special insight into a demonic realm, beyond what little is said in the Bible. The letters of Screwtape merely function as amusing allegories on human frailty, teaching us something useful about how to avoid making bad choices in life. The great irony here is that Lewis was a believer in a literal Satan, despite writing a myth that brought him so close to understanding the mythical nature of that being.

If you suffer from an obsessional behaviour pattern that you find disagreeable or unethical, it may be tempting to ponder the notion that you are inhabited by a demon. While this is not literally what is going on, it can actually be useful to conceptualise your predicament in those very terms. It allows you to name the problem, separate it from your personal identity, examine its demands, and relate to it confrontationally as an enemy of your wellbeing. The "demon" will desire to be fed, but now that it has been spotted, you can try various strategies on it instead of caving in to its every demand. You might try starving it to death; this may be the best strategy in cases where one is suffering an addiction to a physical substance. In other areas of life, a more realistic approach might be to find a means where you and the demon can both live with each other; the demon is allowed to stay, but is kept on a firm leash, not allowed to run amok and ruin your life. Just don't fall into the trap of thinking this is a literal demonic entity. You are modelling an aspect of your psyche in a manner that allows you to understand it and shape it for the better. This is precisely the value of *The Screwtape Letters*.

We need never fear being tempted by Satan, only by our own lusts. Nor should we be so irresponsible as to say, "The devil made me do it." The responsibility for all our thoughts and actions lies squarely within our own nature. The real Satan is *you*.

SATANIC PANIC

S ATAN continues to be a popular object of modern tale-spinning –
stories that are far from harmless to individuals who have an entirely
ethical interest in the occult. I include myself in that category.

When I was fifteen and attending high school, we had one period of
Religious Education per week. For about half of the school year, this lesson
consisted solely of our class reading through *From Witchcraft to Christ*
(1973), the autobiography of Doreen Irvine, allegedly an ex-witch and ex-
Satanist. Today, revisiting the book two decades later, I'm amazed by how
much of the story I remember. You might say it had something of an impact
on me originally; it certainly reinforced my vague Christian beliefs and
coloured my opinion of the occult.

At fifteen I was completely naïve, and when I became a committed
Christian at age seventeen, I wasn't much brighter. Now, however, as an adult
who survived the brainwashing exercise of authoritarian religion and came
out the other side with a razor-sharp intellect, a fresh reading of Irvine's
autobiography makes quite a different impression on me.

There are many elements of her depiction of Satanism that are impossible
to reconcile with what is known about the religion. Irvine describes Satan as a
literal being who also goes by the names Lucifer and Diablos. The erroneous
conflation of Lucifer with Satan we have covered. Diablos is presumably
Diabolus (Greek for devil); the author misspells the word throughout her
account. She refers to the leader of her cult as "the chief Satanist," having
no knowledge of actual titles used in magical orders, such as Magister,
High Priest, or Ipsissimus. At one point, she refers to her organisation as
"the order of Satanism," while at another it's "the most ancient order of
Satanism." Is the order *called* Satanism, or is it an order *of* Satanism? Irvine
herself doesn't seem to know. The details of the ceremonies in which she
participates are scant, as if she hasn't the necessary imagination for the task
of invention required, and so she relies on brief summary. She claims to
have been bestowed with the title "the queen of black witches," which is
completely unheard of in occult lore.

At one point in her story, Irvine had to walk through a bonfire, and as
she did so, the devil walked with her, visibly as a black figure. On several
occasions she talks about seeing Satan physically, hearing his voice audibly,
then later as a Christian she makes the same claims about Jesus. Of course,
there's not a shred of evidence, and the reader is simply expected to take

her word for everything. One night, Irvine is with her witch chums on the moor when several strangers come over the hill. She uses her satanic powers to make the witches invisible and avoid getting caught. Brimming with supernatural power, while devoid of esoteric knowledge. How *does* she do it?

Irvine's errors and complete lack of knowledge of the occult betray her. She describes Satanism in the most uninformed stereotypical terms. To her, a Satanist is one who knowingly worships the actual Satan of the Bible, one who is given supernatural powers by him, one who believes that hell will be a place of pleasure, one who goes out of his way to do evil deeds, one who slaughters animals in ritual. She describes a comical religion fitting for a horror movie.

Throughout the book, she refers to key characters using their forenames only or job titles. Not even her parents' names are provided. She deliberately refrains from giving the exact locations where important events took place. She talks about "Satanist temples," but never gives the reader any clue where they are located. All this is unfortunate, because those details would have allowed her claims to be corroborated. Without them, the reader is left to make an entirely subjective judgement on whether the events she describes really took place. This is especially difficult given the supernatural claims.

Equally hard to swallow is the account of Rev. Arthur Neil's exorcism of Irvine. Demons with names like Doubt and Lesbian are cast out of her. An intelligent reader will understand that doubt is a perfectly healthy psychological response, indicating a lack of conviction based on the absence of sufficient information. To label it a demon is utterly absurd. And to state that Christians can be cured of homosexual impulses by having a demon cast out of them is contrary to any rational examination of sexuality (not to mention contrary to the experiences of those Christians who remain lumbered with unwanted desires, despite their faith). This is all disturbingly reminiscent of the ancient misdiagnosis of epileptic fits as demonic possession.

Once Irvine is on the Christian path, the final quarter of the book is taken up by sanctimonious, melodramatic stories of her early ministry as an evangelist. On one occasion, she sprained her ankle and was forced to cancel an appointment. Satan received the blame for the accident, convenient scapegoat that he is. How thrilling to believe that your little life is at the centre of such cosmic drama.

It's difficult to know how much of Irvine's story is deliberate deceit and how much is down to over-enthusiastic evangelists preying upon a psychologically unstable woman. Irvine's witchcraft experience is either entirely bogus, or at best grossly exaggerated for dramatic effect.

What bugs me is not so much Irvine's tale-telling; it's widespread *credulity*. Christians, already predisposed to accepting the supernatural, have an unfortunate tendency to simply believe without question the startling claims of other alleged Christians. *From Witchcraft to Christ* is a mega-seller. It has been read and believed by countless numbers of wide-eyed Christians, who possess no knowledge of the occult with which to critique it effectively, and no propensity for healthy scepticism. Let the honest Christian reader take note: you should be every bit as concerned as I am to expose people like Doreen Irvine. Liars in your ranks do you no credit.

Interestingly, there's not a single mention of the satanic ritual abuse (SRA) of children, something which became a staple of reports about Satanism in the 1980s and 1990s (the period known as the Satanic Panic). Clearly, in the 1970s, when Irvine wrote her story, SRA hysteria had not yet become part of the zeitgeist.

The first book to be published on SRA was *Michelle Remembers* (1980), co-written by Michelle Smith and her psychiatrist Lawrence Pazder. Over a period of one year, Pazder records hundreds of sessions where Smith allegedly recovers repressed memories of herself as a five-year-old undergoing a prolonged period of ritual abuse at the hands of a satanic cult. She is tortured, sexually abused, locked in a cage, a witness to murders, and painted in the blood of sacrifice victims. At one point, a Satanist sews horns and a tail into Smith's flesh. The scars left by this surgery would have proved invaluable in authenticating the account, but there is no such evidence on Smith's adult body.

The ceremonies were gory and bizarre, and bore no relation to the rituals of the Church of Satan. Nevertheless, Pazder wastes no time in naming this specific organisation as the perpetrator of Smith's abuse. He also states, in total ignorance of known facts: "The Church of Satan is a worldwide organization. It's actually older than the Christian Church." Pazder was forced to withdraw his assertion of the Church of Satan's involvement after the book's publication, when Anton LaVey threatened to sue for libel.

As the story progresses, it becomes clear that Smith's idea of Satanism suffers from the same faulty assumptions as Doreen Irvine's account; she depicts Satanists as worshippers of the literal devil of the Bible. The rituals are filled with pointless, nonsensical, sinister elements and horror movie trappings, including the appearance of a monstrous spider crawling across an altar cloth and a vampire bat with claw-tipped wings perched on the altar's edge. In the final quarter of the book, Satan makes regular appearances in the flesh. And Smith's depiction of him is an all-out horror movie cliché, right down to the horns on his head and the claws on his hands. Curiously, he has a pig's snout and sports a tail that occasionally shape-shifts into a snake. Fire sprouts from his back. Amusingly, Satan insists on continually speaking in rhyming verse throughout the account:

The knife is ready. It is time to begin.
It has been poisoned and sharpened very thin.

I confess that while I was reading the early pages of the book, I seriously considered that this child might have been the victim of some deeply unethical occult group. But by the time I finished, the entire tale had made a nosedive into total religious farce. In addition to enduring the devil's bad poetry, Smith witnesses heads spinning, just like Linda Blair in the movie *The Exorcist* (1973). Jesus, the Virgin Mary, and the Archangel Michael appear to Smith at various points during her dark days in the ritual chamber. Absurdly, Mary sprinkles her sentences with French, which would not have been her native language, nor is it Smith's. The two authors' combined depiction of Satanism seems to be a fusion of their own Catholic prejudices and Pazder's past encounters with unusual religion from his time spent working and living in Africa in the 1960s. He goes as far as drawing this comparison himself in the book. It's hard to see how Pazder maintained any credibility with his peers after publishing this unconscionable mix of psychiatry and superstition as fact.

It also turns out that some of Smith's claims are provably false beyond reasonable doubt. Early in the story, she is allegedly involved in a car crash that is staged to look like an accident, as a means of the Satanists getting rid of a dead body. Conveniently, it happened so long ago that police and hospital records of the event had been destroyed by the time of Smith's therapy. However, Pazder overlooked the fact that it's possible to check newspaper records in library archives. No such incident was reported around the time indicated by Smith's testimony.

The book features a photograph of a mausoleum at Ross Bay cemetery, at which a ritual allegedly took place. However, when this building is snapped from a different angle (as another photographer has since demonstrated), the mausoleum is revealed to be within eyeshot of suburban houses. Maybe the Satanists used one of Doreen Irvine's invisibility spells.

Towards the end of the book there is an eighty-one-day non-stop ceremony. Yearbooks from Smith's elementary school have revealed no indication of her being missing for a lengthy period of time.

There are many more problems with Smith's account that I could raise, but these examples suffice to destroy her credibility. All that remains is to determine whether she is delusional or an outright liar. The coherency and detail in her account compel me to side with the latter.

Even without the evidence against Smith and Pazder, the simple fact that nothing can be corroborated ought to ring warning bells in the minds of readers. But many people have never made the mental effort to learn what criteria they ought to use in separating truth from falsehood. People tend to believe something if it merely *feels* true, or if they simply want to believe. The ability to believe claims in the absence of evidence is how witch-hunts are born. And in this instance, that's exactly what happened.

Michelle Remembers opened the floodgates for countless reports of satanic ritual abuse. Pazder was considered to be an expert. He became involved in the Cult Crime Impact Network and lectured to police agencies about SRA during the late 1980s. By September 1990 he had been consulted in more than a thousand ritual abuse cases.

Closure of the Satanic Panic finally came with the publication of the Lanning Report (1992) by the Federal Bureau of Investigation. Three hundred cases of multi-victim, multi-offender SRA were examined and no physical evidence of abuse could be found; the existence of an underground occult organisation engaging in SRA could not be substantiated. This document can be read in full on the Internet. Even so, conspiracy theorists still like to keep the phenomenon alive. I read this in an online forum: "The Lanning Report is a load of pig shit, if you ask me. Written by the same people it claims 'do not exist.'" Of course, the conspiracy theorist doesn't require actual *evidence* of the FBI's involvement in a cover-up; the mere suspicion of it is enough to warrant firm belief.

During the years of the Panic, the lives of many law-abiding Satanists (and other occultists) were subjected to the judgements of a dangerously ignorant population (including its law enforcement) that was feeding on a diet of sensationalist propaganda.

By contrast, the uncovering of real, verified, widespread child sexual abuse within the Catholic Church has to be one of the most spectacular reversals of expectation in history, as we discover that real evil lies within those who masquerade as the good, rather than those who merely enjoy the glamour of sinister symbolism.

It is ironic that Christians pin such practices as ritualised child sexual abuse, animal sacrifice, and child sacrifice, on occultists, when it was their own God who once required these practices of his people. Yahweh demanded that male babies should suffer pointless genital mutilation in a bizarre religious rite called circumcision (Genesis 17:12). He required the continuous slaughter of animals upon an altar to himself, because he couldn't get enough of the smell of burning flesh; the phrase "an aroma pleasing to the LORD" is repeated throughout the Book of Leviticus. He even ordered Abraham to ritualistically sacrifice his son Isaac (Genesis 22:1-12). He may have relented at the last moment, but the fact that Abraham was willing to subdue his natural compassion to perform this act was praiseworthy in the eyes of this deity (Christians call this level of devotion fanaticism when talking about other religions). Christianity itself is built around the ritual sacrifice of its central character – a sacrifice that is recalled on a weekly basis in a faux flesh-eating, blood-drinking ritual called the Eucharist. Christians need look no further than their *own* religious heritage for the crimes of which they accuse occultists.

I used to think that God sacrificing himself for the sins of mankind was a profound idea. I would not have thought so, had I understood the origin of the practice of sacrifice. Sacrifice exists in many ancient religious traditions, as far off from Judeo-Christianity as the Aztecs and Mayans of the Americas. Why did man come up with the idea of sacrificing to the gods in the first place – a practice that seems bizarre to us? He observed that the corpse of an animal decomposes and fertilises the ground on which it lies, stimulating the growth of plants. Of course, he couldn't perceive it in this modern scientific fashion; his understanding was simply: "From death comes life." The mysterious hidden forces of causation in nature that he calls gods appear to reward death. And so, the idea of deliberately killing animals (and sometimes humans) to please the gods was born. The idea of sacrifice in Judeo-Christianity is much more elaborate than this basic premise, involving the substitution of another's death in place of one's own, to make amends for one's offences against God. However, in considering the sacrifice of Jesus, one cannot escape the outdated quasi-logic from which the whole notion of sacrifice itself sprung.

The present chapter has been peripheral to the main theme of my book, but I felt it was important to raise this information, because I'm about to talk about black magic, and I will not be doing so in a typical spirit of fear and condemnation. Taking such a stance involves risk, because some persons will undoubtedly view me as evil by default. It is dangerous for an individualist to speak out in the midst of a poorly educated population whose minds are filled with unexamined superstitious notions about reality. Take a look at the state of Christianity in Africa if you need confirmation of that. Over there, confused, helpless children are subjected to physical and psychological abuse after being identified as witches by Pentecostal and Charismatic pastors who mix Christianity with African witchcraft beliefs. We are not so poorly educated here, but still, it is too easy for someone in my position to be tarred as the bad guy. And it's not safe to be the bad guy. On the Internet, I have been called everything from demon-possessed to a shape-shifting reptilian alien in human guise. Oh yes, the guy was serious.

The Satanic Panic must never happen again. That will only be possible through the widespread triumph of reason over superstition. And that, reader, is up to you.

MAGIC AND SCIENCE

THE avenue of science has provided us with a great deal of knowledge about the Universe, but science is currently functioning from the standpoint of an inadequate vision of reality, viewing it exclusively in terms of physics. It is my conviction that consciousness should be understood as a property of the Universe every bit as fundamental as matter. When science finally stops disregarding its inability to solve *the hard problem* of why subjective experience exists at all, the deterministic model of the Universe will give way to a fuller understanding of the Universe as *aware of itself* and hence somewhat unpredictable in ways not often noticed.

In delving into this unfamiliar territory, I have discovered that there are some individuals who are slightly ahead of the game. They are modern occultists and their writings provide us with a wider theoretical playground than contemporary science will entertain. When we accuse someone of magical thinking, we tend to mean that he is indulging in superstitious flights of fancy that have no rational backing. That is not the manner in which the term magic will be employed here. Science fiction author Arthur C. Clarke famously said, "Any sufficiently advanced technology is indistinguishable from magic." It's interesting to reverse that statement: "Any sufficiently advanced magic is indistinguishable from technology." You can't divorce science from magic, or magic from science, because they're not two separate aspects of reality. Evolutionary biologist Richard Dawkins wrote a book called *The Magic of Reality* (2011). The author is not an occultist or a believer in anything paranormal, but he uses the term magic to convey the sense of amazement he feels about how the Universe works. You can say, "Science is magical," or "Magic is scientific." Both statements are true. So the kind of magic I'm going to talk about here is both compatible with science and an extension of it. It is distinguished in name only because the current scientific paradigm does not acknowledge its importance.

Let's begin by examining the work of Anton Szandor LaVey. LaVeyan Satanism is often referred to as atheistic Satanism, but this is not quite true and assumes that the only options are the extreme polarities of theism and atheism. When you read between the lines, LaVey's own metaphysical understanding was more akin to deism, the view that "God" is the impersonal creator of an essentially clockwork Universe. LaVey believed in the existence of what he called a "dark force of nature," something which is not conscious, nor interested in human affairs, but which can be tapped using certain methods.

There is an unfortunate tendency among atheistic Satanists to hijack the term LaVeyan Satanism for themselves and to brand theistic Satanists as deluded. The truth is that LaVey deliberately made room for both camps. From my own philosophical perspective, theism and atheism are both imperfect approximations, and I consider LaVey's lack of dogmatism on this issue a strength.

His theory of magic involves the use of dramatic ritual – psychodrama – for the purpose of creating change within oneself. Ritual is deliberately designed to stimulate the emotions, *not* to engage the intellect. This is based on the established understanding in psychology that an extreme emotional state makes the mind suggestible, where the intellect can be bypassed and the psyche programmed. Aldous Huxley, in *Brave New World Revisited* (1958), explains how this is an old trick that fire-and-brimstone preachers have been using for centuries, terrorising congregations with graphic depictions of the torments of hell, then implanting a new belief while the rational mind lies dormant. The difference in satanic ritual is that the participant willingly takes his psyche on a pre-planned emotional journey, in full awareness of the inner change he wishes to achieve. He reprograms himself, rather than being unwittingly programmed by another. Most people are unaware that this kind of black magic is played upon them every day, as they sit entranced by their television sets, dumbly allowing their lives to be guided by emotionally stimulating advertising.

The candles, the attire, the symbolism, the words, the music – none of these details are important except in the effect they have upon the minds of the participants. The correct approach to ritual is to leave the rationalising mind at the door and lose oneself in the drama. LaVey described the use of ritual as an "intellectual decompression chamber" – a place to feel and not to think. The unconscious mind does not rationalise or judge; it merely drinks in experience, looking for patterns to learn. Effective psychodrama therefore requires a suspension of disbelief. The participant temporarily tricks himself into believing that what he is experiencing is real. This is easier than it sounds; you do it naturally every time you become emotionally involved in a movie or novel. To remind yourself it's not real every few minutes is only to spoil your enjoyment. So, simply bring that same attitude into the ritual chamber. Emotion, not reason, is the language of the unconscious. When a psychodramatic experience is infused with emotion, permanent change at a deep level of the psyche can be achieved. You can teach yourself to love something you hate, or hate something you love – to your benefit or detriment.

In Derren Brown's book *Tricks of the Mind* (2006), the author describes a form of self-therapy where a person performs various visualisation exercises in order to change how he feels about something, such as when attempting to cure a phobia. The basic routine works like this: Relax. Begin by remembering something that makes you feel positive and empowered. Exaggerate the memory, if necessary; whatever adds potency to the feeling. While you are immersed in this positivity, picture yourself sitting at the back of an empty cinema. Recall an unpleasant phobia-triggering memory, but present it to yourself in a particular way, as a small rectangle in the middle of the cinema screen. See the movie in fuzzy black and white. Choose a piece of comical music to go with it. When the movie finishes, freeze it on the last frame. Float out of your seat and fly forward into the movie to meet your other self. Congratulate him on being so brave. Move right into his body, so that you are now looking out through his eyes. Change the image from black and white to full colour. Rewind the entire movie at high-speed, as you gaze out from within the eyes of your other self. Finally, open your real eyes. The aim of this whole routine is to associate a new positive feeling with a memory that had been originally linked with fear.

In essence, this is the creation of a ritual chamber within the mind. Is this any different from a physical ritual chamber? Not at all. Consider how one can feel frightened by reading a horror novel as much as by watching a horror movie. In the former, the emotional experience is generated by the pictures evoked in the imagination of the reader; in the latter, it is generated by the tangible pictures on the television screen – which, after entering your eyes, are then experienced within the mind, as with the reader. The only difference is that a reader is given more flexibility than a viewer regarding the precise details of the mental picture he generates in his mind's eye.

It should be noted that Derren Brown is not an occultist, but a skilled mentalist and illusionist, not to mention a firm sceptic of the paranormal. He is the perfect example of how the line between the mainstream and the occult is often blurry. In fact, the division is based on nothing more tangible than the ever changing public perception of what is permissible and forbidden.

Michael A. Aquino, founder of the Temple of Set, in his book *Black Magic* (1975), describes the use of ritual as training wheels for magic. Considering how prone the mind is to wandering, the construction of a physical ritual chamber, instead of a purely mental one, provides an unwavering focus to the operation. A physical ritual chamber will not be necessary for someone who has developed disciplined mental focus.

An obvious, though rarely recognised, example of purely mental psychodrama is romantic infatuation. The would-be lover finds himself repeatedly fantasising about a particular female until he has unwittingly evoked deep change within himself in how he feels about her. Unfortunately, his unconscious makes no distinction between the idealised woman evoked in his imagination and the real woman who only physically resembles this phantasm of the mind. The man is now hopelessly in love with an illusion that he thinks is real, and the woman is hopelessly unable to fulfil his longing for a person who doesn't actually exist. Careless psychodrama can often be the root cause of an unhealthy obsession. So be careful how you employ your imagination. It's all too easy to play tricks on yourself, to your own detriment. Sometimes, in relationships, people think they're in love with each other, when they're actually in love with unreal idealised versions of each other – evidenced by the friction that occurs when the real persons don't live up to a set of expectations they were never even aware of in the first place.

A more unusual aspect of LaVey's magic is the belief that ritual can evoke change outside of the mind, in the world at large. Since such a feat is not currently explainable scientifically, some atheistic Satanists have a tendency to downplay this part of the magical theory, but LaVey was a believer in the paranormal side of magic nonetheless.

At first glance, the two forms of magic appear to be distinct and unrelated to each other, but when one understands the individual mind, not as an isolated unit of consciousness, but as the tip of a great all-encompassing iceberg extending to the entire Universe, then this second side of magic is a natural extension of the first. Under the surface, all mind and all matter are one. Not even the division of mind from matter remains separate. Beyond space-time, everything is connected to everything as a unity. With this theory in place, we begin to understand that creating change within the mind is merely the first step to creating change outside the mind. The unconscious is a gateway to the rest of the Universe. In ordinary experience, this door is closed; consciousness is imprisoned by sensory experience and brain-based thought. Ritual magic is a sort of lock-pick that allows the gateway to be temporarily breached.

Peter J. Carroll, co-founder of the Illuminates of Thanateros, coined the useful term the *psychic censor* to describe this arrangement where consciousness is ordinarily blocked from perceiving beyond the boundaries imposed by the mind and body. See *Liber Null & Psychonaut* (1987).

There are many definitions of magic, but the universal essence of the term is the ability to cause change by obscure methods. LaVey divided these means into *lesser magic* and *greater magic*. The former is the use of known physical laws, such as the tricks employed by a stage magician, or the psychological manipulation of an experienced salesperson. Even the act of a woman dressing seductively qualifies as lesser magic, for she is attempting to acquire the attentions of men by employing methods to raise her own sex appeal. It is no accident that the term bewitch is synonymous with seduce.

Greater magic is of a sort currently unexplainable by science. In *Satan Speaks* (1998), LaVey colourfully stated: "Those who spell magic with a 'k' aren't." This mirrors his disdain for Aleister Crowley, but also I think it speaks of the understanding that science is always moving forward, which means that existing categorisations of magical practices will inevitably change in the future. On the occasions when we gain an understanding of the inner workings of something that is considered paranormal, we then re-file it under normal. The division between the normal and the paranormal is artificial; there are obscure phenomena that we have some understanding of and there are obscure phenomena that we have a severely limited understanding of. It is merely the level of obscurity that determines which category we file a phenomenon under. With this in mind, we can see why occultists and stage illusionists are equally referred to as magicians. Although both roles have vastly different preoccupations, both deal with the obscure. The connection between science and magic is captured by LaVey's statement: "Magic is never totally scientifically explainable, but science has always been, at one time or another, considered magic." A similar way of looking at it is to say that *everything* is magical, while science is merely the portion of magic that lends itself to being highly predictable and replicable.

LaVey criticises the notion of *white* magic. He chooses the colour black for the same reason that he chooses the symbol of Satan – because he is practising something that is condemned by the Christian masses. White magicians are those who, like LaVey, play the adversarial game, but unlike LaVey, refuse to bear the Adversary's name. When Christians condemn Wiccans as evil, these white witches commonly react by redirecting their accusers to everyone's favourite scapegoat: the Satanists. This is the hypocrisy of white magic. The Satanist would say, "If you're going to do something that is perceived as forbidden, better to wear the badge of villain with pride, in defiance of the need for approval."

Social considerations aside, magic is neither white nor black, just as we would never speak of white science and black science. Magic is a tool, just like a syringe is a tool. A syringe may be used to inoculate a person against a disease or fill his veins with poison. Ethics are in the mind of the one who wields the tool, not in the tool itself.

Some may feel that the distinguishing of white magic from black lies not in the morals of the practitioner, but in the nature of the particular deity that is summoned forth in the ritual. This assumes that gods, spirits, or demons are literal entities, some being good and others evil. In the LaVeyan system, it really does not seem to matter which god you call upon to do your bidding, or even whether that god is historically "real," as a deity who was once worshipped in the past. *The Satanic Rituals* (1972) even contains a ritual based on horror author H.P. Lovecraft's entirely fictional Cthulhu mythos. To LaVey, invoking a god was just a psychological mechanism to trigger and direct the will towards a desired goal. LaVey was more concerned with the end result than with understanding quite how it was achieved. In 1975, when Michael Aquino left the Church of Satan after a falling out with LaVey, he formed the Temple of Set, exchanging the Satan of Christianity for Set, the ancient Egyptian god of the desert. He made this transition without any change in personal belief, understanding that both Satan and Set were merely symbolic pointers to a metaphysical mystery, as are all gods. Peter Carroll's deity Thanateros is entirely his own invention, a merging of Thanatos (death) and Eros (sexual love) from Greek mythology.

In the medieval era, before the rise of science, Christianity was the dominant worldview of the Western world. The occultism of that period inevitably reflected Christian ideas. Today, we look upon an unusual phenomenon and think immediately of energy transference and hidden forces, whereas the medieval occultist thought of invisible demons that he could compel to do his bidding. Far from viewing himself as in league with Satan, the occultist of old sought to *protect* himself from the demon through the drawing of a magical circle, words of power, and prayers to Yahweh. See the chapter "Ceremonial Magic and Sorcery" in Manly P. Hall's *The Secret Teachings of All Ages* (1928).

Today, having freed ourselves from the superstitions of Christianity, we may also dispense with an unnecessarily fearful approach to occultism, although we should not recklessly assume that there are *no* dangers involved. For instance, if one attempts something intentionally harmful to another, such as throwing a curse, it stands to reason there is the possibility of the curse failing to hit its target and rebounding upon the magician instead. It's also important to realise that when we use words like energy and force, we are interpreting magic in the context of present science, where there is still no comprehensive model of reality. Whether it is possible to attain a Theory of Everything is uncertain. All philosophy, all religion, and all science provide maps of reality. Some maps are more accurate and more useful than others, but the important point is that they remain forever maps, and the map is not to be confused with the territory. At any time, the Universe might throw you a curveball and show you the inadequacy of your favourite map. It must be admitted that, in the current climate of human understanding, we're still groping in the dark; we only have a slightly better context for grasping what we're dealing with than the occultists of centuries past.

Chaos Magic takes an interesting approach to the issue of man's relationship to truth. Beliefs are like commodities; we use them to accomplish goals. And we can change our beliefs at any time, just like putting on or taking off a coat. A particular belief does not need to be true objectively, it only has to be *useful* within the context we wish to employ it – just like Newtonian mechanics is useful for working with everyday objects, but not with electrons. Consider wave-particle duality. Reality neither consists of particles nor waves, but we might model it in either fashion, depending on what we wish to achieve with our calculations. Even though each model functions effectively in its respective context, they are incompatible with each other. Similarly, in the domain of magic, you can believe there's a hidden realm populated by supernatural beings that you compel to do your bidding, or you can believe in a dark force of nature that permeates all things, or you can believe that the Universe itself is conscious, or you can believe something entirely different. Reality itself does not bow down to our models of reality; the models we construct are merely our shortsighted attempts to scratch the surface of reality. While it is not possible to believe in something irrational (like the existence of the Easter Bunny) by sheer force of will, once you realise that all models of reality are imperfect approximations of the ungraspable, then it becomes possible to play with different models as one sees fit. The Chaos Magician works from the premise "Nothing is true, everything is permitted." This does not mean he believes in nothing; it frees him from attachment, allowing him to experiment with various beliefs in the knowledge that nothing he chooses can possibly model reality itself. Think about the internal combustion engine of a car, kept out of sight beneath the bonnet. If asked, could you draw it on paper? I certainly couldn't. I have an extremely vague idea of what it looks like from the few occasions when I've opened the bonnet to fill the radiator or check the oil. I might as well draw something I saw in the engine room of the Starship *Enterprise*, or a glowing ball of magical energy. But here's the key: driving a car does not require a knowledge of how the car works. Similarly, the success of magic does not require that one understands how it functions.

In studying old-school Western occultism, we encounter numerology, astrology, alchemy, the Tarot, the Kabbalah. Some prominent occultists were John Dee (1527-1608), consultant to Queen Elizabeth I; Eliphas Levi (1810-1875), creator of the Baphomet image later adopted by modern Satanism; Helena Blavatsky (1831-1891), co-founder of the Theosophical Society. The Hermetic Order of the Golden Dawn was a magical order active in the late nineteenth and early twentieth century, founded by three Freemasons: William Robert Woodman, William Wynn Westcott and Samuel Liddell MacGregor Mathers. Aleister Crowley (1875-1947) was a member of the Golden Dawn before forming his own magical order, the A.˙.A.˙. You could spend a lifetime studying these avenues, but a useful primer is *The Black Arts* (1967) by Richard Cavendish.

From my own limited investigation, it's clear that the occultism of the past was a mixture of insight and wishful thinking. There was a time when occult knowledge was kept deliberately secret, but the Internet age has firmly put an end to that endeavour and revealed many secrets to be not quite as profound as legend regards them. The occult is now an open book.

My own approach has been to concentrate my studies on occultists from the second half of the twentieth century to the present. If I were studying science, I might choose to read Isaac Newton, but it would undoubtedly be more productive to read Stephen Hawking. Similarly, if there is anything useful to be synthesised from the occult writings of the distant past, surely the modern voices have already done the hard work on our behalf.

LaVey's opinion of the history of occultism was summarised thus: "With very few exceptions, every tract and paper, every 'secret' grimoire, all the 'great works' of magic, are nothing more than sanctimonious fraud – guilt-ridden ramblings and esoteric gibberish by chroniclers of magical lore unable or unwilling to present an objective view of the subject."

That said, modern occultists are not entirely free from making occasional claims that damage their own credibility. *The Satanic Bible* states: "The amount of energy needed to levitate a teacup (genuinely) would be of sufficient force to place an idea in a group of people's heads half-way across the earth, in turn, motivating them in accordance with your will." Even if it were possible for a skilled magician to perform either of these feats, how could such a comparison between them be drawn? How exactly could LaVey have collected experimental data on something of this nature? By all appearances, his statement is a piece of flimsy guesswork. Carroll, at the close of *Liber Null*, claims that a magician can reincarnate his spirit into a new body: "The adept takes a young, strong female and forms a powerful love bond to her. He impregnates her and then during the early stages of the pregnancy, within the first two months, he voluntarily ends his present existence. The powers of the adept developed in astral travel workings, coupled with the effects of the love bond to the mother, cause a reincarnation into the developing foetus." Do we have records of children who remember living as their own fathers and killing themselves to be reborn? Presumably not. So what is this "spirit" that is being reincarnated, since the personality dies with the brain? And how does Carroll come up with a specific figure of two months? To know that, he would need to have performed numerous experiments and collected data on each one for comparison. In other words, did he observe numerous ritual suicides and study the lives of the respective offspring as they grew up? It's clearly impossible to collect that kind of data. Perhaps Carroll is merely echoing a dubious claim made by a prior occultist. Not his finest moment.

Nevertheless, there appears to be something worth investigating in the overall work of modern occultists. LaVey's magic is kept refreshingly scientific and boils down to five ingredients: desire, timing, imagery, direction, and the Balance Factor.

Desire is self-explanatory; we must *want* the outcome of the ritual to manifest, with a genuine single-minded intent of the will.

Timing relates to the susceptibility of the target. If one is attempting to influence another person, the target's mind is more susceptible while he is asleep, particularly during dream sleep, which normally commences about two hours before waking. 5 a.m. would typically be a good time for a magical working.

Imagery involves the use of a substitute for the target. In the case of a curse, this might be a doll with a photograph of the target attached to the head. By venting all of one's rage upon the doll, while suspending disbelief and allowing oneself to think of it as the actual person, LaVey's "dark force of nature" draws misfortune into the life of the actual target.

Direction refers to accumulating sufficient force and directing it accordingly. During ritual is the time to give vent to one's desire, not before or after. Dwelling upon it outside of the ritual serves to weaken the effectiveness of the magical working. Success depends on putting it out of one's mind, so that desire is not spread thin and diluted.

The Balance Factor is the awareness that there are realistic limitations to a magical working. Magic takes place in the real world, which is subject to physical laws, and it occurs in the heads of real people, who have feelings and expectations. A lust ritual performed by an extremely ugly man is never going to bring him the affections of the beautiful movie star he yearns for. Magic, while metaphysical, is not miraculous. It works by tipping the existing balance in your favour, not by zapping the target with Cupid's arrow.

My use of the word target should not imply that the magician's intentions are always destructive or selfish. LaVey categorised ritual into three types: a destruction ritual, a lust ritual, and a compassion ritual. The latter is an attempt to improve the life of the target. The only warning given to the magician is that he should not regret the potential cost to himself that might result from helping another.

Aquino models the Universe in terms of what he calls the objective universe (OU) and subjective universe (SU). The OU is the Universe in which we all share a common experience. The SU is the world inside our heads, which features the OU filtered through our senses as well as everything we care to imagine. There is only one OU, but each person has his own individual SU. In ordinary experience, the OU is fixed by natural laws, and is unaffected by the SU. But by means of establishing a *magical link* between the OU and SU, an individual's SU may affect the OU. In other words, immaterial imagination can affect material reality.

In the LaVeyan system, emotion appears to be described as a kind of fuel for a magical working. LaVey criticised the white magicians of old for unnecessarily sacrificing animals. He claims that it was not the spilling of blood that aided the working, but the adrenal and bio-electrical energy expended in the death throes of the animal, which was then transmuted into a usable force. The magician should be able to draw such energy from within himself, without destroying life in the process.

Carroll views the role of emotion differently. Magic works by means of altered states of consciousness. One such state is *no-mind*, where all mental chatter is silenced through disciplined meditation. This he calls *gnosis*. The other state is that of extreme emotion, such as stimulating oneself into a berserker rage. The emotion is not an energy source, but a key that temporarily alters consciousness in a manner that permits a magical working. The common denominator in the two states of awareness is a subduing of the thinking mind. Meditation silences thoughts; similarly, passion makes us run on automatic, acting in a driven, unconscious manner.

When I was a Christian, I attended a Pentecostal church for a time. This was a vastly different experience from what I had been accustomed to in the quiet little traditional church I previously attended. The Pentecostals were uninhibited. Church services could turn into emotionally charged outpourings of prayer to God. People got down on their knees, with their hands raised in supplication and *real* tears flowing down their cheeks. Others fell to the ground as if struck by something unseen. Some shook in their seats, seemingly in the grip of a mysterious power. My question today is: how is this any different from the practice of magic? The Christian will, of course, reject such a comparison, arguing that his God is the one true God and all other gods are false. But if you can see beyond such exclusivity, then it becomes clear that the ingredients of magic are indeed present. The Pentecostals were engaged in a focused outpouring of the will, their minds subdued with emotional fervour. As I recall, the passion was heightened through the use of deliberately stimulating music. An intellectual decompression chamber, if ever I saw one.

In my mid-twenties, during the time I was attending this Pentecostal church, I had a strange experience of my own, although it happened in the quietness of my living room, not in the engineered atmosphere of a service. I was with my girlfriend and we were praying together. At one point she said, "Lord, I ask you to come close to Darryl right now." I remember thinking, "Oh, I really wish something like that would happen – that God would touch me." Then, out of nowhere, I started to feel a curious turbulence in my abdomen. The "vibration" gradually increased and lasted several minutes before finally dissipating. During the experience, I was breathing erratically, but grinning with joy, because I was being filled with the Holy Spirit – as I interpreted it. To this day, I don't know what it was, but an experience like this is certainly not unique to Christianity. Similar manifestations are documented in Eastern religious practice. Interestingly, it also bears a resemblance to the physiological sensation that can occur when practising psychokinesis.

Admittedly, a great deal of Christian prayer is ineffective, because the practice isn't understood. Dutiful, passionless requests ending in a humble "Not my will, but thine, be done" are impotent, magically speaking, because there is no desire of any real potency. After hundreds of unanswered requests, the disciple grows weary of the practice in his personal life, while at church he yawns his way through the emotionally flat clichés that are spoken by others, week after week. This certainly happened to me. But on a rare occasion of personal distress, raw need motivated me to a form of prayer that was dynamic. Somehow I intuitively knew that I ought to set aside a particular time to express my desire effectively, otherwise it would be diluted and ineffective. I held my emotions in check until I was able to be alone and undisturbed. Then I ritualistically got down on my knees and directed my heart's desire to God with fervent emotion and tears. And when it was done, there was a sense of having made a transition, having accomplished something and brought it to a successful close.

Consider my experience in light of LaVey's magical ingredients of *desire* and *direction*. Prayer, when it's heartfelt, is indistinguishable from magic. And sometimes these rare rituals of authentic prayer seemed to work. When a Christian says, "I'll pray for you," it probably means he'll mumble a few words to God, so that he can feel he has done his duty. On the other hand, if he is earnest about it, in his own way he might be an accomplished magician, exerting an influence upon your life.

It is ironic that a book which began with a condemnation of organised religion should conclude with an acknowledgement of prayer as a potentially worthwhile act. In my personal experience as a Christian, *real* prayer seemed to yield results. From a religious perspective, answered prayer is often used as the ultimate validation of the supplicant's religion over all other religions. "Christianity alone is true," says the believer, "because of my personal experience of God." Little does he know that the followers of other religions are having the same experience. Such incidents are either valid across the whole spectrum of world religion, or equally invalid in all cases.

From a scientific perspective, positive answers to prayer would naturally be considered coincidences, unless they could be replicated. This would involve a massive statistical analysis over a large period of time, involving multiple subjects. Even if this provided an indication that something unusual was happening, there is still the problem of selective reporting to consider. In other words, successful prayers are reported while failed ones lie forgotten. There is also the difficulty of how to categorise a result that stood a fair chance of happening without the aid of prayer. All this puts us in the unfortunate position of having to consider that prayer might be valid, but is too slippery for the scientific method to confirm. This predicament is equally true of magic. The key question is: are we willing to flirt with the possibility of something being true, in spite of the fact that it resists scientific confirmation? The occultist will answer yes, while the scientist, often someone who treats the scientific method like an unbreakable religious dogma, will usually say no. This is the crux of science's denial of the legitimacy of magic. The key question is: do we live in a Universe that is like a machine running on entirely deterministic principles, or does the Universe have a slippery, mysterious, metaphysical side that is most often hidden from view, resistant to scientific confirmation by virtue of its occlusion? In answering this question as an individual, the value of a single paranormal experience, examined critically and rationally, is priceless.

Learning a thing or two about magic was fascinating, especially in relation to my ongoing interest in psychokinesis. In practising PK, I came to the understanding that success depended on first creating a mental image of what I wanted to occur and pouring strong desire into that image, then clearing the mind of all thought and letting the result manifest. This corresponds neatly to LaVey's ingredients of desire, imagery and direction. The Balance Factor is shown by the difficulty in moving larger objects. PK uses only the available energy; it is not a miracle that breaks the laws of physics. It strikes me that the same underlying "science" is behind both PK and ritual magic. Visualising a psi wheel spinning then witnessing it spin for real – how is that different from sticking pins in a doll that has someone's photo attached to it and manifesting an actual curse in his life? I would suggest it's not.

Look at how PK works. We begin with desire and visualisation, but nothing actually happens until we finish with that stage and enter a state of thoughtlessness. Notice the delay between what you want to happen and the happening of it. This delay makes the resulting PK effect seem non-volitional. It appears that something other than you is working through you. Some might fear that this observation lends credence to the notion that we are inviting demonic entities into our lives, but we need not be so dramatic. Even in the natural movements of the body, there is a brief delay between the will and the fulfilment of an action, as brain, nerves and muscles communicate. The pause is so brief that we don't notice it. In the case of PK, the more pronounced delay lends a ritualistic flavour to the activity. PK is also in keeping with Aquino's theory of the SU affecting the OU, and Carroll's assertion that altered states of consciousness, such as no-mind, are the key to magic.

Thus far, the only LaVeyan ingredient that is missing is timing. This is irrelevant to PK because timing applies to the susceptibility of a target's mind, whereas we are dealing with inanimate objects, which do not sleep or dream. But timing is certainly not irrelevant to psychic phenomena in general. Dean Radin, in his book *The Conscious Universe* (1997), catalogues many scientific experiments relating to psi that took place across the twentieth century. Of particulate note is his report that the results of cross-cultural surveys in the 1960s showed that about half of all spontaneous psi experiences occurred in the dream state. From 1966 to 1972, psychiatrist Montague Ullman and psychologist Stanley Krippner conducted a series of telepathy tests in a dream research laboratory. These involved a sender, who was awake, and a receiver, who was asleep. Over time, when enough sessions had been catalogued, the evidence suggested that the receiver sometimes incorporated images from the sender in his dreams. This is in keeping with LaVey's view that the dream state leaves one more open to magical (telepathic) influence.

Some psychic dabblers wish to make a clear distinction between their own "safe" activities and the "dangerous" practices of the Black Arts. Perhaps they haven't quite managed to disentangle themselves from a lingering belief in Christianity's bogeyman. It's abundantly clear to me that there is no difference between the two fields. Nor is there any fundamental difference between black magic and prayer. Psychokinesis, magic and prayer are all attempts at causing change outside of oneself by ritualistically focusing the will using altered states of consciousness. It matters not whether the will is focused upon an imaginary beam of light projected from the hand, or an imaginary deity, be it Yahweh, Satan, or even Cthulhu. All gods, of all cultures, are nothing more than convenient fictions that provide a means of focusing the will, and they have no independent existence except as intelligible metaphors to aid the will in acting beyond the illusory constraints imposed by body/mind.

Carroll divides conscious existence into two fundamental attributes: will and perception. Will is outward moving, from consciousness into world. Perception is inward moving, from world into consciousness. In everyday experience, the will acts via brain-based thought, which triggers bodily action, which then affects the world at large. Perception works by receiving signals from the world at large into the body via the sense organs. These signals are then transmitted via nerves into the brain, where they are translated into meaningful information in consciousness. All legitimate psychic and magical endeavours are based on the understanding that will and perception may be tuned to other "frequencies" than these. This is why such activities emphasise the stilling of the body and mind.

Music allows us to make a rough analogy. You might listen to a particular song for years, never failing to pick out the catchy bassline, pounding snare drum, energetic guitar, and melodious keyboard harmonies. Then, quite by accident, you notice a subtle hi-hat ticking away in the background, throughout the piece. It had always been there, but the more powerful allure of the other instruments never allowed your attention to focus upon it. Until now, it was as if the hi-hat didn't exist. Later, when you listen to the song again, you forget all about the hi-hat, because you want to enjoy the fullness of the music. Only when you deliberately force your attention away from what it naturally tries to focus upon can you hear the hi-hat. Consciousness is like that. Our attention is naturally focused upon the incessant demands of our five senses and the chattering thoughts in our brains. But when attention is withdrawn from these, we discover subtler aspects of ourselves.

Consciousness only occurs when the two vectors of will and perception are present – will pushing outward and perception pulling inward. Similarly, all psi phenomena can be categorised into these same two basic areas: psychokinesis (outward) and extrasensory perception (inward). PK is merely an extension of will and ESP an extension of perception. In magical terminology, these two vectors are sometimes called enchantment (outward) and divination (inward).

Taking into account the philosophical position of monism argued for in this book, the self that exists as body/mind is not something real, not a thing-in-itself. This limited self, psyche, or mind, is a focused area of limited awareness for the Infinite – which is both everything-that-is and the only real self. The self is ordinarily focused by the activity of body and brain. Magic is the understanding that this focal setting can be adjusted. Sit still and you gain a sense that you are more than just your body; silence the mind with meditation, or bypass it with strong emotion, and consciousness is freed from the boundaries of mind – to perceive things it cannot normally perceive and to act in ways it cannot normally act, as it reaches out into the vast field of itself that is ordinarily focused into an experience of material forms appearing separate from it. The Universe that you see outside of your eyes is not really outside of your eyes; it's *inside* you, because you *are* the Universe. This is the rational basis of magic. All magical systems have this at their core, whether the magicians who developed them realised it or not. Symbols, rituals and gods have no power other than what the magician chooses to invest in them. Use them, or make up your own, or work without them entirely; it doesn't matter, because the magic is in *you*. And the magic is in you because *nothing exists outside of you*.

Magic may be absurd to the material minimalist, but it makes perfect sense when the so-called self is perceived as indistinguishable from the Universe as a whole, and when the brain is understood as a limiting mechanism for the self/Universe. If not for the thinking mind, consciousness would expand to infinite proportions and would not be able to function.

Psi phenomena provide a much firmer basis than a compassion or destruction ritual in obtaining evidence for the reality of magic. Unlike a misfortune that befalls the target of a curse, PK can be witnessed directly and can be repeated with limited success in a controlled environment, albeit on a small scale. Once its reality is established in the mind of the experimenter, and its connection to ritual magic understood, then one begins to suspect that attempting to move larger objects may be a misguided application of this talent – like a bodybuilder attempting to lift a double-decker bus with his bare hands, believing that he will eventually accomplish it, as long as he keeps trying. It's clear that the muscles of the human body are not capable of such an undertaking, and they never will be, regardless of how much time is spent at the gym. Similarly, any successful magical endeavour will be in keeping with the laws of physics; sufficient energy must be available to accomplish whatever is desired. Magic works with the existing flow of life – the Balance Factor.

Magic deserves be taken seriously because its connection to psi phenomena is undeniable. The possibilities and limits of magic will only be known through personal experience (as with psi). How far one is prepared to go, I leave to the individual conscience of the reader. I take no responsibility for your actions or their consequences. Perhaps I am putting a loaded gun in your hands. Even so, the gun is neither good nor evil. *You are.*

Anton LaVey, despite his magical prowess (real or imagined), died in near poverty in 1997. Magic may be far too slippery and unpredictable to be of high practical use, other than perhaps to give one an edge amid life's problems. For me, the greater value of magic is that it provides an empirical basis for the philosophy of monism – not the typical materialistic monism of the present scientific climate, but a true monism that doesn't dismiss the importance of consciousness.

I have described a magical paradigm that is philosophically rigorous, deeply rational, experientially knowable, and yet so mysterious that it makes quantum theory look like the tip of the iceberg. Imagine a dolphin taking one of its characteristic leaps out of the ocean. For a few seconds, as it performs its graceful arc through the air, it catches a glimpse of the night sky, the moon and stars shining bright. Then gravity pulls the creature back into its natural watery habitat. Now picture that same dolphin using this heavily restricted experience to come up with theories about gravitation, elliptical orbits, spiral galaxies, and black holes. I fear that this task for the dolphin may be analogous to the human's curious probing into the mystery of magic. The gateway, at the root of our unconscious mind, is simply too small, too difficult to open, and too prone to snap shut. And the realm beyond is too dark to see anything clearly from here.

Consider the predicament of a goldfish living out its existence in a bowl. The fish's ability to understand the Universe is limited to the point where water meets glass. It might be argued that the fish has a truer appreciation of reality than some humans, for at least it knows that there is a vast, incomprehensible arena of existence beyond its own boundaries. To be fair on poor old *homo sapiens*, the fish does have the advantage of receiving visual confirmation of this, as it watches huge hulking shapes moving about in a bizarre waterless realm. For the most part, the fish's life is predictable, like the human's. But occasionally, something from "outside" decides to interfere with the routine. Something reaches into the water and attempts to snatch the fish. The cause of the interference is a child holding a net, but the concepts *child* and *net* mean nothing to the fish. Its life has been invaded by the unknown. Perhaps the child is removing the fish to clean the bowl, or perhaps he is merely wishing to torment the fish for his own sadistic pleasure. It could be either. All the fish knows is that something new and potentially dangerous, of which it has no understanding, is happening.

The key question is this: are we humans also living in a fishbowl of sorts? We're not so different from the fish, in that we're both products of a single evolutionary ancestor, way back in the mists of time. Despite our differences, we're both entirely reliant on limited senses and cognitive ability. Yet unlike the fish, we have the hubris to imagine that we can explain all of reality in a neat little set of equations. The evolution of the human brain was successful because it aided the survival of the creature, not because it allowed the creature to understand everything about the Universe. Evolution does not know where it is going beforehand; it is not purpose-driven towards a specific goal. Genetic mutations occur and sometimes they provide happy accidents that a creature can make use of to its advantage. Knowing that, it's remarkable that we've been able to understand as much as we have. The human brain happens to be the most complex structure we know of in the entire Universe. Even so, if its complexity turned out to perfectly complement the complexity of the Universe (in the sense that it allowed everything about the Universe to be knowable), this would be a fluke of staggering proportions.

When we are blind to our limitations, we are, in effect, stating: "The human fishbowl is all that exists, so the answer to every question we could possibly ask about reality must be inside our fishbowl." Wait till you have an experience of something that only makes sense when you view it as originating from a higher dimension of existence that you have no ability to fully comprehend or measure. Sadly, the scarcity and unpredictability of such experiences reinforces man's overconfidence in his pursuit of a Theory of Everything.

Science on its own, for all of its accuracy and usefulness, can really only be said to be scratching the surface of reality. Physicists devote their attention to the deterministic side of the Universe and they are often entirely convinced that this is the only side it has. Those who are preoccupied with the quest for a Theory of Everything have no idea just how far from a complete answer they may be.

THE MAGIC OF THE MUNDANE

L ET's play a little psychological game. Imagine darkness all around you, except for a single blinding light directly ahead. The source of the light is obscured by a ship's helm, which appears to you as a blackened silhouette against the glow. Within the disc at the hub of the helm, a stencil in the shape of an inverted pentagram has been cut out, allowing the light to shine through.

I want to use this image as a means of communicating several ideas by symbolic representation. The first idea is that we can't see the light in its totality. The finite cannot grasp the Infinite. In attempting to understand the Infinite, we must resort to approximations, due to the limited nature of our minds and perceptions. All of our hard science must be understood within a metaphysical framework that is, of necessity, abstract. Symbolically, the bright light obscured by an object reminds us of this fundamental blind spot in our awareness. As physical creatures, we must learn to live with, and even appreciate, the impenetrable mystery at the heart of existence.

Why a helm, in particular? Because life is an experience of progress. We are each on an individual voyage of discovery, sailing our ships ever forward. We are never in stasis, never sitting still with perfect understanding, but always progressing towards a total illumination that we never quite reach – always learning, but never privy to the whole story.

A steering wheel is built to be turned. We must have an ever-present readiness to alter our bearing. In other words, we must always be willing to reassess our existing views in light of new information and, when necessary, to change our minds. Otherwise we are merely sailing out into the darkness of delusion.

Notice this is not a wheel from just any vehicle; it is a ship's helm. Life at sea is lonely and dangerous; a sailor's companions are few and he may face stormy seas. In a similar fashion, we must stand apart from the masses, forming our individual opinions and resisting herd mentality. As a consequence, we must be willing to face hurtful interference and even social exile, because our views may not be popular or tolerated by the masses. Don't sail this ship unless you're prepared to accept the risks.

The significance of the inverted pentagram lies in the relationship of the Infinite to the finite, of non-duality to duality. The veiling of the Infinite creates a self-other distinction, which inexorably brings about an adversarial Universe – a *satanic* Universe, to state it theatrically. All things are as they are by virtue of the continual conversion of energy. As creatures, the relationship of predator and prey is unavoidably woven into the nature of our existence. Generally speaking, conflict is a fact of life that must be faced and embraced.

Inevitably, a free-thinker faces hostility for his refusal to fall in line with accepted thinking. Though he may live in a civilisation that tolerates individuality, he must be ready in all circumstances to face opposition with courage. Though he is ethical by his own volition, he may be branded as a villain for his basic non-conformity to established dogmas. He is out in the dark, alone, pursuing the truth.

The human being is a herd animal, and not all men and women are capable, or willing, to step outside of the safety that the herd offers. For this reason, there may always be the exoteric and the esoteric: common beliefs that allow man to be a happy, socially acceptable animal who doesn't have to think too much, and deeper mysteries for those who are self-realised enough to cognise them – secrets hidden in plain sight.

I call this the Dark Wheel. It's not a term I invented. In my early teens, I read a memorable science fiction novella called *The Dark Wheel* (1984) by Robert Holdstock. It was written as a companion to a groundbreaking computer game called *Elite* and its purpose was to add substance to the game's theme of interplanetary trade and piracy, where players progressed from their initial rating of harmless, to dangerous, deadly, and for the skilled few, elite. In Holdstock's story, the Dark Wheel was a secret society of elitists concerned with unravelling the secrets of the Universe. This quest was not fleshed out in any detail, but the sense of mystery made it all the more memorable.

I decided to borrow the term the Dark Wheel, not because Holdstock had something profound to say, but because I can't seem to shake the relevance those words have for my personal philosophical outlook. If it seems childish to use science fiction as a basis for a serious philosophy, one should remember that all the gods and goddesses of antiquity, from which we extract symbolic relevance, are also fictitious.

I designed this symbol in 2011, when I was toying with creating an identity for my worldview. I forgot about the symbol for a while, and when I came back to it at a later date, an interesting effect occurred while gazing at it. I felt inspired. It was as if the symbol was imbued with power and it was working upon me. Of course, there was nothing paranormal afoot; the symbol was exuding power for the simple reason that I had previously empowered it with meaning. I had encoded in it the nature of man's relationship to the Infinite and the most important character traits he requires as a truth-seeker in a hostile world. I saw myself in the symbol and felt a renewed sense of the value of my path.

All symbols work like this. When a Christian chooses to wear a cross pendant, he is doing so because he wishes to identify with the meaning behind the cross. Atheists sometimes mock the symbol as the first century equivalent of wearing an electric chair around one's neck, but to the Christian this is a symbol of great power, reminding him of the sacrifice he believes God made on his behalf. Protestants add an additional layer of meaning by excluding the body of Jesus from the cross. In part, this is due to their rejection of the use of images of God, but it is also a statement that their Christ has risen from the dead.

Some use symbols as charms or talismans. This is not quite as superstitious as it first appears to the rational mind. Wearing a symbol, or gazing at it, gives you a certain feeling, and that feeling affects your behaviour. The mystically minded may be inclined to believe that symbols contain supernatural power, but the nature of that power is merely applied psychology. A pentagram might evoke feelings of revulsion or dread in a Christian, but this is entirely down to the meaning he has chosen to place upon the symbol, a meaning usually formed by exposure to anti-occult propaganda and horror movies. A friend of mine once told me an amusing story about wearing a pentagram ring to work. A Christian co-worker saw it and remarked, "I didn't know you were Jewish" (the Jewish symbol, in case you don't know, is a *six*-pointed star).

When a person gazes at a Christian cross, an inverted pentagram, a Taoist taijitu (yin-yang), or even a big yellow McDonald's M, it evokes a psychological response, depending upon what meaning the observer has attached to the symbol. In the case of McDonald's, the meaning is subliminally injected. One of the company's sustained advertising campaigns involved embedding the statement "I'm lovin' it" into the symbol using a torrent of television advertising that associated the phrase with the symbol. McDonald's restaurants then relied on the prominent display of the company logo on the roofs of their buildings to *charm* passers by into dining there.

This is one example of how we are used and abused by the holders of this esoteric knowledge. But the same knowledge can be used, not only to disentangle oneself from the web of influence that catches the masses, but also for one's own personal empowerment. The practical value of a visual symbol is its ability to condense a variety of ideas into a simple, memorable aesthetic form and to serve as a reminder of them all to the beholder. My symbol, the Dark Wheel, communicates: daring to stand alone, rejecting the conditioning of your past; grasping the fundamental reality of the Infinite as the basis of your existence; integrating the adversarial side of life into this non-dual awareness; appreciating the predicament of living with impenetrable mystery; flowing with the forward motion of knowledge instead of turning present assertions into dogma; admitting the subjective nature of your relationship to truth and being ever vigilant for the tides of change. Without words, the symbol serves to maintain my focus upon all of this. I have simply engineered it as a tool for personal growth.

It's also important to remember that one can be too serious. There is a deliberate sense of fun and rascality intended in giving this symbol an air of the sinister. Branding is important, and nothing attracts attention more than a sense of the forbidden. Like many occultists, I prefer dark aesthetics, both for their theatrical value and because black relates to the obscure, the hidden, the unknown, while white is often the signature colour of purity, and purity is often a mask for hypocrisy.

If you are entirely new to magic, you can use the Dark Wheel as your first conscious magical working. If you resonate with the meaning of the symbol, make it your own. Draw your own version; make changes to it that are more in keeping with your individual worldview, or design an entirely different symbol altogether. Think carefully about what aspects of life you place great importance in, or crystallise a long-term goal that you wish to accomplish. Search for a way to represent this aesthetically.

In choosing or inventing a symbol, listen to your gut feelings. Colours and shapes speak to us on a primal level. In the science fiction movie *The Black Hole* (1979), the good robot and the evil robot are instantly recognisable in their respective roles, even before they speak or act, because of what their physical appearance alone communicates to the viewer. Vincent is grey in colour, has large cartoon-like eyes, and his short, squat body is mostly outlined in friendly curves. Maximillian's metal body is red, tall and broad-shouldered, made up of straight lines and harsh corners. His head is a trapezoid, a shape that evokes a feeling of wrongness because it is like a distorted rectangle or an incomplete pyramid. And his single eye is a soulless horizontal strip that glows an angry bright red. You will see this instinctual aesthetic awareness employed again and again in science fiction films. There is something instantly friendly about C-3PO, but from the first moment you see Darth Vader (assuming you grew up with the original *Star Wars* trilogy), you sense he's evil incarnate.

The same aesthetic principle is at work in nature. Once, while I was walking near a lake, I came across a family of swans resting on the grass by the shore. As I approached, one of the large parent birds started waddling slowly towards me, head lowered, wings extended upwards in an unusual V shape. I intuitively picked up on this as a threat, even though I had never before seen this posture. The bird was clearly saying, "Do not mess with my family." It struck me that the shape the bird was making with its wings was much like horns. It instinctively knew the effect this pose would have, and I instinctively felt that effect. This is the *primal* significance of the inverted pentagram. It evokes a feeling that a traditional pentagram, with its single point facing up, does not.

The best symbol is the kind that nags at you until you embrace it, where it almost feels as if the symbol chose you, rather than you chose it. This illusion is created by the primal draw of the aesthetic form. The fact that I am drawn to identify with an image of horns extended says something important about my character – that I've accepted the hostile aspect of human nature and integrated it into my personality. Whatever symbol you invent or borrow, see that it speaks to you on a primal level. As time goes by, you will experience how your symbol acts as a means of empowerment for the desired direction of your life.

"Wait a minute," you may object. "There's nothing magical about this. You yourself admitted that it was just applied psychology. I want to experience something paranormal." The two sides of magic are not separate, and one of the essential steps in the path of a magician is developing an appreciation that *life is magical*, in an entirely mundane sense. This observation is not easily appreciated in our scientifically oriented culture, where our focus is on understanding life by breaking everything down and labelling the parts. While that approach does yield much knowledge, it's easy to miss the value of examining life as an experience of wholeness. When we stand on a mountaintop and gaze in awe at the view, what we experience in the mind will not be understood by examining the composition of the soil, or by knowing that the water running down the river consists of two parts hydrogen to one part oxygen. As rational Westerners, it is easy to dismiss the term magic because of its mystical heritage, but there is really no better word to describe this side of life experience.

Life casts "spells" upon us all the time. Overcast weather makes us feel gloomy; sunshine makes us feel joyful. A woman who is skilled at using her body can make a man's pulse race with sexual excitement. We are constantly at the mercy of all manner of influences. Being a magician means having a much greater awareness than the average person of the forces that move us. Not only does this empower us to resist the natural currents of life (if we so choose), but it also gives us the power to influence the lives of others. People are generally predictable because they unconsciously go with the flow. This makes them controllable, simply by making subtle adjustments to their circumstances. Having this power does not make a magician evil, any more than having a knife in your kitchen drawer makes you liable to stab a family member. Magic should be undertaken with a great sense of responsibility. For the most part, my own efforts at magic consist of steering my circumstances towards the most productive outcome.

I have a personal axiom: "Act, don't react." This is easy to practise when my ego is in sync with my monistic outlook on life. There is no individual self, so there is no need to react vindictively to anyone. However, I am not always so mindful. Sometimes I really do have to hold back the natural, predictable tendency to lash out verbally. In those circumstances, the only thing stopping me is the development of this useful habit. The energy of my anger exists, but it goes into an internal buffer, waiting for direction from me. I coolly analyse the situation, weighing the consequences of expressing my anger against the consequences of remaining calm. And then I act responsibly, based on what I want to happen, not on what the runaway voice in my head is urging me to do.

"Act, don't react" isn't synonymous with "Suppress, don't express." Suppressed emotion is dangerous, because it is unresolved and tends to trickle out in day-to-day living, adversely affecting all your relationships. The emotional block has to be cleared, and any method that helps you achieve this safely is perfectly valid. "Act, don't react" applies to the whole spectrum of behaviour, not just to anger. The internal landscape of your mind is something to be tended like a garden, not allowed to run amok, overgrown with weeds.

I've had some fun learning to adopt this attitude. In my late thirties, I started riding a bicycle to my job every day. For a particular period, I was subjected to mockery by a group of teenagers on their way to school each morning. They knew my identity because they had previously attended the school where I'm employed. I guess they thought it was novel to be able to poke fun at an employee without consequence to themselves; it wasn't like I could put them in detention. Unfortunately, the geography of my town meant that there was no alternative route I could take. So I endured this treatment silently for a couple of weeks, feeling the anger gradually build up inside me. It was especially frustrating that my position of responsibility at a school meant that I had to appear angelically blameless in public.

Eventually, I decided to risk a strategy that I hoped would solve the matter quickly. I was going to scare the living daylights out of them. The next morning, one of the teenagers was walking alone, and he called out in his usual mocking tone. This time I stopped the bike, turned around, and unleashed a torrent of verbal abuse. It was an abrupt personality shift from the calm, well-mannered man he had known in his previous school, into a thug. I don't recall much of what I said, but the underlying impression I intended to leave with him was this: "You don't really know me, and you've no idea what I'm capable of doing." Before I had finished three sentences, he had turned away from me and scampered off with his tail between his legs. I dared to think: Result! But that was just the beginning; I had severely miscalculated.

Once word got to the rest of the gang, their torments multiplied; now that they had successfully got a rise out of me, they thought it would be great fun to have a repeat performance. In my ineptitude, I tried the same ruse again, which naturally failed. After that, I made a promise to myself: "No matter what they do, they will never, *ever* get another reaction from me." They tried and tried, but I kept my cool. The only real solution for me was to change the time I cycled to work in the mornings. I hated doing that, because I was letting them win. Notice how active my ego is throughout. I wish I could tell you I handled the situation by informing my ego that it doesn't have to triumph because it isn't the real me. I wish I could say I endured the boys' taunts without feeling any need to get my own back. But my sense of self (or non-self) wasn't sufficiently developed at the time. Even so, I knew my own limits, so I took the only action I could take to defuse the situation. I still encountered the teens now and again, when coming home from work in the afternoons. And they continued to holler at me, for months, even – a little too simple-minded to realise I was on to their game. Eventually they found something better to do with their time, as was inevitable. So, that's an example of a failed application of magic, for your amusement. But a lesson learned the hard way is a mistake that won't be repeated. And I learned a lot from that episode – about predicting behaviour in others, about becoming aware of my own limits, and about defusing an emotional time bomb.

Greater magic is best applied in situations where there is no lesser magical alternative. To throw a curse sounds objectionable, but that's a bit like saying a police officer should never, under any circumstances, fire his gun. What if you find yourself stuck in a life situation where you are continually at the mercy of a physically abusive person and there is no viable exit? Wouldn't it be appropriate to curse him, if there's nothing else you can do to free yourself? Is this even any different from a Christian who prays for God's help with the situation, then thanks him after the abuser ends up being run over by a car?

It also sounds somewhat nefarious to perform a lust ritual to attract the attentions of a woman. But when females commonly dress in a manner that broadcasts a mating signal to all males in their vicinity, the question must be asked: who is really working magic on whom? This illustrates the entwined nature of lesser and greater magic. Life is magical. It's beside the point whether normal or paranormal influences are used as an aid to achieving a goal. Either way, it's witchery, seduction, manipulation – whichever synonym you prefer.

Before I secured a publishing contract for this book, I was considering self-publishing it. That meant it would be my responsibility to prepare an eye-catching cover. Not being a professional artist, I ploughed through thousands of stock images online, looking for one that had just the right psychological effect on me. This effect would hopefully be reflected into the minds of my intended audience. Make no mistake: my aim was to do everything in my power to bewitch you into lifting this book off the shelf (or, as is now most often the case, clicking on its image on a website). I planned to use the obscure powers of aesthetics to influence how you felt, and I intended that feeling to drive you to action in keeping with my will. That is magic. Don't be offended; this is how the world works. If you search your own motivations with great honesty, you will find many examples of how you have played these tricks upon others. It can be as simple as grooming yourself in front of a mirror in the morning, or choosing a particular outfit from the wardrobe, because you want the aesthetics of your body to have a particular effect upon those you will encounter during the day ahead. Denying this side of life is like asking a peacock to stop showing off its feathers.

When I put on my motorcycle jacket, this causes me to feel different about myself, because it changes the shape of my body. It also alters others' perceptions of me. The armour in the shoulders causes me to appear more physically powerful, while also making my waist appear narrower by contrast. When I ride the bike down the street and a little kid sticks his thumb up at me in greeting, he is doing so because I have become cool in his estimation. Bike and rider are not separate, in his eyes. For the duration of the encounter, the animalistic growl of the engine becomes an aspect of who I am, more so even than my face, which is obscured behind a helmet visor. Had I been walking down the street in ordinary clothes, I would not have been saluted, let alone noticed, by the youngster. The magical effect lies in the combination of obscure separate elements that create an aesthetic whole.

My interest in magic originally stemmed from dabbling in psychokinesis, which is, of course, causing change by obscure means – the definition of magic. I remember the perspective I had when I was just starting out, prior to any successful experimentation – the sense that life would never be the same if I could just break through. While that consequence proved to be true, it may surprise the uninitiated to learn that even something like PK eventually becomes mundane when practised often enough. Every experience, no matter how initially mind-blowing, is eventually integrated as a part of everyday life. My interest in PK was philosophical, and once I had extracted the clues that PK provided about the nature of reality, my will to obsessively practise it diminished, as did any further progress. I know my dismissive attitude is hard for someone on the outside to understand, but no experience of life holds its thrill forever, not even this. PK provides no greater a repository for endless excitement than skydiving holds for someone who has jumped from a plane five hundred times. The true value of PK is the long-term life-changing benefits of such an initiation into a new perspective on the Universe.

A magician is commonly thought to be one who is exclusively preoccupied with the paranormal, but he is actually one who is equally interested in the magical nature of ordinary life. Life is magical because it is filled with obscurity. The magician's "sixth sense" is a highly developed awareness of the commonly unnoticed aspects of life, and this elevated vantage point allows him to influence life to a greater degree than the average person. To what end? That depends on you. The path of the magician can be a descent into egocentric madness, or one's self-centred motivations can be counterbalanced with selfless love. It all depends on what the word *I* means to you.

CONCLUSION

THE cornerstone of this book is the case for monism. I have made my arguments on rational and empirical grounds. I began by overturning two widely held paradigms (religious dogmatism and material minimalism) that are hurdles to the view I propose. I essentially rebooted the mind, minus the typical conditioning that is put in place in the West through religious and secular education.

I sought to understand the Universe afresh with a philosophical blank slate. I backed up my insights with carefully articulated logic. The central pillar supporting everything else was an appreciation of the fundamental reality of the Infinite, the Immeasurable, the Formless – call it what you will – a level of reality that is undoubtedly real, but ungraspable from the perspective of a creature. The Infinite is what we encounter when we probe such avenues as the underlying essence of matter and consciousness. At the root of all our finite measurements and categorisations is an ungraspable infinity – an unbound singularity from which a Universe of apparent multiplicity springs.

I have been careful to avoid presenting monism as a form of salvation – a new gospel – like so many spiritual teachers. While it is certainly true that there is no essential need to embrace this worldview, it must be understood that one's personal philosophy, whatever it may be, determines his whole outlook on life, including his psychological health, ethical values, and experiential goals.

Consider these words, from a stranger who wrote to me online, having watched some of my video lectures: "I wanted to say that I agree, there's no duality, that 'duality' is about living in the now. But life is nothing but suffering and will always be suffering. I can't enjoy my 'now' with suffering going on all around me. I'm not going to stay and watch other human beings hurt each other, and that's why I will be committing suicide soon. Sorry to be defeatist. There will be a time in the future in which human beings will live in harmony, and if I am given the opportunity to come back from the formlessness (and I believe I can; reincarnation is our existence), I will. See you on the other side."

If you think beliefs don't matter, think again. Here's a person whose beliefs are driving him to take his own life. I don't wish to be cruel to someone who is clearly suffering, but it needs to be said: he thinks the problem is in the world around him, but the real source of the problem is in his head.

His understanding of life is unrealistic, and so he makes an unrealistic demand of life: the expectation that there ought to be harmony. And when that demand isn't met, he wants to escape. His belief in reincarnation makes the suicide more palatable, because he thinks he can come back later, when conditions are more to his liking – a bit like taking a nap until the storm blows over.

If this person saw life a little more clearly, he would notice that there is never harmony between the lion and the gazelle, between the immune system and the invading virus, between the planet and the asteroid that's on a collision course. So what right has a human being to a life free from suffering? None! Notice that you don't see gazelles jumping off cliffs because they're tired of being chased by predators. Why not? Because non-human animals are not tortured by the twists and turns of human philosophy. Furthermore, even though this person denies believing in duality, he still thinks of his identity as a self separate from the Universe – a soul that can exit from life and return later. But if life is non-dual, there can be no exit, ever. You can't truly commit suicide, because you're alive in all the other suffering creatures. All life is the Universal Self in manifold guises.

Do you see how erroneous beliefs, even seemingly harmless "spiritual" ones, can be utterly pernicious? Sometimes what you believe really is a matter of life and death. Adhering to wrong beliefs never led me to such extremes, but I can speak from the personal experience of having been a Christian, whose life was crippled by unnatural life-denying rules. I was also an atheist, whose happiness was poisoned by nihilism. What, then, does monism do for my outlook on life?

Non-dual awareness is not some sort of cosmic consciousness that is off-limits to all but the spiritual elite among us. It is the awareness you possess right now, except that it recognises the world of the senses and the mind as a veneer over a more fundamental reality. Beneath the surface of appearances, the whole Universe is a formless, incomprehensible unity, where nothing is separate from anything, including your identity from the whole. In other words, you are IT.

Consider the far-reaching implications of monism in relation to the space-time experience of apparent separateness in which we all participate:

1. There has never been, nor will there ever be, anything other than *you*.

2. There has never been, nor will there ever be, any other moment but *now*.

3. You exist, now, in an eternal flow of change.

These three principles will seem utterly alien to anyone who has not properly grasped monism. But when they sink in at a deep level, the practical outworking in one's life is profound. Again I speak from personal experience.

There is no room for nihilism, because you are eternal. There is no place for greed, because the inevitability of change means that no accumulation of wealth or power can ever truly last. There is no need for a reliance on spiritual pipe dreams concerning the soul and the afterlife, because you have already arrived at the centre of eternity: *now*. In grasping this, you are seeing the truth behind the ideas that religions have been intuitively approximating through the ages. Your grip on the importance of your ego is loosened, removing much of the terror from the anticipation of death and allowing you to take life a lot less seriously, because you understand that your individual consciousness is only a finite manifestation of the real you. You grow older without the sense of urgency that your time is running out, because all life is you in other guises. Where once you experienced restless cravings, you now experience playful desires, because no matter what you strive to achieve or obtain with your "time," the destination is always the same as the origin: now. You learn to relax into the now at all times, since it's the only moment you know. And your capacity for love is deepened through your awareness that you are metaphysically inseparable from everyone and everything.

Consider these attitudes: "As long as I'm all right, I don't care about anyone else." "It's not my problem if I overhear my neighbour beating his wife senseless." "The world's oil reserves might be running out, but I'm happy as long as there's enough to last the rest of my lifetime." "Why should it matter to me that I'm polluting the planet? The next generation can deal with it; I'll be dead and gone long before any of that affects me." These stances are the logical result of dualistic thinking, where the self is viewed as something alienated from what it perceives as other-than-self. Such attitudes are impossible to hold when non-dual awareness develops, because the sense of separation is replaced by a sense of unity. This example gives a taste of how monism, if understood *en masse*, could dramatically impact the world for the better.

If there is any enlightenment to be obtained in life, it is only in the sense of an improvement to the quality of consciousness. Historically, we might say that Christian spirituality was an improvement over Roman materialism. We might also say that scientific reasoning is an improvement over Christian authoritarianism. The non-dual perspective that I defend here is an improvement over the mind-body dualism common among theists and atheists today.

Existence remains impenetrably mysterious, but for those willing to do the hard work of de-conditioning and re-educating themselves, life becomes a delicious mystery that is stripped bare of misdirection, and we find ourselves freed from the psychological problems spawned from our erroneous beliefs. As a result of my own journey, I am imbued with a sense of awe and wonder about life, the likes of which I haven't experienced since childhood.

Life is a dance of energy. The dance feels brief and insignificant when the ego misidentifies itself as a separate entity from the whole. But in reality, every manifestation of that dance, across the entire Universe, for the duration of an unending present moment, is *you*.

When a human being truly comes to recognise himself as the Universe peering out through a pair of eyes, the most natural reaction is laughter. And when the laughter subsides, a light-hearted, playful spirit, born of an enriched awareness, remains.

ACKNoWlEDGEMENTS

Learning requires not just thinking your own thoughts, but carefully examining the musings of others, too. The more you read, the more you know. And there is never enough time to read everything. Nevertheless, out of the many books that I have consumed in life thus far, I would like to shine a light on a few authors who were particularly influential in helping me synthesise my own worldview.

The first is David Icke. I don't subscribe to his theories about a global conspiracy, or shape-shifting reptilian entities that look human, or the moon being an artificial construction projecting a fake reality to the Earth. I think Icke, as a researcher, has made countless wrong turns, relying on "channelled" information from alleged psychics, running on pure intuition with little rational support, placing confidence in unverifiable testimonies, trafficking in rumour, and wallowing in unrealistic levels of paranoia. You might wonder what I could possibly gain from the writings of a man with so flimsy a grasp of epistemology. Two things:

Icke, for all his flaws, was the first example I came across of what might be called *spirituality with balls*. Through my Christian conditioning, I had equated spirituality with the "virtues" of humility and obedience. Through Icke, I quickly learned that rebellion was not something unspiritual or unethical. In fact, it was necessary, as my own sheep-like spirituality was not working as a positive force in my life. Icke, who went through a period of massive public ridicule in the early 1990s for making some outlandish claims on public TV, picked himself up, weathered the storm, and ended up becoming a more empowered person because of it. Regardless of what I can't accept about Icke's views, I never fail to be inspired when he talks about being yourself, not caring about what anyone thinks of you, refusing to conform to what you know is wrong; he is a man talking from hard-earned experience.

The second thing I gained was my first inkling of monism. His metaphysics was streets ahead of Christian monotheism, which was all I knew at the time. In reading his books, I was seeing the vague shape of where the truth lay. Nowadays, my own philosophy differs substantially from Icke's, but I have to give him credit as the man who helped me hit the ground running at a time in my life when I was very confused. The book that started it all for me was *I Am Me, I Am Free* (1996).

The next major influence on my life was Anton LaVey, the founder of the Church of Satan and author of *The Satanic Bible* (1969). Ironically, one of the reasons I began studying Satanism was to see whether Icke's claims about a satanic conspiracy had any merit (they didn't). I never expected to discover a philosophy that resonated with me. LaVey was a visionary for his time, seeing human nature with a great deal of clarity and packaging his insights in the form of an outrageous myth that ensured his popularity long after his death. LaVey, for me, was a grounding force that kept me mindful of the harsher realities of physical existence, since so much of my studying consisted of metaphysics books. Without LaVey, I might not have clearly seen the errors that many spiritual teachers fall prey to – those that talk about removing low-vibrational energy (whatever that is) and expressing universal love. LaVey was all about seeing the world as it is, not indulging in wishful thinking. I didn't agree with his philosophy in its entirety. It was better suited to dualism than to monism, which explains its continuing popularity with atheists. But what I gained from studying Satanism I would have been hard pressed to find elsewhere.

Someone who took LaVey's philosophy and attempted to develop it into something better is Jason King, author of *Postmodern Satanism* (2009). King, like myself, is a monist, and his book was invaluable in helping me to integrate non-dual awareness with a sense of realism about the predicament of creaturely existence. I don't think King and I join all the dots in exactly the same places, but his influence permeates my book. *Postmodern Satanism* provided a much needed balance against the unrealistic love-and-light spirituality expressed by many teachers of non-duality.

Stephen Hawking's popular physics book *A Brief History of Time* (1988), while difficult to read, proved to be a delightful antidote to years of ill-informed Christian propaganda about cosmology. Through this work I started to see how science could be successfully integrated with a rigorously thought-out monism and could even enhance that metaphysical perspective in unexpected ways.

Lastly, I was delighted to discover Alan Watts, author of *The Book: On the Taboo Against Knowing Who You Are* (1966) and many others works. Watts took my appreciation of monism to even deeper levels with his ability to communicate the insights of Eastern philosophy (Hinduism, Buddhism and Taoism) in a language and structure suitable to our preconditioned Western brains. When I am asked to summarise my personal philosophy, I sometimes say, "It's what you would get if Buddha and Satan sat down and worked out their differences."

I could talk about many more invaluable minds, but those are the big ones that triggered significant changes in my thinking. No doubt there are further treasures to discover, as I continue to joyfully explore the many avenues of human knowledge.

I, Universe was written from 2009 to 2018. During its development, many of my online "followers" offered helpful criticisms and corrections. My thanks to all of you; it's a better book because of your input. Thanks also to the folks at Skylight Press for taking a chance on my labour of love.

SUGGESTED READING

The following list by no means constitutes a complete programme of study; it is only an inventory of what I consider to be the most important books from the many titles I have read in recent years. I do not endorse every claim made by every author. Often it's important to get both sides of a story and to formulate your own personal synthesis from opposing viewpoints. The following titles simply contain useful information over a wide variety of fields. It is up to the individual reader to assert his own critical thinking.

Michael A. Aquino: *Black Magic* (1975)
John D. Barrow: *Impossibility: The Limits of Science and the Science of Limits* (1998)
Howard Bloom: *The Lucifer Principle: A Scientific Expedition Into the Forces of History* (1995)
Derren Brown: *Tricks of the Mind* (2006)
Joseph Campbell: *Myths to Live By* (1972), *The Power of Myth* (1988)
Peter J. Carroll: *Liber Null* (1978), *Psychonaut* (1982)
Richard Cavendish: *The Black Arts: A Concise History of Witchcraft, Demonology, Astrology, and Other Mystical Practices Throughout the Ages* (1967)
Sean Connelly: *The Psion's Handbook* (2004)
Brian Cox & Jeff Forshaw: *The Quantum Universe: Everything That Can Happen Does Happen* (2011)
Richard Dawkins: *The Blind Watchmaker* (1986)
James Fallon: *The Psychopath Inside: A Neuroscientist's Personal Journey Into the Dark Side of the Brain* (2013)
Charles Fort: *The Book of the Damned* (1919)
Tim Freke: *The Mystery Experience: A Revolutionary Approach to Spiritual Awakening* (2012)
Robert Greene: *The 48 Laws of Power* (1998)
Dan Harris: *10% Happier: How I Tamed the Voice in My Head, Reduced Stress Without Losing My Edge, and Found Self-Help That Actually Works* (2014)
Sam Harris: *The Moral Landscape: How Science Can Determine Human Values* (2010), *Waking Up: A Guide to Spirituality Without Religion* (2014)
Stephen Hawking: *A Brief History of Time* (1988), *The Grand Design* (2010) [with Leonard Mlodinow]
Phil Hine: *Condensed Chaos: An Introduction to Chaos Magic* (1995)

Aldous Huxley: *The Doors of Perception* (1954), *Heaven and Hell* (1956), *Brave New World Revisited* (1958)

David Icke: *I Am Me, I Am Free: The Robots' Guide to Freedom* (1996)

Jason King: *Postmodern Satanism* (2009)

Paul McKenna: *The Hypnotic World of Paul McKenna* (1994)

Anton Szandor LaVey: *The Satanic Bible* (1969), *The Satanic Witch* (1971) [originally published as *The Compleat Witch*]

Elaine Pagels: *The Origin of Satan: How Christians Demonized Jews, Pagans and Heretics* (1995)

Dean Radin: *The Conscious Universe: The Scientific Truth of Psychic Phenomena* (1997) [published in the UK as *The Noetic Universe*], *Entangled Minds: Extrasensory Experiences in a Quantum Reality* (2006), *Supernormal: Science, Yoga, and the Evidence for Extraordinary Psychic Abilities* (2013)

Wilhelm Reich: *Listen, Little Man!* (1948)

Bertrand Russell: *A History of Western Philosophy* (1945)

Carl Sagan: *The Demon-Haunted World: Science as a Candle in the Dark* (1995)

Christopher Ryan & Cacilda Jetha: *Sex at Dawn: The Prehistoric Origins of Modern Sexuality* (2010)

David Self: *The Lion Encyclopedia of World Religions* (2008)

Upton Sinclair: *Mental Radio* (1930)

Brad Warner: *Hardcore Zen: Punk Rock, Monster Movies, and the Truth About Reality* (2003), *Sit Down and Shut Up: Punk Rock Commentaries on Buddha, God, Truth, Sex, Death and Dogen's Treasury of the Right Dharma Eye* (2007)

Alan Watts: *The Book: On the Taboo Against Knowing Who You Are* (1966), *The Philosophies of Asia* (1995)

Colin Wilson: *A Criminal History of Mankind* (1984)